REA's Test Prep Books Are The Best!

(a sample of the <u>hundreds of letters</u> REA receives each year)

" I did well because of your wonderful prep books... I just wanted to thank you for helping me prepare for these tests. "
Student, San Diego, CA

" My students report your chapters of review as the most valuable single resource they used for review and preparation. "
Teacher, American Fork, UT

" Your book was such a better value and was so much more complete than anything your competition has produced — and I have them all! "
Teacher, Virginia Beach, VA

" Compared to the other books that my fellow students had, your book was the most useful in helping me get a great score. "
Student, North Hollywood, CA

" Your book was responsible for my success on the exam, which helped me get into the college of my choice... I will look for REA the next time I need help. "
Student, Chesterfield, MO

" Just a short note to say thanks for the great support your book gave me in helping me pass the test... I'm on my way to a B.S. degree because of you! "
Student, Orlando, FL

" The gem of the book is the tests. They were indicative of the actual exam. The explanations of the answers are practically another review session. "
Student, Fresno, CA

(more on next page)

(continued from front page)

" I just wanted to thank you for helping me get a great score
on the AP U.S. History... Thank you for making great test preps! "
Student, Los Angeles, CA

" Your *Fundamentals of Engineering Exam* book was the absolute best
preparation I could have had for the exam, and it is one of the major
reasons I did so well and passed the FE on my first try. "
Student, Sweetwater, TN

" I used your book to prepare for the test and found that the advice and the
sample tests were highly relevant... Without using any other material, I earned
very high scores and will be going to the graduate school of my choice. "
Student, New Orleans, LA

" What I found in your book was a wealth of information sufficient to shore up
my basic skills in math and verbal... The section on analytical ability was
excellent. The practice tests were challenging and the answer explanations
most helpful. It certainly is the Best Test Prep for the GRE! "
Student, Pullman, WA

" I really appreciate the help from your excellent book. Please keep
up with your great work."
Student, Albuquerque, NM

" I used your *CLEP Introductory Sociology* book and rank it 99% — thank you! "
Student, Jerusalem, Israel

" The painstakingly detailed answers in the sample tests are the most helpful
part of this book. That's one of the great things about REA books. "
Student, Valley Stream, NY

The Best Test Preparation and Review Course

PATENT BAR EXAM

For Registration to Practice before the U.S. Patent Office

By Staff of Research & Education Association

Research & Education Association

61 Ethel Road West • Piscataway, NJ 08854

http://www.rea.com

The Best Test Preparation and Review Course for the Patent Bar Exam

Printed in the United States of America

Library of Congress Catalog Card Number 00-132020

International Standard Book Number 0-87891-329-7

Research & Education Association
61 Ethel Road West
Piscataway, New Jersey 08854
Email: info@rea.com

About Research and Education Association

Research and Education Association (REA) is an organization of educators, scientists, and engineers specializing in various academic fields. Founded in 1959 with the purpose of disseminating the most recently developed scientific information to groups in industry, government, high schools, and universities, REA has since become a successful and highly respected publisher of study aids, test preps, handbooks, and reference works.

REA's Test Preparation series includes study guides for all academic levels in almost all disciplines. Research and Education Association publishes test preps for students who have not yet completed high school, as well as high school students preparing to enter college. Students from countries around the world seeking to attend college in the United States will find the assistance they need in REA's publications. For college students seeking advanced degrees, REA publishes test preps for many major graduate school admission examinations in a wide variety of disciplines, including engineering, law, and medicine. Students at every level, in every field, with every ambition can find what they are looking for among REA's publications.

Unlike most Test Preparation books that present only a few practice tests which bear little resemblance to the actual exams, REA's series presents tests which accurately depict the official exams in both degree of difficulty and types of questions. REA's practice tests are always based upon the most recently administered exams, and include every type of question that can be expected on the actual exams.

REA's publications and educational materials are highly regarded and continually receive an unprecedented amount of praise from professionals, instructors, librarians, parents, and students. Our authors are as diverse as the subjects and fields represented in the books we publish. They are well-known in their respective fields and serve on the faculties of prestigious universities throughout the United States.

Acknowledgments

We would like to thank the following for their contributions:

Raj V. Abhyanker, BSEE, MBA,
Registered Patent Agent at Law, for the formidable task of developing and writing a comprehensive summary of the MPEP.

Dr. Max Fogiel, BME, MME, Ph.D. (EE)
Registered Patent Agent at Law, for his overall guidance which has brought this publication to completion.

Carl Fuchs, BA, MBA
Chief Editor, for writing the Introduction for this book and his management of the editorial staff through every phase of development, from design to final production of the book.

Michael Tomolonis, BA
Editorial Assistant, for coordinating the development of this book and his meticulous proofreading of the manuscript and text.

CONTENTS

Contents

Patent Examination I   131

Patent Examination II   209

Guide for the Preparation of Patent Drawings   289

How this Book Will Help You

Patent law has grown into one of the most interesting and highly-paid legal specialties with job opportunities exceeding many other professions. The continuous development of new technology in computers, software and biotechnology keeps the patent profession humming.

You most probably picked up this book because you are preparing for the patent bar exam or you are already in the patent field and want a comprehensive summary on patent procedures. This book will serve both purposes very well.

The book is a self-study course and review that will help patent bar candidates pass the very difficult patent exam. Two actual and recently administered patent exams with explanations are included along with test tips and strategies. Since much of the exam is based on the massive MPEP — Manual of Patent Examining Procedure, candidates for the patent bar will find this book's quick and detailed review of the MPEP a great time-saver and fabulous resource. Practicing attorneys, agents, inventors, law firms, and anybody associated with the patent field will also find the MPEP summary a useful resource in their daily practice.

For both exam candidates and those already associated with patents, the book contains up-to-date and practical information in the following areas of the patent field:

- Career opportunities as a patent attorney or agent
- Detailed information on the Patent and Trademark Office (PTO)
- Important publications of the PTO

- The difference between patents, trademarks, and copyrights
- What makes an invention patentable
- The functions of the PTO
- The role of the patent examiner
- Rules governing patent attorneys and agents

About the chapters:

The chapter titles in this book correspond to the actual chapter designations in the MPEP. The MPEP is a massive 3000 page book on which the patent bar exam is based. It is a federal publication which can be obtained in any law library or downloaded (a massive file) from the website: http://www.uspto.gov/web/offices/pac/mpep/index.html.

Reference annotations have been added throughout the MPEP review in this book. This will help you look up concepts in the voluminous MPEP should you require further detail or clarification. (e.g. You will see MPEP 702, MPEP 1244, etc. marked throughout the MPEP Review.)

The chapter on preparing Patent Drawings is included because it is useful for anyone preparing a patent application. However, candidates for the exam should understand that the subject of patent drawings is not a part of the Patent Bar Exam.

Carl Fuchs
Chief Editor

The Best Test Preparation and Review Course

PATENT
BAR
EXAM

Introduction

Introduction

Patent Law is a Great Profession

Not only is patent law one of the best specialties in the legal field, it also ranks at the top of many professions. Excellent starting salaries, limitless opportunity, intellectual challenges, and the opportunity to work almost anywhere makes the patent profession hard to beat. Moreover, it is one of the few legal specialties where demand continues to outpace supply. Lawyer glut is not an issue with patent law remaining one of the few still growing legal professions. The lack of a science/technical background and the difficult patent bar exam keep most otherwise qualified out of this field. Patent attorneys enjoy all the benefits of the legal profession minus the stress, minus the competition, and minus the bad lawyer jokes.

Starting salaries for patent attorneys can easily range from $50,000 to $100,000. Experienced patent attorneys in large law firms make much more. Patent attorneys also have many choices in terms of how and where they work in the field, offering something for all personalities and styles. For those who like the excitement of the courtroom, there are plenty of patent cases to litigate. Others will find the technical side of formulating the patent application more low-key and intellectually stimulating. For the technically devout, it is a great way to stay current in science and technology. By being exposed to a wide variety of inventions, the patent attorney stays on the cutting edge of technology and sees the latest innovations before almost everyone else.

Introduction

While many legal specialties are often associated with high stress and thankless tasks, the patent field is just the opposite. Patent prosecution (written and oral arguments to obtain a patent for an invention in the patent office) is generally non-confrontational. Working with inventors on drafting the patent application and prosecuting the invention often results in a special collaborative bond between the inventor and attorney. A newly issued patent is a highly rewarding accomplishment.

There is also a wide choice in the workplace between a firm that specializes in patents and intellectual property or a general practice firm with a separate patent department. In recent years, large law firms have been far more aggressive about adding patent departments since there's so much money to be made and they want to get in on the action. Patent attorneys are not limited to practicing in law firms, since many attorneys find great jobs and great pay in business and industry. For those who like to travel or work overseas, patent attorneys can find exciting jobs in many countries by joining multinational companies.

The Future is Bright and Rosy

The patent profession has always been a financially rewarding field but recent years have produced even greater opportunity and the future looks just as promising. There are several reasons for this growth. First, technology that didn't exist a few years ago has added considerably to overall patent application filings in computer hardware, software, and biotechnology. Second, patent applications filed by foreign entities have grown exponentially in the past two decades. Foreign applications now account for about half the total filings in the U.S. with Japan contributing 25% of the U.S. total. These foreign companies seek out American representation. Third, U.S. businesses have become far more aggressive in protecting their intellectual property and view patent protection as tantamount to protecting their business from competition. The courts have also become far "friendlier" to patents than in past years when there was greater anti-monopoly / pro-competition sentiment and patents were easier to challenge or overthrow. Finally, with much of U.S. manufacturing taking place overseas, businesses are far more vulnerable to getting ripped off by cheap foreign copies. When the copies are marketed here, patent protection allows U.S. businesses to sue the infringing foreign companies in U.S. courts in front of friendly juries.

It Began with the U.S. Constitution

With extraordinary insight, the framers of the Constitution recognized the importance of including laws to encourage technology and innovation in the newly formed United States. The Constitution gives Congress the power to enact laws relating to patents, in Article I, section 8, which reads "Congress shall have power . . . to promote the progress of science and useful arts, by securing for limited times to authors and inventors the exclusive right to their respective writings and discoveries." Under this Constitutional power, Congress has enacted various patent laws. The first patent law was enacted in 1790. The law presently in effect is a general revision which was enacted July 19, 1952, and which came into effect January 1, 1953. It is codified in Title 35, United States Code. Patent law specifies the subject matter for which a patent may be obtained and the conditions for patentability. The law establishes the Patent and Trademark Office to administer the law relating to the granting of patents, and contains various other provisions relating to patents.

The Function of the Patent and Trademark Office

The Patent and Trademark Office (PTO for short) is an agency of the U.S. Department of Commerce. The role of the PTO is to grant patents for the protection of inventions and to register trademarks. It also advises and assists the bureaus and offices of the Department of Commerce and other agencies of the Government in matters involving "intellectual property" such as patents and trademarks. Through the preservation, classification, and dissemination of patent information, the Office aids and encourages innovation and the scientific and technical advancement of the nation.

In discharging its patent related duties, the Patent and Trademark Office examines applications and grants patents on inventions when applicants are entitled to them; it publishes and disseminates patent information, records assignments of patents, maintains search files of U.S. and foreign patents, and maintains a search room for public use in examining issued patents and records. It supplies copies of patents and official records to the public. Similar functions are performed relating to trademarks.

Introduction

Know the Difference Between
Patents, Trademarks, and Copyrights

Patents, trademarks, and copyrights are often confused. Although there may be some similarities among these kinds of intellectual property protection, they serve different purposes.

A patent for an invention is the grant of a property right to the inventor, issued by the Patent and Trademark Office. The term of a new patent is 20 years from the date on which the application for the patent was filed in the United States or, in special cases, from the date an earlier related application was filed, subject to the payment of maintenance fees. US patent grants are effective only within the United States, US territories, and US possessions. If you want protection in other countries you must file an application in those countries under their rules of practice.

The right conferred by the patent grant is, in the language of the statute and of the grant itself, "the right to exclude others from making, using, offering for sale, or selling" the invention in the United States or "importing" the invention into the United States. What is granted is not the right to make, use, offer for sale, sell or import, but the right to exclude others from making, using, offering for sale, selling or importing the invention.

A trademark is a word, name, symbol or device which is used in trade with goods to indicate the source of the goods and to distinguish them from the goods of others. A servicemark is the same as a trademark except that it identifies and distinguishes the source of a service rather than a product. The terms "trademark" and "mark" are commonly used to refer to both trademarks and servicemarks.

Trademark rights may be used to prevent others from using a confusingly similar mark, but not to prevent others from making the same goods or from selling the same goods or services under a clearly different mark. Trademarks which are used in interstate or foreign commerce may be registered with the Patent and Trademark Office.

A copyright is a form of protection provided to the authors of "original works of authorship" including literary, dramatic, musical, artistic, and certain other intellectual works, both published and unpublished. The 1976 Copyright Act generally gives the owner of copyright the exclusive right to reproduce the copyrighted work, to prepare derivative works, to distribute copies or audio of the copyrighted work, to perform the copyrighted work publicly, or to display the copyrighted work publicly. The copyright protects the form of expression rather than the subject matter of the writing. For example, a description of a machine could be copyrighted, but this would only prevent others from copying the description; it would not prevent others from writing a description of their own or from making and using the machine. Copyrights are registered by the Copyright Office of the Library of Congress.

Ideas are Not Patentable

In the language of the statute, any person who "invents or discovers any new and useful process, machine, manufacture, or composition of matter, or any new and useful improvement thereof, may obtain a patent," subject to the conditions and requirements of the law. The word "process" is defined by law as a process, act or method, and primarily includes industrial or technical processes. The term "machine" used in the statute needs no explanation. The term "manufacture" refers to articles which are made, and includes all manufactured articles. The term "composition of matter" relates to chemical compositions and may include mixtures of ingredients as well as new chemical compounds. These classes of subject matter taken together include practically everything which is made by people and the processes for making the products.

The Atomic Energy Act of 1954 excludes the patenting of inventions useful solely in the utilization of special nuclear material or atomic energy for atomic weapons.

Note that the patent law specifies that the subject matter must be "useful." The term "useful" in this connection refers to the condition that the subject matter has a useful purpose and also includes operativeness, that is, a machine which will not operate to perform the intended purpose would not be called useful, and therefore would not be granted a patent.

Interpretations of the statute by the courts have defined the limits of the field of subject matter which can be patented. Thus, it has been held that the laws of nature, physical phenomena and abstract ideas are not patentable subject matter. A patent cannot be obtained upon a mere idea or suggestion. The patent is granted upon the new machine, manufacture, etc., as has been said, and not upon the idea or suggestion of the new machine. A complete description of the actual machine or other subject matter for which a patent is sought is required.

The Importance of Nonobvious and Other Conditions for Obtaining a Patent

In order for an invention to be patentable it must be new as defined in the patent law, which provides that an invention cannot be patented if: "(a) the invention was known or used by others in this country, or patented or described in a printed publication in this or a foreign country, before the invention thereof by the applicant for patent," or "(b) the invention was patented or described in a printed publication in this or a foreign country or in public use or on sale in this country more than one year prior to the application for patent in the United States . . ."

If the invention has been described in a printed publication anywhere in the world, or if it has been in public use or on sale in this country before the date that the applicant made his/her invention, a patent cannot be obtained. If the invention has been described in a printed publication anywhere, or has been in public use or on sale in this country more than one year before the date on which an application for patent is filed in this country, a patent cannot be obtained. In this connection it is immaterial when the invention was made, or whether the printed publication or public use was by the inventor himself/herself or by someone else. If the inventor describes the invention in a printed publication or uses the invention publicly, or places it on sale, he/she must apply for a patent before one year has gone by, otherwise any right to a patent will be lost.

Even if the subject matter sought to be patented is not exactly shown by the prior art, and involves one or more differences over the most nearly similar thing already known, a patent may still be refused if the differences would be obvious. The subject matter sought to be patented must be sufficiently different from what has been used or described before that it may be said to be nonobvious to a person having ordinary skill in the area of technology related to the invention. For example, the substitution of one material for another, or changes in size, are ordinarily not patentable.

The PTO Receives over Five Million Pieces of Mail Each Year

Congress established the United States Patent and Trademark Office (PTO) to issue patents on behalf of the Government. The Patent and Trademark Office as a distinct bureau may be said to date from the year 1802 when a separate official in the Department of State who became known as "Superintendent of Patents" was placed in charge of patents. The revision of the patent laws enacted in 1836 reorganized the Patent and Trademark Office and designated the official in charge as Commissioner of Patents and Trademarks. The Patent and Trademark Office remained in the Department of State until 1849 when it was transferred to the Department of Interior. In 1925 it was transferred to the Department of Commerce where it is today.

The Patent and Trademark Office administers the patent laws as they relate to the granting of patents for inventions, and performs other duties relating to patents. It examines applications for patents to determine if the applicants are entitled to patents under the law and grants the patents when they are so entitled; it publishes issued patents and various publications concerning patents, records assignments of patents, maintains a search room for the use of the public to examine issued patents and records, supplies copies of records and other papers, and the like. Similar functions are performed with respect to the registration of trademarks. The Patent and Trademark Office has no jurisdiction over questions of infringement and the enforcement of patents, nor over matters relating to the promotion or utilization of patents or inventions.

The head of the Office is the Assistant Secretary of Commerce and Commissioner of Patents and Trademarks, and his staff includes the Deputy Assistant Secretary of Commerce and Deputy Commissioner of Patents and Trademarks, several assistant commissioners, and other officials. As head of the Office, the Commissioner superintends or performs all duties respecting the granting and issuing of patents and the registration of trademarks; exercises general supervision over the entire work of the Patent and Trademark Office; prescribes the rules, subject to the approval of the Secretary of Commerce, for the conduct of proceedings in the Patent and Trademark Office, and for recognition of attorneys and agents; decides various questions brought before him by petition as prescribed by the rules;

and performs other duties necessary and required for the administration of the Patent and Trademark Office.

Albert Einstein was a Patent Examiner

In 1902, at the age of 23, Einstein took a job as a patent examiner for the Swiss patent office in Bern. Three years later, he published three ground-breaking papers in physics.

The work of examining applications and determining whether an invention is patentable is divided among a number of examining groups, each group having jurisdiction over certain assigned fields of technology. Each group is headed by a group director and staffed by examiners. The examiners review applications for patents and determine whether patents can be granted. An appeal can be taken to the Board of Patent Appeals and Interferences from their decisions refusing to grant a patent, and a review by the Commissioner of Patents and Trademarks may be had on other matters by petition. The examiners also identify applications that claim the same invention and initiate proceedings, known as interferences, to determine who was the first inventor.

In addition to the examining groups, other offices perform various services, such as receiving and distributing mail, receiving new applications, handling sales of printed copies of patents, making copies of records, inspecting drawings, and recording assignments. At present, the Patent and Trademark Office has about 5,700 employees, of whom about half are examiners and others with technical and legal training.

Patent applications are received at the rate of over 200,000 per year. Over 6,000,000 patents have been issued.

Rules Governing Patent Attorneys and Agents

While the law allows inventors to prepare their own applications and file them in the PTO and conduct the proceedings themselves, most inventors employ the services of registered patent attorneys or patent agents. The law gives the Patent and Trademark Office the power to make rules and regulations governing conduct and the recognition of patent attorneys and agents to practice before the

PTO. Persons who are not recognized by the PTO for this practice are not permitted by law to represent inventors before the PTO. To be admitted to the register of the PTO, a person must comply with the regulations prescribed by the Office, which require a showing that the person is of good moral character and of good repute and that he/she has the legal, and scientific and technical qualifications necessary to render applicants for patents a valuable service. Some of these qualifications are demonstrated by the passing of the patent bar examination. Those admitted to the examination must have a college degree in engineering or physical science or the equivalent of such a degree.

The Patent and Trademark Office registers both attorneys at law and persons who are not attorneys at law. The former persons are referred to as "patent attorneys" and the latter persons are referred to as "patent agents." Insofar as the work of preparing an application for a patent and conducting the prosecution in the Patent and Trademark Office is concerned, patent agents are usually just as well qualified as patent attorneys, although patent agents cannot conduct patent litigation in the courts or perform various services which the local jurisdiction considers as practicing law. For example, a patent agent could not draw up a contract relating to a patent, such as an assignment or a license, if the state in which he/she resides considers drafting contracts as practicing law.

Some individuals and organizations that are not registered advertise their services in the fields of patent searching and invention marketing and development. Such individuals and organizations cannot represent inventors before the PTO since they are not subject to Patent and Trademark Office discipline. The PTO does not recommend any particular attorney or agent, or aid in the selection of an attorney or agent.

In employing a patent attorney or agent, the inventor executes a power of attorney or authorization of agent which must be filed in the Patent and Trademark Office and is usually a part of the application papers. When an attorney or agent has been appointed, the Office does not communicate with the inventor directly but conducts the correspondence with the attorney or agent since he/she is acting for the inventor thereafter although the inventor is free to contact the Patent and Trademark Office concerning the status of his/her application. The inventor may remove the attorney or agent by revoking the power of attorney or authorization of agent.

The Patent and Trademark Office has the power to disbar, or suspend from practicing before it, persons guilty of gross misconduct, etc., but this can only be done after a full hearing with the presentation of clear and convincing evidence concerning the misconduct. The Patent and Trademark Office will receive and, in appropriate cases, act upon complaints against attorneys and agents. The fees charged to inventors by patent attorneys and agents for their professional services are not subject to regulation by the Patent and Trademark Office. Definite evidence of overcharging may afford basis for Patent and Trademark Office action, but the Office rarely intervenes in disputes concerning fees.

Important Publications of the Patent and Trademark Office

The specification and accompanying drawings of all patents are published on the day they are granted and printed copies are sold to the public by the Patent and Trademark Office.

Printed copies of any patent, identified by its patent number, may be purchased from the Patent and Trademark Office. The current fee schedule is available on by accessing PTO's Web site at http://www.uspto.gov/ or by calling PTO General Information Services at 1-800-786-9199 or 703-308-4357.

Future patents classified in subclasses containing subject matter of interest may be obtained, as they issue, by prepayment of a deposit and a service charge. For the cost of such subscription service, a separate inquiry should be sent to the Patent and Trademark Office.

The Official Gazette of the United States Patent and Trademark Office is the official journal relating to patents and trademarks. It has been published weekly since January 1872 (replacing the old "Patent Office Reports"), and is now issued each Tuesday in two parts, one describing patents and the other trademarks. It contains a claim and a selected figure of the drawings of each patent granted on that day; notices of patent and trademark lawsuits; indexes of patents and patentees; list of patents available for license or sale; a list of Patent and Trademark Depository Libraries (PTDLs); and much general information such as orders, notices, changes in rules, changes in classification, etc. ***The Official Gazette*** is sold on subscription and by single copies by the Superintendent of Documents, U.S. Government Printing Office, Washington, D.C. 20402.

The illustrations and claims of the patents are arranged in ***The Official Gazette*** according to the Patent and Trademark Office classification of subject matter, permitting ready reference to patents in any particular technology. Copies of ***The Official Gazette*** are available in the PTDLs and public libraries of other cities.

Index of Patents - A two-part publication which summarizes for a given calendar year the classification and inventor/assignee information at the time of issue for utility, Design, Reissue, and Plant Patents; Reexamination Certificates, and Statutory Invention Registrations published weekly in ***Index of Patents.*** Part I, List of Patentees comprises an alphabetical listing of every patentee and assignee recorded at the time the patent document was issued. Part II, Index to Subjects of Inventions comprises a listing of all patents for the year according to U.S. Patent Classification class and subclass designation at the time the patent document was issued. It is not an index of subjects, per se. Sold by the Superintendent of Documents.

Index of Trademarks - An annual index of registrants of trademarks. Sold by the Superintendent of Documents.

Index to the U.S. Patent Classification System - An alphabetical list of approximately 65,000 common, informal headings or terms which refer to specific classes and subclasses in the ***Manual of Classification*** used to categorize patents. It is intended as a means for initial entry into the Classification System and should be especially useful for persons not familiar with the system as well as those who may not be familiar with any particular technology under study. Sold by the Superintendent of Documents.

Manual of Classification - A loose-leaf manual containing a list of all the classes and subclasses of inventions in the Patent and Trademark Office classification systems, a subject matter index, and other information relating to U.S. patent classification system. Each subclass has a short, descriptive title often arranged in a specific hierarchical order designated by dots for indentation levels. Substitute pages are issued from time to time. Annual subscription includes the basic manual and substitute pages. Sold by the Superintendent of Documents.

Classification Definitions - Gives a detailed definition for each class and official subclass included in the ***Manual of Classification.*** The definitions indicate the subject matter to be found in or excluded from a class or subclass; they limit or expand in precise manner the meaning intended for each subclass title; they serve as a guide to users of the ***Manual of Classification*** to refer to the same subclass for patents on a particular technology by eliminating, as much as possible, subjective and varying interpretations of the meanings of subclass titles. The "notes" illustrate the kinds of information that can be found in a subclass and direct the searcher to other related subclasses which may contain relevant information. Subscription service consists of a basic full set of definitions and semiannual sets of updated definitions for an indeterminate period. Sold by the Superintendent of Documents.

Title 37 Code of Federal Regulations - Includes rules of practice for Patents, Trademarks, and Copyrights. Available from the Superintendent of Documents.

Attorneys and Agents Registered to Practice Before the U.S. Patent and Trademark Office - An alphabetical and geographical listing of patent attorneys and agents registered to practice before the U.S. Patent and Trademark Office. Sold by the Superintendent of Documents.

Manual of Patent Examining Procedure (MPEP) - A looseleaf manual which serves primarily as a detailed reference work on patent examining practice and procedure for the Patent and Trademark Office's Examining Corps. Subscription service includes basic manual, periodic revisions, and change notices. Sold by the Superintendent of Documents. (The MPEP is also available in electronic form from the PTO's Office of Electronic Information and as an Internet information file.)

Guide for the Preparation of Patent Drawings - A collection of the most pertinent rules from Title 37 of the Code of Federal Regulations pertaining to patent drawings with interpretations of those rules and examples. Sold by the Superintendent of Documents.

PTO Products and Services Catalog, Information Dissemination Organizations (IDO) - This compendium describes the products and services available from the Patent and Trademark Office (PTO) and provides ordering information. Many items are available free of charge from the Information Dissemination Organizations (IDOs). The catalog lists products and services available from the three IDO offices responsible for public records; electronic products/services; general information; PTO's public search facilities in Arlington, Virginia; and the network of 80 Patent and Trademark Depository Libraries (PTDLs) in 49 states, the District of Columbia, and Puerto Rico. Included are detailed descriptions of data available on magnetic tape, diskette, or CD-ROM. A number of products can be ordered in paper form, including PTO forms and patent or trademark copies, as well as Technology Assessment and Forecast (TAF) statistical reports and research publications. Available from the PTO General Information Services at 1-800-786-9199 or 703-308-4357.

Many publications listed above, as well as other Patent and Trademark Office products and services are available electronically from IDO or on the PTO's Web site. Call General Information Services for more information at 800-786-9199 or 703-308-4357.

About the Patent Bar Exam

In order to practice before the Patent Office as a registered patent attorney or agent you must fulfill the following requirements:

Prove that you possess the legal, scientific, and technical qualifications that will enable you to provide "valuable service" to applicants for patents. The Patent Office prefers an undergraduate degree in science or engineering but two years of college level science will often be enough to meet this requirement.

(The end of this chapter includes information from the PTO General Requirements Bulletin on requirements for admission to the exam and cities around the United States where the exam is administered.)

Demonstrate that you are competent to advise and assist applicants for patents in the presentation and prosecution of their applications before the Patent Office. For almost everyone, this means passing the Patent Bar Exam. The examination may be waived for someone who has actively served for at least four years in the patent examining corps of the Patent Office.

Passing the Patent Bar Exam

The Patent Bar Examination consists of a three hour morning session and three hour afternoon session. Both sessions are required and you must answer at least 70% of the questions correctly on the entire examination in order to pass. You get one score for the examination. Each session comprises approximately 50 multiple choice questions covering the same topics in both the morning and afternoon. This is in contrast to past years when the morning session was comprised of multiple choice questions and the afternoon session was a subjective section devoted to patent claim drafting. The Exam is generally administered in November and April.

It's an Open Book Test but that Won't Help You

While the test is open book, forget about looking things up. One hundred questions in six hours translates into about 3.5 minutes per question and you will not have enough time to look for answers you don't know. Books, notes, or other written materials are permitted but past exam questions and/or answers are not permitted into the exam room. The questions are considerably longer and more involved than they were in the past. You will use most of the time to analyze the question and then find the correct answer. How difficult is the exam? Very difficult—recent pass rates have been less than 40% of examinees. You need sound preparation and that is what this book is designed for. Prepare to devote a considerable amount of time to studying for this exam. Begin studying about 4 months before the exam and plan on setting aside between 10 and 15 hours of focused study time per week. There is a major amount of information to memorize and you can't cram all this information in a few weeks. If you try to cram you will be one of the 60% who does not pass the exam.

The examination's multiple-choice questions are designed to test your knowledge of PTO rules, practices, and procedures; your understanding of claim drafting and your ability to properly analyze factual situations and properly apply the rules of the preparation and prosecution of patent applications. The examination may also include questions dealing with standards of ethical and professional conduct applicable to registered patent attorneys and agents.

You will need to study and know the patent statutes; the U.S. Patent and Trademark Office rules of practice (Parts I and 10 of Title 37 of the Code of Federal Regulations), and most importantly the procedure and policy set forth in the Manual of Patent Examining Procedure (MPEP.) The second part of this book contains an excellent and extensive review of the MPEP concentrating on topics that are usually covered on the exam. Since much of the exam focuses on the MPEP you will need to devote much of your study time on the MPEP and our review. Refer to the previous section on PUBLICATIONS for obtaining the MPEP and other important sources you'll need to study for the exam.

Detailed Admissions Requirements (From the PTO General Requirements Bulletin)

Requirements for Admission to the Examination

Unless the examination has been waived pursuant to 37 CFR ß 10.7(b), you must take the examination for registration. To be admitted to the examination for registration, you must demonstrate that you possess the scientific and technical training necessary to enable you to render applicants for patents valuable service. You bear the burden of showing that you possess the requisite scientific and technical training. This showing must satisfy one of the following categories, A, B, or C, below.

Category A. Bachelor's Degree in a Recognized Technical Subject. You will be considered to have the necessary scientific and technical training if you show that you received a Bachelor's degree in one of the following subjects from a United States college or university of recognized standing, or the equivalent to a Bachelor's degree in one of the following subjects from a foreign university:

* Biology	* Biomedical
* Biochemistry	* Ceramic
* Botany	* Chemical
* Electronics Technology	* Civil
* Engineering	* Computer
* Aeronautical	* Electrical
* Agricultural	* Electrochemical

* Engineering Physics
* Geological
* Industrial
* Mechanical
* Metallurgical
* Mining
* Nuclear
* Petroleum
* Food Technology

* General Chemistry
* Marine Technology
* Microbiology
* Molecular Biology
* Organic Chemistry
* Pharmacology
* Physics
* Textile Technology
* Computer Science*

*The computer science program for which your degree was awarded must be accredited by the Computer Science Accreditation Commission (CSAC) of the Computing Sciences Accreditation Board (CSAB) on or before the date your degree was awarded.

If you have a Bachelor's degree in one of the above identified subjects, you must furnish an original official transcript from the college or university from which you received your degree. A copy of your diploma will not be accepted. An official transcript from your college or university issued to you, as a student is acceptable provided it includes an original college or university stamp or seal.

If you have a Master's or higher level degree in one of the subject areas listed above, but do not have a Bachelor's degree in that subject, you must qualify under Category B below. Degrees such as Biological Sciences, Pharmacy, and Mechanical Technology, not listed above, must qualify under Category B.

Category B means that you have a Bachelor's Degree in another Subject. If you have a Bachelor's degree in a subject other than one of those listed in Category A, you must establish that you possess scientific and technical training equivalent to that received for a Bachelor's degree in one of the subjects listed in Category A. To establish such equivalence, you must submit a showing that you have satisfied one of the following options.

If you need to make a showing to establish your scientific and technical training, it is strongly recommended that you file your showing at least two months prior to the closing date for filing your application to afford an adequate time to present a supplemental showing which the Office of Enrollment and Discipline may require.

Option 1: 24 semester hours in physics. Only physics courses for physics majors will be accepted.

Option 2: Combination of 24 semester hours in biological sciences and either 8 semester hours of chemistry (two sequential semesters, each semester including a lab) or 8 semester hours of physics (two sequential semesters, each semester including a lab). Only biological science courses for biological science majors will be accepted and only chemistry and physics courses for chemistry, biology, or physics majors will be accepted.

Option 3: 30 semester hours in chemistry. Only chemistry courses for chemistry majors will be accepted.

Option 4: Combination of 40 semester hours of chemistry, physics, the biological sciences, or engineering. The courses relied upon must include at least 8 semester hours of chemistry (two sequential semesters, each semester including a lab) or 8 semester hours of physics (two sequential semesters, each semester including a lab). Only chemistry, biological sciences, and physics courses for majors in chemistry, physics, biology, or engineering will be accepted.

For each college or university where you took a course for which you are requesting credit under Category B, you must furnish an "official transcript."

For each course relied upon in Options 1, 2, 3, or 4 above, you must furnish an official course description which is concurrent with the year in which you took the course, and you must furnish an original official transcript from the college or university where you took the course. You must also submit copies of the catalog cover page showing the year, the page(s) describing the requirements for your major, and complete pages describing the courses you want considered. Only courses in which you received a grade of C- or better will be accepted. Please highlight the courses you want considered. To convert quarter hours into semester hours, multiply quarter hours by

2/3. Certified English translations of foreign language transcripts and course descriptions must be furnished.

Under Option 4, up to four semester hours will be accepted for courses in design engineering or drafting. Also, under Option 4, computer science courses which stress theoretical foundations, analysis, and design, and include substantial laboratory work, including software development will be accepted. Such courses include the representation and transformation of information structures, the theoretical models for such representations and transformations, courses that provide basic coverage of algorithms, data structures, software design with a laboratory, programming languages with a laboratory, and computer organization and architecture. Other acceptable courses in computer science include artificial intelligence and robotics, networking, linear circuits, logic circuits, operating systems, and software methodology and engineering.

The following typify courses which are not accepted as demonstrating the necessary scientific and technical training: science courses for non-science majors; astronomy; paleontology; anthropology; ecology; courses in public health; mathematics courses; high school level courses; one day conferences; patent law courses; continuing legal education courses, political science courses, behavioral science courses such as psychology and sociology; courses relating technology to politics or policy; courses offered by corporations to corporate employees; courses in management, business administration and operations research; courses directed to data management and management information systems; repair and maintenance courses; computer courses which are directed to business applications; courses on how to use computer software; vocational training courses; radio operator licenses; courses taken on a pass/fail basis; audited courses; home or personal independent study courses; correspondence courses; courses to develop manual, processing or fabrication skills (e.g. machine operation, wiring, soldering, etc.); economics of technology; courses in the history of science, engineering and technology; field identification of plants and/or animals; work study programs; college research or seminar courses where the course content and requirements are not set forth in the course descriptions; and courses which do not provide scientific and technical training in patentable subject matter. Also not accepted are courses that repeat, or which are substantially the same as, or are lesser included courses for which credit has already been given.

Other factors will also be considered on a case-by-case basis with respect to scientific and technical training.

The Office of Enrollment and Discipline will consider expertise in scientific and technical training which is equivalent to that of a Bachelor's degree listed in Category A. Applicants without a degree listed in Category A have the burden of establishing possession of sufficient training and expertise in science or engineering to be equivalent to that of a Bachelor's degree in a subject listed in Category A. Demonstration that training is equivalent to training received in courses accepted under Category B will help establish such equivalency. Also see Category C below. Although the Office of Enrollment and Discipline will not evaluate and award credit for military service, credit may be granted for technical courses taken pursuant to military training. The applicant has the burden of showing the semester hours credit each course relied upon would be accorded toward a degree at an accredited U.S. university or college. Applicants should consult the Guide to Evaluation of Educational Experience in the Armed Services, which is available through the American Counsel on Education, Military Evaluation Program, 1 Dupont Circle, Washington, DC 20036.

Category C refers to Practical Engineering or Scientific Experience. If you are relying on practical engineering or scientific experience or if you cannot qualify under A or B above, you may establish that you possess the required technical training by taking and passing the Fundamentals of Engineering (FE) test. The FE test is a test of engineering fundamentals.

The FE test is developed and administered by a State Board of Engineering Examiners in each State or comparable jurisdiction. The test is not administered by the U.S. Patent and Trademark Office or any other U.S. Government agency. If you desire to take the FE test, direct your inquiries to the Secretaries of the appropriate State Boards.

The exam may be taken in major cities across the United States:

* Albuquerque, NM
* Anchorage, AK
* Atlanta, GA
* Baltimore, MD
* Bangor, ME
* Boston, MA
* Chicago, IL
* Concord, NH
* Dallas, TX
* Dayton, OH
* Denver, CO
* Detroit, MI

* Ft. Snelling, MN
* Hartford, CT
* Honolulu, HI
* Houston, TX
* Indianapolis, IN
* Kansas City, MO
* Los Angeles, CA
* Memphis, TN
* New Orleans, LA
* New York, NY
* Oklahoma City, OK
* Orlando, FL
* Philadelphia, PA

* Phoenix, AZ
* Pittsburgh, PA
* Raleigh, NC
* Salt Lake City, UT
* San Antonio, TX
* San Francisco, CA
* San Jose, CA
* San Juan, PR
* Seattle, WA
* St. Louis, MO
* Syracuse, NY
* Washington, DC

The Best Test Preparation and Review Course

PATENT
BAR
EXAM

MPEP Review

The chapter titles in this review correspond to the actual chapter designations in the MPEP.

MPEP Review - Chapter 100
Secrecy, Access, National Security and Foreign Filing

Access (MPEP 101, 103)

1. ***Who can see issued patents?***

   - Everyone can see issued patents (no fee, copying charge only)

   - Everyone can see re-issued and re-examined patents (no fee, copying charge only)

2. ***Who can see pending or abandoned patents? (MPEP 104)***

   - These patents are held in confidence

   - Any inventor can see the patent unless assignee has requested otherwise in writing

   - Any inventor who was named but did not sign (Rule 1.47(a), Rule 1.48(b))

   - Any assignee (entire or partial interest)

   - A licensee of entire interest (not partial interest)

   - An attorney or Agent of Record, or anyone given written authorization from an inventor

3. **What major changes will occur relating to utility patent applications filed after December 2000?**

   - Utility Patent applications filed after this date will be published 18 months after being filed

   - Applicant can opt out of this publication provided that no foreign applications have been or are going to be filed in order to preserve trade secret nature of an invention

   - This law does apply to applications filed after December 2000, but patent applications filed before December 2000 are held in confidence

4. **When can one see an interference file?**

   - After an award of priority has been made

   - After the interference has been terminated (no fee, copying charge only)

5. **How long is the power to inspect good for?**

   - If assigned by agent, inventor, or attorney, indefinite unless otherwise stated

   - If assigned by Patent Office, limited because circumstance may change

Status (MPEP 102)

6. **What are the three types of application status?**
   - Pending
   - Abandoned
   - Issued

7. **What is necessary before the PTO will tell status of an application?**

   - Access must be obtained

   - Application must be identified by serial number and filing date

- A patent must be in the national phase of an international (PCT) application

---

8. *What is a CIP patent application?*

- It is a Continuation-In-Part patent application
- The first application must be copending and the CIP retains the earlier filing date
- The CIP contains new matter over the patent application

---

9. *What is an EPO patent application?*

- It is a European Patent Office application (an application filed in the European Patent Office)

---

10. *What is a PCT patent application?*

- It is an international patent application (Patent Cooperation Treaty)

---

11. *When will the status of any parent application be disclosed?*

- When a continuation, CIP or division qualifies to have its status disclosed

---

12. *Under what conditions can one obtain access to an abandoned application?*

- If it is referred to in a U.S. patent
- If it is referred to in a U.S. application open to the public
- If it claims the benefit of a filing date of a U.S. application open to the public
- A petition and fee are not required (copying charge only)
- Other special circumstances may require fee (1.53(d) CPA)

---

13. *How can someone get special permission to access a pending application file?*

- File petition for access

- Pay petition fee
- Give copy of petition to applicant/owner directly or through patent office

---

14. What special circumstances are acceptable when seeking access to pending applications?

- When owner is using the patent application to interfere with a competitor's business
- When the application is referred to in an issued patent
- When a patent relies upon the application for priority

---

15. What is the purpose of service (telling applicant/owner) to seek access to a patent application?

- The purpose is to give the applicant/owner a chance to protest access to whole file

---

16. When is service not required?

- When the application is incorporated in whole or part into an issued U.S. patent
- Normally a copy of the application is filed, when preserved in secrecy, but the file itself can not be obtained without service

---

17. What is the Patent Term Guarantee?

- As of the December 1999 rule changes, the Patent Office guarantees that a first action will be made within 14 months, a reply to an official action or an appeal brief within four months, and to issue within four months after the issue fee is paid

Foreign Filing Licenses (MPEP 140)

18. When is a foreign filing license required?

- Before filing an application in another country (if invention is made in the U.S.)

19. ***What are 3 ways that a person can get a foreign filing license?***

- By waiting 6 months after filing any U.S. application
- After the date shown on filing receipt indicating effective date
- By asking for one through a petition

20. ***When is a foreign filing license not required?***

- If the invention is made outside of the U.S. (even by an American)

21. ***Can a foreign filing license be obtained retroactively?***

- Yes, it can be obtained provided that illegal foreign filing occurred by mistake and without deceptive intent
- A detailed explanation must be provided to explain mistake
- It can be obtained with a large penalty fee

MPEP Review - Chapter 200
Types, Cross-Noting and Status of Application

Differences between PCT Applications and National Applications (MPEP 201)

1. *What is the difference between the treatment of national and national stage applications?*

    - Restrictions practice (Chapter 800) only applies to national applications, whereas unity of invention practice applies to national stage applications

    - There is a filing date awarded without oath or declaration with national applications

    - There is no filing date until oath or declaration is submitted and the fee is paid

2. *Can international (PCT) applications be filed for design or plant patents?*

    - No, only for utility patents

3. *What is the difference between a foreign priority application and domestic priority application?*

- The date of a prior art U.S. patent under §102(e) is its filing date

- The date of prior art for a foreign filing is not its filing date until the patent is issued

4. *Are omitted claims considered prior art under §102(e) in a U.S. filing that issues as a patent?*

- No, not under §102(e)

- Omitted claims under §102(a) will be considered prior art as of the issue date of the patent

5. *What is the difference between 35 USC §119 and 35 USC §120?*

- 35 USC §119 has to do with determining priority for foreign applications

- 35 USC §120 has to do with determining priority for domestic applications

6. *What happens if the deadline to file an application for a foreign priority application falls on a weekend or holiday?*

- The deadline is automatically extended to the first business day following the weekend or holiday

7. *When is the deadline for filing a design patent originally patented in a foreign country?*

- Six months

8. *When is the deadline for filing a utility patent originally patented in a foreign country?*

- One year

9. *Does the date that a U.S. patent becomes prior art under §102(e) move back as a result of a foreign priority?*

- No, it does not

10. *Does a filing in a foreign country that is withdrawn, abandoned, or otherwise disposed of preclude priority based upon a subsequent application filed under 35 USC §119?*

- In some cases it does not (e.g. If an application is modified in another country because of incompleteness, then the one year term for filing in the U.S. begins when the application is fully complete, not the original filing date)

11. *What must an applicant do to preserve foreign priority? (MPEP 201.14)*

- Ask that he or she be given the benefit
- File a certified copy of the original foreign application

12. *What is an EPO application?*

- European Patent Office application

13. *Can all countries be eligible for obtaining foreign priority?*

- No, a list of eligible countries is provided in MPEP 201.13

Inventorship and Rule 1.48

14. *What are the two magic phrases when dealing with correction issues?*

- "Without deceptive intent"
- "With written consent of assignee"

15. *Can inventorship be changed in issued patents? (MPEP 201.13)*

- Yes, pursuant to rules 1.48(a) and 1.48(b)

16. What does Rule 1.48(a) say?

- An error occurred, and inventorship was wrong from the beginning

17. What does Rule 1.48(b) say?

- Inventorship was initially correct, but amendment or cancellation of claims deletes the contribution of one or more inventors

18. What does Rule 1.48(c) say?

- If an application having unclaimed subject matter invented in whole or part by unnamed inventors is claimed, then an amendment of the application should be made to add the unnamed inventors

19. What must a 1.48(a) filing be accompanied by?

- A petition including statement of lack of deceptive intent (no proof req.) signed by each person being added and each person being deleted
- Oath or declaration executed by actual inventors
- The required fee
- A required written consent of assignee

20. What must a 1.48(b) filing be accompanied by?

- A petition including statement that the inventor's contribution is no longer being claimed
- The required fee

21. What must a 1.48(c) filing be accompanied by?

- A petition including statement of lack of deceptive intent (no proof req.) signed by each person being added
- An oath or declaration by the actual inventors
- The required fee
- A written consent by the assignee

22. ***What do Rules 1.48(d) and 1.48(e) state?***

    - Errors of inventorship in provisional applications

    - In 1.48(d), inventors can be added

    - In 1.48(e), inventors can be deleted in provisional applications

23. ***Is a new oath or declaration required when correcting inventorship in a provisional application?***

    - No, because oaths or declarations are not filed in provisional applications

24. ***What documents in patent applications determine inventorship?***

    - The oath or declaration in a non-provisional application, and by inventors listed on the cover sheet in a provisional application

25. ***What does the patent office recommend when at least one named inventor is correct? (MPEP 201.13)***

    - File a continuing application under Rule 1.53(b)

26. ***In which three 1.48 rules is no new oath or declaration required?***

    - Rule 1.48(b), 1.48(d), 1.48(e)

Provisional Applications

27. ***What happens if the 1 year due date to replace a Provisional Application falls on Saturday, Sunday, or a holiday?***

    - The due date is the first working day after the holiday or weekend

28. *Are IDS's permitted in provisional applications?*

- No, they are not

29. *Can non-provisional applications be converted to provisional applications?*

- Yes, they can within the first year of filing

30. *What is necessary in Provisional Applications? (MPEP 201.04(b))*

- A specification satisfying first paragraph of §112
- A necessary drawing
- A fee is required
- No oath or declaration is required

31. *Can an application replacing a provisional application be filed by Express Mail on Saturday, Sunday, or a Holiday?*

- Yes, provided your post office will accept it
- As of the December 1999 rule change, you can also wait to file first day after the holiday

32. *What does a complete provisional application comprise of? (MPEP 201.04(b))*

- A cover sheet identifying the application as a provisional application
- It comprises of the name of inventor, residence of each inventor, title of invention, name and registration number of the agent or attorney, the docket number of the filer, and correspondence address
- A specification as prescribed by 35 USC §112
- A drawing when necessary to understand invention
- A required filing fee

33. What happens if the cover sheet is missing or incomplete or the filing fee is not paid in a provisional application?

- A Notice of Missing Parts is sent
- Two months are given to complete filing or else it is abandoned

34. What is an application without a proper cover sheet identifying it as a provisional application treated as?

- It is treated as a non-provisional application

35. Does the time that the provisional application is pending count against the twenty year from effective filing date term of a U.S. Patent?

- No, it does not
- The term "parent" is not used to describe a provisional application, but solely in conjunction with 35 USC 120 domestic priority

36. Can a provisional application be filed for a utility patent? For a design patent? Plant patent?

- A professional application can be filed only for a utility patent

37. What are seven things you cannot do for Provisional Applications

- Claims
- Oaths/declarations
- Examination or amendment
- Weekend/holiday extension
- Design applications
- Claim for priority
- IDS statements

Applications after Initial and Continuation

38. *Is a substitute application a copending application?*

- No, a substitute application is an entirely new application

---

39. *What are four types of applications made after the initial?*

- Continuation
- Continuation-In-part
- Substitute
- Divisional

---

40. *What is a Continuation?*

- Second, third, etc. application by the same applicant for the same invention
- Typically filed to restart prosecution after a Final Rejection rather than appeal
- Fresh papers with new oath (1.53(b))
- Based on parent application using same file (1.53(d))
- Filed before parent application becomes abandoned

---

41. *What is a Continuation in Part?*

- Repeats some substantial portion of all of the earlier applications
- Adds new matter
- Can be filed only with fresh set of papers with new oath (1.53(b))
- Filed before parent application becomes abandoned

---

42. *What is a Substitute application?*

- Same disclosure as an earlier application
- Not copending with other application

43. ***What is Divisional application?***

- It can be filed for a distinct or independent invention carved out of a pending application and claiming only subject matter disclosed in the earlier parent invention

44. ***What is a CPA?***

- This is a Continued Prosecution Application
- This is defined by Rule 1.53(d)
- This has same serial number as its parent and no reference to the parent is inserted into the specification

45. ***What claims are excluded from being carried over in a CPA application?***

- The election of the parent application

46. ***Can CPAs be filed for provisional applications or PCT applications?***

- They cannot be filed for provisional applications
- They can be filed for PCT applications only if they are in a national stage

MPEP Review - Chapter 300
Ownership and Assignment

Inventorship verses Ownership

1. Can inventorship be changed?

- No, inventorship is a legal determination which cannot be changed by an agreement

2. What does ownership mean?

- Ownership refers to the party who has controlling interest in a patent or a patent application
- Patents can be bought and sold like property
- Owners can be either corporations or individuals

3. Can an owner control patent prosecution and exclude the inventor from gaining access?

- Yes, but if the ownership is under dispute, court interpretation may be required to decide who is the actual owner

4. ***What does inventorship mean?***

- It is a legal definition of true inventors of a patent
- If inventorship is wrong, a patent is invalid unless correctable and corrected
- It can be excluded from participation if assigned and owner requests
- The Patent Office can determine inventorship
- It must be a person or persons; not a corporation or other entity

5. ***What is the difference between ownership and inventorship?***

- While ownership can be changed, inventorship is a legal definition
- While ownership can be a company, inventorship must only be a human being
- While ownership must be determined by courts, inventorship can be determined by Patent Office

Recording Assignments (MPEP 302)

6. ***Are you required to record assignments in the PTO?***

- No, recording is voluntary, but it does serve as proof in case of future problems

7. ***What must a document contain in order to be recordable?***

- It must be in English
- It must be identified by an application number or patent number and filing date
- It must include the name of each inventor
- A required fee
- One-sided paper only
- It must have cover sheet conveying necessary information (MPEP 302.07)

8. *Can multiple patents or applications be listed on an assignment?*

- Yes, multiple patents or applications can be listed

9. *Does a continuation require a separate application? Does a CIP require a separate application?*

- A continuation and divisional application does not require a separate application, but a CIP does require a separate application

10. *What restrictions do employees of the Patent Office have in terms of applying for or acquiring any interest in a patent?*

- Employees are forbidden during their period of employment and one year thereafter
- The only exception is when patents are inherited or bequested

11. *When can a second buyer take title to a patent over a first buyer?*

- If first buyer fails to record the assignment within three months prior to second assignment, whichever is later
- When the second buyer took it for consideration (it was not a gift or bequest)
- When the second buyer did not know of the first sale (i.e. was without notice and acted under color of title)

12. *If a granddaughter inherits a patent that is sold, but the sale is not officially recorded, does the granddaughter own the patent?*

- No, the granddaughter does not own the patent because it was given to her without consideration (as gift)

13. *Must a legal assignment be in English?*

- No, it need not be in English or be recordable to legally transfer title

14. *In the case of Joint Owners, who can carry out acts that would otherwise infringe the patent? Assume an absence of an internal agreement between the two parties.*

   • Either inventor

MPEP Review - Chapter 400
Representative of Inventor and Owner

Disclosure Requirements, Representation, Power of Attorney (MPEP 402)

1. *Who has the duty of candor and good faith to disclose information to the patent office?*

   - Everyone associated with the filing including inventor, attorney, and associated people has the duty

   - Duty does not extend to corporations

2. *What is the definition of materiality?*

   - Definition is crudely "but for"

   - For example, the examiner would not have issued the patent unless he had known the invention

   - Rule 1.56(a) describes this closer

3. *What does Rule 1.56(a) say?*

   - This rule describes materiality as information which :

     1. Establishes a *prima facie* case of nonpatentability

2. Refutes or is inconsistent with a position taken by the applicant in opposing an argument for unpatentability advanced by the Patent Office

---

4. *If prior art can be sworn back under Rule 1.131, must it be submitted if it has a prior art date before the earliest effective filing date?*

- Yes, it still must be submitted

---

5. *Who can represent themselves before the Patent Office?*

- Any Inventors
- One inventor to represent all of them
- Registered Patent Attorney or Agents in good standing
- Only individuals, not firms, can be given power of attorney

---

6. *Must a practitioner personally sign every paper filed by an agent?*

- Yes, a practitioner must personally sign except those requiring signature of applicant (very few documents)

---

7. *Can a practitioner execute a disclaimer or terminal disclaimer?*

- Yes, a practitioner can execute a disclaimer or terminal disclaimer

---

8. *Who can revoke power of attorney? (MPEP 402.05)*

- Any party may revoke the power of attorney for any reason

---

9. *When is revocation effective?*

- The date it is received by the PTO

10. ***Can less than all inventors revoke the power of attorney? If so, what is required? (MPEP 402.10)***

- Yes, but a petition giving good and sufficient reason is required
- Required fee

11. ***What is required before a patent attorney or agent revokes power of attorney?***

- Must be filed with at least thirty days remaining before the last possible date for response

12. ***If a continuation is filed, what date determines the term of the patent if issued?***

- The original filing date of the parent
- Term will be reduced

13. ***What does Rule 10.18(b) say?***

- It deals with ethical requirements

14. ***Must papers used to establish facts be signed under oath?***

- Papers which are signed by persons other than attorneys and purporting to establish facts no longer must be signed under oath or with declaration with some exceptions

15. ***Can a duly appointed agent or attorney appoint another agent or attorney to represent?***

- Yes, in such a case the patent office will communicate only with the associate attorney unless instructed to the contrary

16. ***What happens if the inventor is dead, insane or otherwise legally incapacitated? (MPEP 402)***

- The application can be made on the original applicant's behalf

17. *Unless a power remains given by a co-inventor, must a new power be obtained?*

   • Yes, in case of death a new power must be obtained

18. *Will a Notice of Allowance be granted even if a death occurs?*

   • Yes, a Notice of Allowance will still be granted

19. *When an inventor is unavailable or refuses to sign, can an oath or declaration be signed on behalf of the non-signing inventor? If so, by whom?*

   • Another inventor can sign

   • A person demonstrating proprietary interest

   • An assigned party

   • A petition and fee are required

   • It must state the last known address of inventor

   • A notice will be forwarded to the missing inventor

20. *Can a signing field be left blank by one of the inventors? (MPEP 409.03)*

   • Yes, in this case, the application will be treated as having been completed by the other inventors on behalf of the non-signing inventor

21. *Can the Assignee revoke power of attorney? What other rights do Assignees have? (37 CFR 3.73)*

   • Yes, they can revoke the power of attorney

   • They must establish title or refer to a recorded assignment

   • They can exclude inventors from access to file

MPEP Review - Chapter 500

Receipt and Handling of Mail and Papers

Filing Date, Certificate of Mailing and Dates Acknowledged by PTO

1. *What date are papers treated as being acknowledged by the PTO?*

   - The date on which they are received at the PTO

---

2. *Name four kinds of papers that cannot be filed via facsimile? (MPEP 502.01, 502.02)*

   - Any certified document
   - Drawings
   - Request for reexamination
   - International application

---

3. *What happens if you use a Certificate of Mailing or a Certificate of Transmission*

   - The filing date is based on the time sent, rather than received

4. Can the Certificate of Transmission procedure be used for CPA applications?

- No, it cannot be used for CPA Applications

5. Can an application be returned to an applicant after receiving a filing date?

- No, an application cannot be returned after filing, but it can be abandoned

6. What is not required before receiving a filing date? (MPEP 503)

- An oath or declaration
- A fee
- It need not be in English
- A transaction can be filed late

7. What is required before a filing date is issued?

- Specification
- One or more claims
- Drawings are required to understand specification

8. When is a filing receipt issued? What does it tell the applicant?

- It is received when the application is complete
- It tells the applicant whether or not a foreign filing license is granted

9. What happens when an application is incomplete? What is it treated as? (MPEP 506)

- It becomes abandoned unless the Notice of Missing Parts is addressed
- It is treated as a provisional application
- Generally, you will receive a two month extendable Notice of Missing Parts

10. Does a patent application need to be in English?

- No, a patent application need not be in English to receive a filing date

- A translation and the fee can be submitted later

Things that do not Require Paying a Fee, Procedures of Fee Collection

11. What 11 things do not require paying a fee? (MPEP 509)

- Protest filing

- Petition to make special

- Access for abandoned patents

- Timely response to Official Action

- Timely filing of an IDS

- Requesting an Interview

- Certificate of Correction for PTO mistake

- Supplemental Declaration/Supplemental Amendment

- Petition requesting withdrawal of abandonment decision

- Response to Examiner's Reasons for Allowance

- Citation of Prior Art under 35 U.S.C. 301

12. What happens if there are insufficient funds in a deposit account? (MPEP 509.01)

- A stiff surcharge will be applied

- Additional extensions of time may be required

13. What is the methodology for calculating the filing fee? (MPEP 608.01)

- Basic fee in amount of $B

- Independent claim in excess of 3 ($I per excess claim)

- Independent or dependant claims in excess of twenty, $E

- Surcharge of $M for any multiple dependant claims

- Surcharge for late filing of oath, declaration, or filing fee

Fees Reduced for Small Entities and Discount Requirements

14. ***What are some common fees that are not reduced for small entities? (MPEP 509.02)***

- Petition and processing fees EXCEPT revival
- Document duplication fees (paper copying,etc)
- Certificate of Correction
- Reexamination request fee
- Miscellaneous fees and charges
- PCT Application fees (international application fees)

---

15. ***Do small entities get a discount on fees? If so, how much?***

- Small entities get half off

---

16. ***Who can obtain small entity status?***

- Independent inventor, who has not assigned, granted, conveyed or licensed, and is not under obligation to do so
- Small business as defined by Small Business Administration (less than 500 employees)
- Non-profit organizations

---

17. ***Who can/cannot sign a Statement declaring small entity status?***

- The owner or officer can sign
- An attorney cannot sign

---

18. ***If you are a small business, do you still get a discount if you license to the federal government or one of its agencies?***

- Yes, and there is no discount to large corporations other than government

19. *For how long can refunds be obtained on filing fees by small businesses?*

    • For up to an unextendable 2 months after a full fee is paid

20. *Are fees due retroactively if status changes during prosecution?*

    • No, future payments are calculated under the new status

21. *Is a new statement declaring small entity status required for continuing applications?*

    • No, it is not required for continuing applications
    • The payment of a fee as a small entity confirms statement made in parent

When Certificate of Mailing Cannot be Used (MPEP 512)

22. *What are four exceptions in which a Certificate of Mailing cannot be used?*

    • New patent applications (either Rule 1.53(b) or 1.53(d) including Continuations, CIPs, & Divisions)
    • Papers filed in an interference which are directed to be filed by hand
    • Agreements settling an interference
    • Any PCT papers

23. *When one sends something via Express Mail, is a separate Certification of Mailing required?*

    • No, the "date in" on the Express Mailing label is taken as the filing date

24. What happens if the "date in" as mailed and claimed is on a Saturday, Sunday or Holiday?

- It is still maintained as the "date in"

25. What date is used for calculating further due dates?

- The date of receipt will be used and NOT necessarily the "date in"

26. Can a facsimile be used for addressing Rule 1.53(b)

- No, it cannot be used

27. Can a facsimile be used for addressing Rule 1.53(d)

- Yes, it can be used for 1.53(d)

28. Can a Certificate of Mailing be used for any 1.53 rule?

- No, a Certificate of Mailing cannot be used for any 1.53 rule

29. When can Express Mail not be used for filing a paper? (MPEP 513)

- Express Mail can always be used for filing papers with the PTO

MPEP Review - Chapter 600

Parts, Forms and Content of Application

Oaths and Declarations

1. **What is the difference between an oath and a declaration? (MPEP 602)**

   - An oath is sworn to be true before a notary or its equivalent

   - A declaration is a statement with a warning that willful false statements are punishable by law

2. **What must an oath or declaration certify? (MPEP 603)**

   - The inventors believe that they are the first inventors

   - The inventors understand the contents of the application

   - The duty to disclose all information known to be patentable

3. **Does an oath or declaration need to be in English?**

   - No, it does not need to be in English

4. *What is a Supplemental oath or declaration? (MPEP 603)*

- It is submitted to replace an original oath or declaration that is defective

5. *Is filing a supplemental oath or declaration a matter of right, and can one be filed after allowance?*

- Yes, it is a matter of right
- It can be filed after allowance

6. *Is a brand new oath required for a continuation filing?*

- No, under Rule 1.53(b) and Rule 1.53(d)

7. *Is the order of the inventor names on a declaration of legal consequence? (MPEP 605.04(f))*

- No, but it is the order of the inventors that will be listed on the patent

8. *Can the order for shifting names on an issued patent be made?*

- Yes, but it is very rare under 37 CFR 1.183

9. *Can anyone alter an application after the declaration or oath has been executed? (MPEP 608.01, Rule 1.52 Cr)*

- No, nobody can alter an application after an oath
- Prior to execution, an inventor can alter the application by hand provided all changes are initialed by all inventors

10. *Can a patent attorney or agent sign an oath? (MPEP 506)*

- No, even if a previous oath was obtained the same day

Preliminary Amendments, Notice
of Omitted Items, Notice of Missing Parts

11. What is the advantage and what is a preliminary amendment? (MPEP 506)

- It is filed with an application, but is limited to cancellation of claims

- This is typically done to eliminate informal claims and reduce filing fees

- If it is filed on same day, but not referred to in oath, then it is not part of original disclosures

12. Does each inventor need to make a contribution to each claim?

- No, only one can claim

- Inventorship is determined claim by claim

- Inventors who are ignorant of each other and their concepts cannot be joint inventors

13. When does the PTO award a filing date from 1997 onwards after receiving Notice of Omitted Items? (MPEP 601.01)

- The original submission date of the incomplete application, unless a petition is filed and fee paid

14. What is a Notice of Missing Parts?

- It relates to an application that has received a filing date but is missing either the oath, translation, or fee

- The oath, translation, and fee can be submitted late in a patent application

- Receiving a Notice of Missing Parts is a normal occurrence because, sometimes, a patent attorney wants to preserve the inventor's place in line at the PTO, but has not yet received an executed oath, translation or fee from the inventor

14. What is a Notice of Omitted Items?

- This relates to an application missing a critical page that has been numbered

- For example, if pages 24 and 26 are missing in an application that has 30 pages, then a Notice of Omitted Items is sent

15. What is the difference between Notice of Omitted Items and Notice of Missing Parts?

- If you receive a Notice of Omitted Items this is a bad thing, versus receiving a Notice of Missing Parts which is a normal thing

16. Why is receiving a Notice of Omitted Items a bad thing?

- If you receive a Notice of Omitted Items, the filing date can change to the date the figure or page is submitted as opposed to a Notice of Missing Parts, in which there is no possibility to change filing date

- Missing a filing date can cause you to permanently lose your patent rights in some instances by moving your filing date forward

17. What two options does an applicant have upon receipt of a Notice of Omitted items?

- File a petition and fee, together with omitted items, a copy of the Notice, and a request that the later filing date be awarded

- Do nothing in response to the Notice of Omitted items, in this instance the original filing date of the incomplete application will be maintained

18. What is a patent right?

- The patent right is the right to exclude, not a right to practice

- It is the right to prevent others from making, using, selling, offering for sale, or importing

---

19. *What is a necessary distinction between a provisional and non-provisional patent application?*

- A non-provisional patent application has at least one claim

Claim Drafting Inclusions and Language (Jepson, Markush, etc.)

20. *How many words can be added and any number deleted by a simple direction to do so in non-reissue applications?*

- Five words can be added in non-reissue applications

---

21. *What word in a claim is capitalized?*

- Only the first word in a claim

---

22. *What does the preamble in a claim contain?*

- Describes things or steps and a body that sets forth the elements or steps and limitations of the claims
- A claim is divided by a colon (:) which generally describes the things or steps

---

23. *What does comprising mean?*

- Comprising means that the list of elements and limitations that follows defines the minimum for infringement and there still can be infringement if an alleged infringing thing or method has more

---

24. *What does consisting mean?*

- The list that follows defines the exact combination that must be present in order for something to be infringing
- There is no infringement if more elements are present

25. What ends every claim? What separates each "paragraph" of a claim?

- A period (.) ends every claim

- Either a semicolon (;) or comma (,) separates each paragraph

- The last step should have an "and" after the semicolon (; and)

26. What is a Means Clause as defined by the 6ᵗʰ paragraph of §112?

- The "means" elements are defined as covering the corresponding elements in the specification or its equivalent

27. What is the difference between a Method and an Apparatus?

- An apparatus claims a combination of elements
- A method claim covers a combination of steps

28. What is a Markush Group? (MPEP 2.13.05(b))

- A Markush group is used to define a claim limitation where there is no generic term to describe a group of things

29. What two phrases often define a Markush group?

- "chosen from the group consisting of"
- "chosen from the group consisting essentially of"

30. What is a Jepson Claim? (MPEP 212.9)

- A Jepson Claim has a preamble (introduction) that defines what is old, a body defining what is new, and a transition phrase such as "the improvement comprising of"

31. *What are the three Rules in allowable Multiple Dependant Claims?*

- Cannot depend on another multiple dependant claim

- Cannot depend on more than one previous claim

- Each proper multiple dependant claim counts as the number of claims on which it depends in calculating multiple dependant claims in calculating fees

Essential and Nonessential Claims

32. *An application may incorporate "essential" material by reference to what?*

- An issued U.S. patent

- A pending U.S. application

33. *What essential material cannot be incorporated from? (MPEP 608.01(p))*

- A foreign patent or application

- A publication

- A U.S. patent that incorporates by reference the material from another patent

34. *Can nonessential subject matter (background material) be incorporated from publications or foreign patents?*

- Yes

35. *When is material said to be essential?*

- If it is necessary to comply with statutory requirements of disclosure

36. *Is there a mandated form for a patent application?*

- No, there is no mandated form for a patent application

37. **The patent office recommends that a patent be divided in terms of:**

- Title
- Cross reference to related applications
- Brief summary of the invention
- Brief description of the drawings
- Detailed description
- Claims
- Abstract of the disclosure
- Oath of declaration
- Drawings

38. **What are the implications resulting from the fact that the "Abstract" is part of the application as far as §112 is concerned?**

- Material disclosed in the Abstract can be amended into the specification without violating the forbidden new matter rule

39. **Can a Substitute Specification be filed?**

- Yes, if it contains no new matter
- Additions and deletions are not underlined or bracketed in the submitted substitute

40. **Can a Substitute Specification be filed in a reissue?**

- No

41. **Can color photographs and color drawings be accepted for filing? (MPEP 608.02)**

- Yes, a required fee applies
- Three sets of each are required

IDS Filing Requirements and Techniques (MPEP 609)

42. *When must an IDS be filed?*

- Either within three months or before the first action

- If after first action, but before final action, either a statement or fee must be provided

- If after final action or allowance, but before payment of issue fee, a statement, a petition, and fee are required

43. *When must an IDS be filed in a reissue?*

- Within two months of filing

44. *What must a Statement say in filing an IDS? (Rule 1.97)*

- Each item disclosed was cited in a communication from a foreign patent office less than three months before the date of the IDS

- No item was cited in a communication from a foreign office and no item was known to anyone having a duty to disclose more than three months before the date of the IDS

45. *What are the eight things that every IDS must have*

A list of the individual items submitted with patents identified by:

- Patentee
- Number
- Issue date
- Publications by author
- Title
- Relevant pages
- Date and place of publication
- Copy of every patent, publication or other information being submitted

---

46. ***Who has a duty to file an IDS?***

- Everyone associated with a prosecution

---

47. ***Can the time for filing an IDS be extended? What happens to noncomplying IDS's?***

- No, it cannot be extended
- Noncomplying IDS's will be placed in a file, but not considered

MPEP Review - Chapter 700
Examination of Applications

Rejection Practice (MPEP 706)

1. *Can you respond to some rejections or objections and defer others for some future time?*

   - No, you cannot do this

   - Responses must be complete and address each rejection and objection

2. *What is the difference between a rejection and an objection?*

   - If the subject matter is said to be unpatentable, it is considered a rejection

   - If the form of the claim, specification, or drawing is improper, an objection is made

3. *What are usually reasons for a rejection?*

   - Anticipation (35 USC §102)

   - Obviousness (35 USC §103)

- Lack of subject matter
- Written Description, enablement and best mode (35 USC §112)
- Lack of utility (35 USC §101)

4. ***How can someone test an objection?***

- First, ask examiner for reconsideration
- Second, file a petition to the Commissioner

5. ***How can someone test a rejection?***

- First, ask examiner for reconsideration
- Second, pursue appeal to the Board of Patent Appeals and Interferences

Concept of Prior Art, §102, and §103

6. ***In an official action, what are the three things that an examiner can do to a claim?***

- Object
- Allow
- Reject

7. ***What is swearing back? (Rule 1.131)***

- It is when you claim that the invention date is before the date of reference
- It must be done on a claim by claim basis
- It is when different claims can also have different filing dates

8. ***What can someone do to overcome a rejection because of prior art?***

- Swear back
- Amend claim
- Argue claim

9. *Name seven separate circumstances under which a patent cannot be obtained under §102?*

   • Prior publication anywhere in the world

   • Prior patent anywhere in the world

   • Abandonment of invention

   • Prior sale or offer for sale in the United States

   • Prior use in the United States

   • Prior public or general knowledge in the United States

   • Prior invention in the United States

10. *How does NAFTA change definition of prior art? (MPEP 715.07(c))*

    • Since Dec 8, 1993, one has been allowed to establish earlier date to defeat prior art in Mexico or Canada

11. *How does WTO change the definition of prior art? (MPEP 715.07(c))*

    • After January 1,1996, allows one to establish earlier date to defeat prior art in European countries

    • Both WTO and NAFTA laws do not move back the date of the applicants invention was filed

12. *Can prior art be established by acts in other countries?*

    • No

13. *To which act does public knowledge, publication, patent obtained, and use by others relate to? What are the stipulations of each?*

    • This act refers to USC §102(a)

    • Public knowledge: U.S. only

    • Publication: Anywhere in the world

    • Patent obtained: Anywhere in world

    • Use by others: U.S. only

14. *If an invention made in the U.S. is not filed before someone in another country files and is awarded a patent, what happens?*

- The foreign invention is not prior art because it was patented after the U.S. invention

15. *What does §102b say?*

- It says that an invention filed more than a year ago in another country cannot ever be filed in the United States

16. *What is an another?*

- Inventors listed who are not exactly those that invented the actual work. If A,B,C invented something, and A,B are listed on the application, the application is invalid since C should also be listed

17. *Does a sale offer have to go through? Can a sale offer be private?*

- No, it does not have to go through, but it must be an offer made in the U.S.
- Yes, the sale offer can be private

18. *What is the difference between "offer for sale" verses "offers to sell rights" (MPEP 2133.03(b))*

- An offer for sale is the actual product or invention
- Offers to sell rights is a license, not a sale of product

19. *If something is invented in the U.S. more than one year ago, can the inventor file a patent?*

- No, the invention must have been made within one year

§102(a), §102(b), and §102(e) Contrasted

20. *What is the difference between §102(a) and §102(b)?*

- §102a is referenced against the invention date, while §102b is referenced against the filing date

---

21. *A patent application is filed in Italy on 2/3/87. Bill invents the same patent independently on 3/4/89 in the U.S. The Italian application is published on 3/21/89. Bill files for a patent on 1/6/90 in the U.S. The Italian patent is not yet awarded. What can Bill do?*

- Swear back that his original date of invention was 3/4/89, before the Italian idea was published

---

22. *What does §102(c) say?*

- If an invention is abandoned, it cannot be patented
- If 10 years pass, for example, an inventor cannot suddenly decide to file for patent

---

23. *What does §102(d) say? (MPEP 2153.2135.01)*

- You cannot file an application in the U.S. for a patent that you filed in another country more than a year ago when the patent was issued

---

24. *What does §102(e) say? (MPEP 2136/706.02(f))*

- If "another" makes an invention, like the first pending one, then instead of a provisional rejection before filing, a §102(e) will be issued
- The "another" may swear back to an earlier invention date in an attempt to overcome this however

---

25. *What does §102(f) say? (MPEP 2137)*

- This rule bars patenting subject matter that an applicant did not invent

26. *What is the national phase?*

- It is the stage of a PCT (international filing) that enters into the U.S.

- The date of national phase is treated as the filing date

- When U.S. patents issue, they become prior art on the date they were initially filed

27. *When given a question with lots of dates, what should you do first?*

- Read the question and make a timeline

28. *Which §102 statute relates to the invention date and which relates to the filing date?*

- §102(a) relates to the invention date, while §102(b) relates to the filing date

29. *What does §102(e) say regarding prior art?*

- U.S. patent applications become prior art when they issue as of their filing date not their issue date

30. *If you, yourself did not invent something, you are barred from patenting the subject matter under which §102 rule ?*

- §102(f)

31. *What are the three critical components of §102(g)*

- Prior invention must have been made in the U.S.

- The prior invention must not have been abandoned, suppressed, or concealed

- A partial exception is made for commonly owned inventions

32. *What is §102(g) the basis for?*

- Interference practice in the United States

---

33. *What is the §102(f) and §102(g) exception?*

- If an invention was owned by the same entity or subject to an obligation to assign to the same entity, it is not obvious under §103 if both inventions were made simultaneously

---

34. *What are three different ways that prima facie can be established?*

- Prior art must have:

  1. A suggestion in reference or prior art to modify or combine teachings

  2. A chance of success in combining teachings of the references

  3. Taught all of the claim limitations

---

35. *What are two arguments that can be made against an obviousness rejection?*

- A person skilled in the art would not see the combination suggested by the examiner as obvious

- The resulting combination is not the claimed invention

---

36. *When can new matter be added?*

- Never, a new application (CIP) must be filed if new matter is to be entered

---

37. *What constitutes patentable subject matter under §101? (MPEP 706.03(a))*

- Process or method
- Machine (defined as a collection of elements)
- Article of Manufacture
- Composition of matter

38. *Are scientific principles and mathematical discoveries patentable?*

- No, such things are not patentable

- However, methods of using such principles and devices embodying the principles are patentable

Avoidance of Abandonment, Amendment, Final Rejection Practice

39. *What can be done to avoid an application becoming abandoned in response to a Final Rejection? (MPEP 714.12)*

- A response must be filed which places the application in condition of allowance

- A Notice of Appeal is filed

- The examiner converts the action to a non-final one on his own

40. *If you file an amendment after Final Rejection, what can happen to the amendment? (MPEP 714.12)*

- It can be kept in a file, but not considered as far as further proceedings are concerned

41. *What does filing a Notice of Appeal right before the deadline for a Final Rejection accomplish? (MPEP 713.09)*

- It keeps the file open, and therefore helps to prevent abandonment

42. *When is there a right to an interview? (MPEP 713.09)*

- Anytime, except after Final Rejection

- However, interviews are generally granted after Final Rejection

43. *What kind of amendments are always permissible after Final Rejection?*

- Those canceling claims or complying with requirements as suggested by examiner

44. *Before June 8, 1995, what was different about final rejection practice?*

- It was permissible to file a transitional first response to a Final Rejection upon payment of a fee

45. *What is the difference between practice after Final Rejection and First Action?*

- If final rejection, no right to interview, amend, submit affidavits, else all permissible
- If final rejection, filing response does not end deadline unless application is allowable else first response ends deadline
- If final rejection, can file a Notice of Appeal, else cannot file appeal
- If final rejection, advisory action follows response, else next Official Action or Notice of Allowance follows

Condition to Make Special and Exceptions

46. *What is an application that is made special?*

- It is considered by the patent office as a priority, before the usual first come first serve queue

47. *What four categories have no fee in a petition to make special?*

- Illness
- Environment
- Energy
- Age

48. **What eight categories can be made special but may carry with them a fee?**

- Prospective manufacture
- Infringement
- Safer DNA
- HIV/AIDS and Cancer
- Superconductivity
- Countering Terrorism
- Biotech Applications filed by small entity
- Anything else asked for

49. **When can a petition to make special be filed?**

- Anytime during application process, even when the application is pending before the Board of Appeals

50. **When can a petition to suspend not be filed?**

- When there is an action outstanding, no matter how good the reason is

51. **What are the implications of a petition to suspend? (MPEP 309)**

- Required fee
- Maximum six month suspension

Due Date Extensions – for Cause and Automatic

52. **What are two types of due date extensions permissible under §1.136(a) and §1.136(b)**

- Automatic extensions §1.136(a)
- Extensions for cause §1.136(b)

53. ***What are the most important rules under 1.136(a), 1.136(b) concerning extending due dates?***

- Total automatic extension cannot be greater than five months

- Six month statutory time limit requirement for all responses to Official Actions cannot be extended, else: abandonment

- Extensions of time are frequently necessary to make an application copending with its continuation or division to maintain the effective filing date

54. ***Is filing an appeal brief statutory? How long can an extension be obtained?***

- Filing an appeal brief is not statutory, a five month extension can be obtained

55. ***What are six instances in which an Automatic extensions cannot be obtained?***

- Where the official action so states
- A Reply Brief (reply to Examiners Answer in an Appeal to the Board of Patent Appeals and Interferences)
- A request for oral hearing in an appeal
- Responding to a decision by the board
- Anything in an interference
- Due dates in a reexamination

56. ***Due dates cannot be extended even for cause in which instances? (Rule 1.135)***

- IDSs
- Any due date set by statute as the six month absolute deadline
- The issue fee can be paid late, but cannot be extended
- Deadline for responding to a Notice of Omitted Items
- Two month deadline to obtain a refund for a fee paid as a large entity

57. *Can the period to complete a bona fide, but incomplete reply to a non-final action be extended?*

- Yes, it can be extended with an automatic extension of time

Due Date Particulars

58. *From which date are due dates calculated?*

- Due dates are calculated from the mailing date of the PTO office, which is stamped on the action. Date of receipt by the attorney is irrelevant

59. *When must all responses to Official Actions be filed?*

- Within six months of the mailing date

60. *Does a notice to require filing of missing parts before the completion of an application constitute an official action?*

- No, and therefore there are no limits to the extension of time that apply

- The maximum this can be extended is a total of seven months (two given initially, five asked)

61. *What does the PTO normally statutorily set for extension time for a restriction requirement, Ex Parte Quayle action, and other official actions? (MPEP 710.02)*

- One month for restriction requirement

- Two months for Ex Parte Quayle action (formal action)

- Three months for most other official actions

62. *How can an automatic extension be obtained when the Patent Office sets a shorter period to respond?*

- By simply asking for an extension and paying a fee

63. ***Can automatic extensions of time be obtained retroactively?***

- Yes, extensions of time can normally be obtained retroactively.

64. ***What happens if the due date falls on Saturday, Sunday, or a Federal Holiday?***

- The due date is the next working day the Patent Office is open even though this may be more than 6 months after the mailing date

65. ***What happens when there is no such date in the month when the filing is due? (eg. Feb)***

- Then the due date is the last day of the said month

66. ***What happens if an Advisory Action is not received within the six-month window from Final Rejection?***

- If there is lateness in receiving an advisory action from the PTO after a Final Rejection, the due date is moved back to one month from receiving the advisory date

67. ***Can you ask for an extension of time to pay for an issue fee?***

- No, but you can pay the issue fee late. §1.137
- Other associated requirements such as new drawings can automatically be extended

68. ***Do small businesses pay less of an amount in filing an extension fee?***

- Extension fees can be reduced 50% if proper documentation is filed

69. ***When is the Appeal Brief due?***

- One month after proper Notice of Appeal is received by the PTO

70. *What is the last time of the day papers can be filed?*

- Papers can be filed in person, by fax, or by mail until midnight on the day due

71. *What does one month exactly mean? (MPEP 710.02(b))*

- It means not less than 30 days and, therefore, if a restriction is mailed by the PTO on 2/17/98 setting a one-month time limit, then a response on 3/19/98 is timely

72. *What is the deadline on appeals?*

- There is a two month deadline on appeals

Revival Practice (MPEP 711)

73. *Can an intentionally abandoned application be revived?*

- No, it cannot

74. *What must be filed along with a Petition to Revive application?*

- All other outstanding issues must be addressed

75. *What are the fundamental differences between unavoidable and unintentional revival practice?*

- IF unintentional, fee large else fee small
- IF unintentional, statement required else proof required

76. *How are the filings of unavoidable and unintentional revivals the same?*

- Both require proposed response and fee
- No time limit for both but require Terminal Disclaimer

77. *When is an interview a matter of right? (MPEP 713)*
    - After first filing
    - After final rejection at the discretion of the Examiner
    - Interviews after Appeal Brief are normally granted

When amendments are a matter of right

78. *Amendments after allowance are not a matter of right, and require what "4 Why's" to be answered? (MPEP 714.16)*
    - Why is the amendment needed
    - Why no new search or consideration is required
    - Why any amendment or new claims are patentable
    - Why the amendments were not presented earlier

79. *What is a preliminary amendment?*
    - One made after or the time of filing, but before an action is issued

80. *What can be done to change the words in claims?*
    - Cancel the claim, and start with the next unused number
    - Amend existing claims by <u>underlining</u> added words, and bracketing deleted ones []

81. *When can a simpler amendment be made?*
    - When five or fewer words are being added and any number deleted, the change can be made by a simple direction to do so

82. *Swearing back (§1.131) can be used for §102(a) and §102(e) by showing of what?*
    - Date of actual reduction to practice
    - Conception and diligence from the critical date to filing date

83. *What are secondary considerations under §1.132?*

- Submit facts to rebut a prima facie showing of obviousness

84. *What are two ways that a 3rd party can challenge whether a pending application should issue?*

- Protest and a Public Use Proceeding (show that the invention was on sale or in public use and therefore prior art)

MPEP Review - Chapter 800

Restriction in Applications Filed under 35 USC 111: Double Patenting

Independent and Distinct Claims and Other Claim Restrictions (MPEP 803)

1. *Can a nonelected invention be pursued in a divisional application?*

    • Yes, it can

2. *What cannot be rejected on the basis of Double Patenting?*

    • Divisional applications filed as a result of a nonelected invention

3. *When will the examiner request the application to select one species for search? (MPEP 806.04(b))*

    • When the application has a generic (broad) claim and other claims to each one of more than one species

4. *What happens if the broad concepts of the generic claim are allowed?*

- Then, claims covering a reasonable number of the species will automatically be allowed as well

5. *What happens when only one species is allowed?*

- Nonelected claims must be pursued on divisional applications

6. *What are linking claims?*

- These are claims which belong in one or more inventions or species

7. *Under what two circumstances will an application be properly restricted?*

- When the inventions are able to support separate patents
- When the inventions are independent or distinct

8. *What does independent mean?*

- Two subjects are unconnected in design, operation, or effect

9. *What does distinct mean?*

- It means two things which are capable of separate manufacture, use, or sale as claimed AND are patentable over each other

10. *What applications can avoid a restriction requirement? (MPEP 803.03(b))*

- Those applications which were pending at least 3 years as of June 8, 1995
- Fee required and parent application cannot have restriction requirement prior to April 8, 1995

- This can happen provided that Applicant has not caused restriction on his/her own actions

---

11. **What does the MPEP say a generic claim is?**

- One which includes no material limitation in addition to those recited in the species and "must comprehend within the confines of the organizations covered in each of the species"

Restriction Practice, Apparatus vs. Process

12. **What happens if one species is an intermediate product, useful only to make the final product?**

- The species are not distinct
- Restriction of species is not proper in such an instance

---

13. **If a gear is defined as a subcombination to a car and bicycle, is it a generic claim?**

- No, such a subcombination is not a generic claim

---

14. **In order to restrict between a combination and a subcombination, what two kinds of distinctiveness must be shown? (MPEP 806.04(c))**

- The combination does not require the particulars of the subcombination
- The subcombination can be shown to have utility by itself

---

15. **When can a process and apparatus be shown to be distinct?**

- The process as claimed can be practiced on another apparatus
- The apparatus can be used to practice a materially different process

16. When can an apparatus and process be shown to be distinct? (MPEP 806.05)

- The apparatus is not the obvious apparatus for making the product and can be used to make other products
- The product claimed can be made by another materially different apparatus

Traversed Claim Practice

17. Is an election required even if a restriction is traversed (wrong and objected)?

- Yes, an election is still required

18. When is the term "traverse" used? (MPEP 818)

- In connection with trying to get the examiner to change or withdraw a restriction requirement
- Not used in connection with responding to official actions

19. What must a traverse include?

- It must set forth all objections
- Simply stating that the examiner is wrong and the restriction is traversed is not sufficient

20. What does filing a traverse preserve?

- The right to petition after the examiner restricts the restriction requirement

21. What 1.53 subsection rule cannot be filed if the parent is not being abandoned?

- 1.53(d) cannot be filed (CPA)
- 1.53(b) can be filed even if parent is not being abandoned (Continuation, CIP, divisional)

Double Patenting Rejections and Terminal Disclaimers

22. *In the absence of a restriction requirement, can the Examiner reject the claims filed in a voluntary divisional application on the basis of double patenting? (MPEP 804)*

- Yes

- There is no protection against this if there is not a restriction requirement

23. *When can two species be allowed?*

- If after the Examiner allows the generic parent claim after search, then two species will be allowed

24. *Can method claims, which were not filed initially, be introduced?*

- No, a continuation or divisional must be filed to introduce the new method claims, since a restriction can only apply if the methods were mentioned initially

25. *If inventors are not the same but the patent or application has the same owners, is a double patenting rejection allowable?*

- Yes, it is

26. *What is the difference between double patenting rejections of obviousness and same invention type?*

- Same invention type rejections cannot be overcome

- Claims being cited are exactly in scope to an existing patent

- Obviousness type rejections can be overcome by filing a terminal disclaimer

27. ***What does a terminal disclaimer give up?***

- Part of the patent grant which extends beyond the expiration date of the other patent application

28. ***Is a double patenting rejection of the obviousness type allowable if the second application of the is a division of the first and the Patent Office issued a Restriction Requirement which resulted in the division?***

- No, it is not allowable if a Restriction Requirement was placed initially

29. ***What is the difference between a provisional 102(e) and provisional double patenting?***

- If 102(e), swear back possible, else if obvious double patenting, terminal disclaimer
- If Restriction, double patenting focus, else if 102(e), nothing to do with restriction
- If 102(e) can be avoided by filing 2 applications on the same day or through CIP, else if provisional double patenting, can be avoided by restriction requirement
- If 102(e) focus on what is disclosed, else if provisional double patenting, focused on what is claimed

MPEP Review - Chapter 900
Prior Art, Classification, Search

Prior Art, Classification, Search

This chapter is not usually tested on the Patent Bar Exam. It has to do with how examiners do their job.

MPEP Review - Chapter 1000

Matters Decided by Various PTO Officials

Matters Decided by Various
Patent and Trademark Office Officials

This chapter is not usually tested on the Patent Bar Exam.

MPEP Review - Chapter 1100
Statutory Invention Registration (SIR)

SIR Practice

1. ***What is a Statutory Invention Registration?***

   - Hybrid between patent and publication
   - Considered prior art under §102(e)
   - Does not confer any rights to exclude
   - Part of an interference to defeat attempt by another to obtain patent

2. ***Who mainly uses Statutory Invention Registrations (SIRs)?***

   - Mostly used by the federal government

MPEP Review - Chapter 1200
Appeal

Appeal Practice after Final Rejection

1. **How does filing an appeal after final rejection work?**

   - Notice of Appeal filed with PTO

   - Fee paid before or after filing

2. **What is an Appeal Brief and how long do you have to file it?**

   - It is a response to an appeal and is given by the PTO

   - You have two extendable months from their receipt date of the Notice of Appeal

3. **Does the Notice of Appeal need to identify claims being appealed?**

   - No, it does not

4. **Can the Notice of Appeal not be signed?**

   - The Notice of Appeal does not need to be signed

5. How many copies of the Appeal Brief must you provide? (MPEP 1205)

- You must provide three copies

6. What must the Appeal Brief set forth? (MPEP 1206)

- Identification of party in interest
- Related appeals or interferences
- Status of the claims
- Status of all amendments
- Summary of invention
- Arguments directed to **every** rejection
- Appendix containing all claims appealed

7. What can the Examiner's Answer set forth? (MPEP 1206)

- It may no longer set forth new grounds of rejection except to claims entered after final rejection, but may reopen ex parte prosecution

8. If reinstatement or prosecution is elected by the examiner, is a second fee for the Notice of Appeal or Appeal Brief required?

- No, it is not required

9. How quickly may an oral hearing be requested?

- Within two months of the date the Examiner's Answer is sent
- Fee required
- Extendable for cause only

10. Does the six-month rule apply to appeal dates?

- No, the six month rule does not apply to appeal dates

11. *Is a Reply Brief after the Examiner's Answer a matter of right?*

- Yes, but the examiner can choose to act on it or not

Board of Appeals Procedure (MPEP 1213)

12. *What can the Board of Appeals do in its decision?*

- Affirm or reverse examiner
- Find new ground of rejection

13. *If the Board of Appeals issues its own rejection, what can the applicant do?*

- Submit an appropriate amendment of the claims so rejected
- Have matter reconsidered by the examiner

14. *If examiner again rejects the claims, the applicant can do what?*

- Appeal to the Board again
- Have new rejection reconsidered by the Board

15. *Following a decision by the Board, how long does the applicant have to request a rehearing?*

- Two months

16. *What recourse does an appellant have if dissatisfied with the decision of the Board?*

- May seek review by the Court of Appeals for the Federal Circuit or U.S. District Court

17. *Can an appellant withdraw an appeal?*

- Yes, at any time
- Unless there are claims allowed, such withdrawal results in abandonment of the application

18. *When can a rejection be appealed?*

- When it is a final rejection or has been given twice

19. *Must a request for oral argument be filed in writing? Is a fee required?*

- Yes, it must be filed in writing and a fee is required

20. *Does a request for a rehearing require a fee?*

- No, a request for rehearing does not require a fee

21. *Does filing an Appeal to the CAFC (federal court) require a fee?*

- Yes, this requires a fee

22. *Does filing a Reply Brief require a fee?*

- No, filing a Reply Brief does not require a fee

23. *When the board makes a new ground for rejection, who reviews the response?*

- The appellant may ask either the Examiner or Board to review the response

Allowance and Issue

Payment of Fees after Notice of Allowance and Issue Requirements (MPEP 1306)

1. *How long do you have after receiving the Notice of Allowance for payment of the issue fee? Can this time window be extended?*

    - You have three months

    - No, it cannot be extended but the fee can be paid late

2. *Can filings of documents be extended after Notice of Allowance?*

    - Yes, they can be automatically extended under Rule 1.136(a)

3. *How long can issuance of a patent be deferred after Notice of Allowance?*

    - Generally for one month, absent showing of super extraordinary circumstances

4. **What are some reasons for which applications can be withdrawn from Issue?**

   - Mistake by patent office
   - Violation of the duty to disclose
   - Unpatentability of a claim
   - Interference
   - Abandonment to consider an IDS

Patent Term Extensions (MPEP 1309.01)

5. **After what magic date can patent terms be extended past the 20-year after filing limit as a result of delays because of secrecy orders, interferences, and successful appeals to the Board?**

   - June 8th, 1995

6. **How long can patents be extended because of appeals after June 8th 1995?**

   - Up to five years

7. **What two things can cause this extension window reduced?**

   - In cases when the appellant did not act with due diligence
   - The date of filing an appeal is within a three year window from the date of filing

8. **What does due diligence mean?**

   - It means "given forth an effort"

9. **What does rule 1.137 talk about?**

   - This rule discusses paying an issue fee late
   - Paying issue fee late has same procedure as that for reviving abandoned applications
   - Unavoidable or unintentional routes

10. **What is the difference between rule 1.137 and rule 1.317 (MPEP 712)**

- 1.317 comes into effect only when the amount paid is insufficient because there was a price increase when the fee was received by the PTO

MPEP Review - Chapter 1400
Correction of Patents

Reissue Patent Requirements (MPEP 1401)

1. *What happens if an inventor "changes his mind" regarding intentional abandonment?*

    -   The application cannot be reopened

---

2. *What must someone show in order to file for Reissue of an issued patent?*

    -   One must show that mistakes made in the initial patent application were either "unintentional" or "unavoidable"

    -   One must show that the mistakes in the initial patent application were made without "deceptive intent"

---

3. *What happens when a patent is requested to be Reissued?*

    -   Rights to the original patent are given up

    -   New application is treated as entirely new (all fees still apply)

    -   Written assent of all assignees is required

4. What grounds can be cited as reason for Reissue? (MPEP 1402)

- Claims are too broad or too narrow
- Disclosure contains inaccuracies
- Applicant failed to perfect a claim for priority
- Applicant failed to make proper reference to copending applications

5. Can a patent which is not enabling or which does not disclose the best mode be corrected by reissue? (MPEP 1412.02)

- No, such a patent is fatally defective

6. Can broader claims be sought in a Reissue?

- Yes, if the reissue is filed within two years of the issue date of the patent

7. What does assembling a Reissue refer to? (MPEP 1411)

- Mounting and cutting up copies of the original patent, one column per page

8. What requires fees in a Reissue? (MPEP 1415)

- Each claim in addition to the independent claims in the original patent requires a fee
- Each claim in addition to 20 and in addition to the number of claims in the original patent similarly requires a fee

9. How are referencing changes in a Reissue different than filing second amendments?

- In a second amendment, a non-reissue application will omit words that were bracketed in the first amendment and will not underline words added by underlining in a first amendment

- In a reissue, a second amendment will bracket words deleted by an earlier amendment
- A new claim added by amendment is entirely underlined

10. **Is filing an IDS required with a Reissue? (MPEP 1441)**

- No, but it is strongly encouraged

11. **How long after filing are Reissue applications examined by the PTO? (MPEP 2276)**

- Two months after publication of reissue in Official Gazette

12. **Can an examiner restrict a reissue application? (MPEP 1451)**

- No, but the examiner can request that separate patents issue where the original patents contain independent and distinctive inventions

Difference Between Reissue and Reexamination

13. **What is the difference between a Reissue and Reexamination in terms of ability to file continuations?**

- Continuation can be filed in a Reissue under rule 1.53(b) or 1.53(d)
- A Reexamination is not an application, so continuation filing does not apply

14. **What is the difference between a Reissue and Reexamination?**

- If a reissue, only patent owner can file else anyone can file
- If a reissue, any prior art considered else limited to patents and printed publications
- If a reissue, broadening claims allowed in first 2 years, else no broadening claims allowed

- If a reissue, mistakes are required, else no mistakes are required

---

15. What are intervening rights? (MPEP 2293)

- If claims are broadened, entities that were carrying out acts or planning to carry out acts that would otherwise be infringement may have the right to continue those acts

- Any prior liability for past infringement may be wiped out

---

16. What are Certificates of Correction? (MPEP 1480)

- Minor mistakes on the part of the Patent Office or applicant (typos) can be corrected by a Certificate of Correction

---

17. Can inventorship be corrected through a Certificate of Correction?

- Yes, if filing was made without deceptive intent

---

18. Can correction for failure to claim priority be filed with a Certificate of Correction?

- Yes, if filing was made without deceptive intent

---

19. What are two different kinds of Disclaimers and what is the difference? (MPEP 1490)

- Terminal Disclaimer: patent becomes invalid after certain date

- Disclaimer: gives up completely one or more claims in a patent

---

20. How can a Disclaimer be caused by the conduct of an applicant?

- If claims are made to suggest interference (copied from another patent to suggest interference)

- Failure to respond to a rejection or appeal a rejection of a claim copied for interference

---

21. *Can claims in pending applications be disclaimed?*

- No, they cannot be disclaimed, only cancelled

MPEP Review - Chapter 1500
Design Patents

Design Patent Satisfaction Requirements (MPEP 1502.01)

1. ***What rules must design patents satisfy?***

   - Must be ornamental
   - Must contain enough information to practice the invention §112
   - Must be novel §102
   - Must be unobvious §103
   - Must be acceptable for patent §101

2. ***How many claims do design patents have and what do they say?***

   - One claim only that refers to the drawing

3. ***How is the numbering system on design patents and utility patents different?***

   - Design patents begin with a "D" before the number

4. *Which type of patent requires a preamble? What does the preamble state?*

   - If utility, preamble stating the inventors name and title of the invention else not required

5. *How long do design patents last for?*

   - Design patents last 14 years from issue instead of 20 years from date of filing as with post 6/8/95 utility patents

6. *When are the maintenance fees due on design patents?*

   - There are no maintenance fees due on design patents

7. *What stipulation is different under §102(d) for design patents?*

   - Six months maximum other country patent rather than one year as in utility patents

8. *Are design patents allowed a provisional priority?*

   - No, only utility patents are allowed a provisional priority

9. *Can double patenting exist between two or more design applications? Between design applications and a utility application? (MPEP 1504.06)*

   - Yes, but double patenting rejections may be given that carry the same effect as utility applications

10. *What is necessary before photographs and color drawings are entered in design patents? (Rule 1.152)*

   - Petition
   - Required fee
   - Three sets of photographs/color drawings

MPEP Review - Chapter 1600
Plant Patents

Plant Patent Rules (MPEP 1603)

1. *All plants are patentable except?*

   - Bacteria or tuber propagated
   - Plants that are not invented or discovered in a cultivated state and asexually reproduced
   - Plants that are not obvious

2. *Can a plant reproduced by seeds be patented?*

   - No, it must be asexually reproduced initially

MPEP Review - Chapter 1700
Miscellaneous

Document Disclosure Program Particulars

1. What is the Document Disclosure Program?

- It is a document that an inventor can submit with a separate cover sheet and paper describing the invention

- The paper will be retained for two years

- It can serve as proof of the conception of the invention

- It is legally given no more weight other than proof

MPEP Review - Chapter 1800
PCT Applications

Stages of PCT Applications and Definition

1. ***What are the four main phases of an international PTO application?***

    - Step 1: Filing of the international application by the applicant, and its processing by the Receiving Office

    - Step 2: Establishment of the international search report by one of the "International Search Authorities"

    - Step 3: Publication of the international application along with the international search report

    - Step 4: Optional fourth step: Establishment of an international preliminary examination

2. ***What is a PCT application?***

    - It provides a mechanism whereby an applicant can file one application in one language called an "international application"

    - Filing will be recognized in as many member countries as the applicant elects

3. Who can file a PCT application in the U.S.?

- Any U.S. national or resident
- Application must be in English

4. What are the two main phases of a PCT application?

- Phase I: Filing of an international application "international phase"
- Phase II: Entry into local prosecution phase in PTO member country "national" phase

International Search Report Requirements

5. When is the International Search Report (Step 2) generally established?

- About 16 months from the priority date

6. When does publication of an international patent generally occur (Step 3)?

- About 18 months from the priority date

7. When must an applicant make a "demand" for the optional international preliminary examination (Step 4)?

- No later than 19 months from the priority date

Requirements to Enter National Stage (MPEP 1893)

8. What must an applicant do before entering the national phase in the U.S.?

- Pay the required national fees
- Provide translation
- Submit oath or declaration

9. *Is the due date for filing a copy with the U.S. PTO for a PCT application extendable?*

- No, it is not extendable

Oath, Translation and PCT Due Dates

10. *Can the oath and translation be submitted late in filing a PCT application in the U.S.?*

- Yes, up to one month if accompanied by appropriate fee

11. *When will most national offices examine an international application?*

- Generally, after the expiration of 20 months from the priority date.

12. *What happens if the optional international preliminary examination is demanded by the 19th month? (MPEP 1801, MPEP 1864)*

- The 20 month period for entry in the national stage is generally extended to 30 months

13. *What must all international applications contain? (MPEP 1812)*

- Request
- Specification, claim and drawing
- Abstract

14. *Can an Abstract be submitted late in a PCT filing?*

- Yes, it can
- Time limit prescribed later

15. *What must a Request contain? (MPEP 1821)*

- Title of invention
- Applicant name (inventor or owner)
- Representing agent
- Designation of at least one Contracting State

Designations and Precautionary Designations on PCT Applications

16. *Can country Designations in PCT filings be made later? (MPEP 1817.01)*

- No, they cannot

---

17. *Why would one file a Precautionary Designation?*

- Fees are less initially
- Precautionary designations cost 50% more than regular designation if activated later

---

18. *How long does an applicant have to convert a Precautionary Designation to an active one?*

- 15 months from the priority date

---

19. *What is a priority claim of a PCT? (MPEP 1828)*

- Indicates the country in which the earlier application was filed, the date on which it was filed, and the number under which it was filed
- A certified copy of the earlier (priority) application must be submitted by the applicant before 16 months from the priority date to the International Bureau or the Receiving Office
- The copy must be certified by the authority with which the earlier application was filed

Unity of Invention Requirements (MPEP 1875)

20. *What is the Unity of Invention requirement for PCT?*

- Restriction procedures for international applications

---

21. *What happens to international applications that lack unity of inventions?*

- Will be subject to additional fees

22. *Can international PCT applications be amended? (MPEP 1853)*

- Yes, they can be amended once
- Must be in language of original international application

23. *How long can one take before filing an appeal in a PCT application?*

- 16 months from the priority date or two months after the date of mailing of the search report whichever expires later

24. *What exactly must be given to the U.S. PTO before the end of the 20th month?*

- Copy of international application
- National filing fee

25. *Can a PCT application claim domestic priority from an earlier U.S. application if it is filed within 1 year of the filing date of that US application?*

- Yes, it can

26. *Can a PCT application that does not designate the U.S. be filed by an assignee?*

- Yes, an attorney or agent given Power of Attorney may file on behalf

27. *Does a PCT replace regular filings in the respective countries?*

- No, it does not

28. *Are PCT filings cheaper than filing national filings individually?*

- No, they are not
- Initially they may be, but in the end they may cost more than if countries are pursued individually

Prior Art Date of PCT, and
Content Requirements of PCT

29. *When does a PCT application become prior art under §102(e)?*

- When the fee has been paid
- When the declaration or oath of the inventor has been filed
- When the translation has been submitted

30. *How does the filing date affect the term of a U.S. patent?*

- A U.S. patent is 20 years from the filing date of the international application, not the date it enters the national phase.

31. *What are the five parts that every international application must contain?*

- At least one applicant who is a U.S. national or legal resident
- An English description (specification, claims, drawings)
- A request
- A designation of at least one country
- A priority claim

32. *Can the fee and oath be submitted late in a PCT filing?*

- Yes, they can

33. *What does an "Applicant" mean in a PCT filing?*

- It means the inventor or owner

34. *Can a priority claim be added late in a PCT filing?*

- No, it cannot be added late

35. *Do standards for Restriction apply for PCT applications?*

- No, a separate Unity of Invention rules apply

Protest

Protest Particulars (MPEP 1901)

1. ***Who can file a protest against the issuance of any application?***

    - Any member of the public can file
    - An attorney can file protest without naming his or her client

2. ***When is a protest entered into an application file?***

    - If it properly identifies the application
    - If it is submitted before Final Rejection or Allowance
    - If it is served upon the applicant

3. ***Is a fee required in a protest filing?***

    - No fee is required in a protest filing

4. ***What must a protester give to the PTO?***

- Copies of all references
- A listing of references
- Translation of non-English papers
- Concise explanation of relevance

MPEP Review - Chapter 2000
Duty of Disclosure

Duty of Disclosure and Rule 1.56(a)

1. Who has a duty of candor and good faith to disclose information to the patent office? (MPEP 2002)

- Everyone associated with the filing including inventor, attorney and any associated people

- Duty does not extend to corporations

---

2. What is the definition of materiality?

- Definition is "but for"

- For example, the PTO would not have issued the application but for noted prior art

- Rule 1.56(a) describes this closer

---

3. What does Rule 1.56(a) say?

- This rule describes materiality as information which :

    1. Establishes a <u>prima facie</u> case of nonpatentability

    2. Refutes or is inconsistent with a position taken by the applicant

3. If prior art can be sworn back under Rule 1.131, must it be submitted if it has a prior art date before the earliest effective filing date?

- Yes, it still must be submitted

MPEP Review - Chapter 2100
Patentability: Happenings at Patent Office

Living Matter, Method Claims and Patentability (MPEP 2105)

1. ***Can microorganisms be patented?***

   - Yes, microorganisms can be patented

---

2. ***If something is naturally occurring, can it be patented?***

   - No, it must be "something modified under the sun by man"

---

3. ***Must an invention have practical application?***

   - Yes, it must also be unobvious and novel

---

4. ***Can computer programs be patented? (MPEP 2106)***

   - Yes, but mere instructions cannot
   - They must either be a method that is novel, or a system that instructs a computer to perform in a particular action

5. ***Can a product be claimed by describing the process used to manufacture it? (MPEP 2113)***

- Yes, this is especially useful when filing patents for products that are hard to describe

- However, the end product must be unique

- If process or method is unique, than you need to file a patent on the method or process not the product

Prior Art and Publication Particulars (MPEP 2128.01)

6. ***Does anyone have to look at a printed publication for it to be valid?***

- No, it does not have to be proven that the document was read by anybody

7. ***What is generally accepted as the date of publication? (eg. Date at the printery)***

- The date the publication is received by a member of the public, not the printing date or mailing date

8. ***If an inventor tells you that something is prior art (admission), is it automatically considered prior art even if it is not true? (MPEP 2129)***

- Yes, because admissions by the applicant are automatically to be treated as prior art

9. ***What is the difference between constructive and actual reduction to practice?***

- Constructive reduction of practice is the date of filing at Patent Office

- Actual reduction to practice is the date it can be proven that the invention was sufficiently tested to its intended purpose

10. **If an inventor discovers a new best mode, must she file an amendment to correct filing?**

   - No, best mode only refers to best-known mode at the time of filing

   - This would be adding new matter, and new matter can never be added to a patent application and keep the earlier filing date

11. **What statute refers to an application being fatally deficient and not enabling?**

   - §112

Citation of Prior Art and Reexamination of Patents

Reexamination Requests and Components of Reexaminations

1. ***Who can request a reexamination? (MPEP 2209)***
   - Anyone including the patent owner for unexpired patents
   - Anyone including patent owner until six years after patent has expired
   - Fee required
   - Must be based on prior art in the form of either printed publications or patents

2. ***What does filing a Citation of Prior Art do? Is there a fee?***
   - It places evidence of prior art in patent file
   - A copy must be served to patent owner
   - It says that no further action is necessary unless application for reexamination
   - It says that no fee is extracted
   - Anyone can file
   - A submitter may request that his or her identity be confidential

3. **What components must a request for reexamination include? (MPEP 2214)**

- Statement pointing out every new question

- Detailed explanation and identification of every claim sought

- Copy of every publication or patent referred to

- Certification that patent owner has been served with a copy of request

- While fee can be paid later, reexamination date is the date the complete fee is received

New Questions and Extension Practice in Reexaminations (MPEP 2240)

4. **What does the patent office do when a new question is brought forth?**

- If it is a substantial new question, patent owner needs to file a statement within two months else 80% refund

5. **What can a substantial new question not be based upon?**

- It cannot be based upon prior art expressly relied upon by the examiner

- It cannot be prior art which was actually discussed

6. **Can a third party who initiates a reexamination still participate after a substantial new question is confirmed?**

- Yes, but the real party of interests must be identified

7. **What kind of extension is available in reexamination?**

- Extension for cause only, automatic extensions are not available

8. Are continuations permitted in a reexamination?

- No, a reexamination is not an application, so no continuations are permitted

- A reexamination cannot be canceled after filing

9. Can new claims be added in a reexamination?

- Yes, but not broader claims

- However, broader claims are permitted in a reissue if the reissue is filed within two years from issue

10. Can the final decision of the examiner be appealed in a reexamination?

- Yes, the final decision can be appealed by the patent owner only

11. What does filing a response in a reexamination do in terms of deadlines?

- It automatically extends the deadline by one month

12. What is the difference between an ex-party and inter-party Reexamination proceeding?

- An ex-party reexamination can be initiated anonymously by a third party, if ex-party then a third party cannot participate in any way in the prosecution

- An inter-party reexamination requires the disclosure of the real party in interest, if inter-party then patent owner has to serve any paper filed on a third party requestor, who can file comments within 30 days

13. Can a third party requestor appeal any decision favorable to the patent owner in a reexamination proceeding?

- Yes, a third party may appeal to the Board of Appeals and CAFC. (Dec. 1999 rule change)

MPEP Review - Chapter 2300
Interferences

Interference Particulars

1. ***What is interference?***

- Proceeding in PTO between two applications or an application and a patent.

- Used to determine which inventive entity is entitled to obtain claims covering an invention both seek to patent

- Never between two patents that are issued

2. ***Which party prevails during interference?***

- The party that can establish the earlier :

    1. Reduction to practice

    2. Date of conception coupled with diligence

    3. Earlier filing date, parent filing date, or foreign filing date

3. ***What is the claim being fought over called?***

- A count

4. ***What procedure does the interference have? What does it resemble?***

- Resembles a lawsuit
  1. Motions
  2. Discovery Briefs
  3. Hearing
  4. Appeal

5. ***What is one way to initiate interference?***

- One way is to initiate copy claims from a patent into an application.

- PTO emphasizes that patent and claim number must be identified in this case

MPEP Review - Chapter 2400
Biotechnology

Biotechnology

This chapter is not usually tested on the Patent Bar Exam.

Maintenance Fees

Maintenance Fee Particulars (MPEP 2504)

1. ***What schedule are maintenance fees based on?***

- They are based upon the schedule for the original utility application

2. ***When must maintenance fees be paid after issue of patents?***

- Maintenance fees must be paid 3.5, 7.5 and 11.5 years after issue in order for patents filed on or after December 12,1980 to remain in effect

3. ***Do Design and Plant patents have maintenance fees and how long is their term?***

- There are no maintenance fees for these patents
- These patents have a 14 year term

4. *Can patents whose maintenance fee is intentionally not paid be revived?*

- No, intentionally abandoned patents cannot be revived, but unavoidably abandoned patents can be revived

5. *After the six-month grace period (With surcharge), maintenance fees can be revived for how long? What are the implications that this lapse period may have? (MPEP 2540)*

- 24 months
- Someone else using the patent or offers to sell in what would otherwise be infringement is immune from prosecution during this lapse

MPEP PTO Rules
Part 10

Rule 10.18(b) and Ethics Practice

1. ***What does Rule 10.18(b) say?***

   - Signing a document and filing with PTO acknowledges that such a paper is subject to the provisions of 18 USC §1001 concerning willful false statements

   - The filing party believes that claims are true and not being filed for improper purpose

2. ***Can you divide fees with another practitioner who is not a partner or associate without full disclosure to the client? (Rule 10.48, 10.49)***

   - No, the fee must be reasonable and the division must be proportional to the services performed by each

3. ***Can an agent or attorney acquire an interest in a patent or application as part of a reasonable contingent fee?***

   - Yes, but the patent agent may not take an interest in a litigation or proceeding

4. *If someone other than the client discloses information to you, do you have a duty to maintain confidentiality? (Rule 10.59)*

   - No, but client/attorney confidentiality does apply

5. *Which Rules primarily cover ethics?*

   - Rules Part 10

6. *What can a patent agent not do that an attorney can?*

   - Litigate in federal or state courts
   - File trademark applications

7. *How must funds belonging to an agent be handled? (Rule 10.112)*

   - They must be placed in a separate bank account
   - They cannot be commingled with those funds of the attorney or agent

35 USC §102: Defines Prior Art:

Each §102 Rule Summarized

8. *What does §102 (a) say?*

   - It asks if the invention was used in the U.S.
   - It asks if it was printed anywhere or patented anywhere in the world
   - It says to always use timeline in all these patent questions

9. *What does §102 (b) say?*

   - It asks if the invention was public or patented anywhere else in the world
   - It asks if it was on sale in this country, or in public use

- It says that filing dates are always on the timeline
- It says plug in facts

---

10. What does §102 (c) say?

- Abandoned inventions cannot be patented, meaning that you can't wait for an extended period of time (such as 10 years) after you invent something to file for a patent
- §102(c) has never been tested on the patent bar, but you should still know this rule

---

11. What does §102 (d) say?

- It says that if you have an invention that you filed for patent more than a year ago in a foreign country and that patent application in a foreign country issued as a patent, it is barred from filing in the U.S. after the issue date of the foreign patent (See the two examples below)

Example 1:

- If you filed for patent in Germany on 6/23/98 and the patent issued on 10/1/99 in Germany, you cannot file for protection in the U.S. on 10/12/99
- You must have filed for protection in the U.S. before 10/1/99

Example 2:

- If you filed for patent in Germany on 6/23/98 and the patent has not yet been issued in Germany, you can file for protection in the U.S. on 10/12/99 since the German patent has not yet been issued

---

12. What does §102 (e) say?

- It explains if there is a U.S. patent that is before our date of invention
- U.S. patents are treated specials and §102(e) date is the filing date
- Compare 102(e) date with applicant's date of invention then take the first as the date of invention

• When application is filed, we have record of invention being filed, we have an invention date

---

13. What does §102 (f) say?

• Application is rejected by 102(f) if all inventors not listed

---

14. What does §102 (g) say?

• Inventor did not abandon, suppress, or conceal that idea

---

15. How many paragraphs are in §102

• Seven separate paragraphs define prior art in §102

Concept of Another, §101, §103, §112

16. What is the Concept of another?

• If application is in different name of application

---

17. What does §101 deal with?

• §101; patentable subject matter

---

18. What does §103 deal with?

• §103; obviousness of invention

---

19. What does §112 deal with?

• §112; adequacy of describing the invention

---

20. Which §102 sections mention date of invention?

• A, e, g mention date of invention which must be analyzed.
• When you deposit paperwork, the U.S. patent office assumes that your filing date is your date of invention

---

21. What does the PTO use as the Date of Invention?

- When you deposit paperwork, the U.S. patent office assumes that your filing date is your date of invention

---

22. ***Which statute deals with obviousness?***

- Obviousness is located in §103

- If there is a single piece of prior art that qualifies look under §102 and if not the concept as a whole is rendered obvious under §103

---

23. ***Can the Date of invention be moved under USC §131?***

- Date of invention must be analyzed

- When you deposit paperwork, the PTO assumes that the filing date is your date of invention

- Patent Attorney is to show that actual invention is before filing date under Affidavit §131

- Show research notes, evidence, lab notebook, notes, etc.

- Applicant is able to swear behind under 102(e)

- Examiner assumes filing date is our invention date

- Is there proof to show that your filing date is before the other person's filing date? If so, examiner will withdraw.

The Best Test Preparation and Review Course

PATENT BAR EXAM

Patent Examination I

Name _____

U. S. DEPARTMENT OF COMMERCE
UNITED STATES PATENT AND TRADEMARK OFFICE
REGISTRATION EXAMINATION
FOR PATENT ATTORNEYS AND AGENTS

APRIL 21, 1999

Morning Session (50 Points)   **Time: 3 Hours**

This session of the examination is an open book examination. You may use books, notes, or other written materials that you believe will be of help to you *except* you may not use prior registration examination questions and/or answers. Books, notes or other written materials containing prior registration examination questions and/or answers *cannot* be brought into or used in the room where this examination is being administered. If you have such materials, you must give them to the test administrator before this session of the examination begins.

All questions must be answered in SECTION I of the Answer Sheet which is provided to you by the test administrator. You must use a No. 2 pencil (or softer) lead pencil to record your answers on the Answer Sheet. Darken *completely* the circle corresponding to your answer. You must keep your mark within the circle. Erase *completely* all marks except your answer. Stray marks may be counted as answers. No points will be awarded for incorrect answers or unanswered questions. Questions answered by darkening more than one circle will be considered as being incorrectly answered.

This session of the examination consists of fifty (50) multiple choice questions, each worth one (1) point. Do not assume any additional facts not presented in the questions. When answering each question, unless otherwise stated, assume that you are a registered patent practitioner. Any reference to a practitioner is a reference to a registered patent practitioner. The most correct answer is the policy, practice, and procedure which must, shall, or should be followed in accordance with the U.S. patent statutes, the PTO rules of practice and procedure, the Manual of Patent Examining Procedure (MPEP), and the Patent Cooperation Treaty (PCT) articles and rules, unless modified by a subsequent court decision or a notice in the *Official Gazette*. There is only one most correct answer for each question. Where choices (A) through (D) are correct and choice (E) is "All of the above," the last choice (E) will be the most correct answer and the only answer which will be accepted. Where two or more choices are correct, the most correct answer is the answer which refers to each and every one of the correct choices. Where a question includes a statement with one or more blanks or ends with a colon, select the answer from the choices given to complete the statement which would make the statement *true*. Unless otherwise explicitly stated, all references to patents or applications are to be understood as being U.S. patents or regular (non-provisional) utility applications for utility inventions only, as opposed to plant or design applications for plant and design inventions. Where the terms "USPTO," "PTO," or "Office" are used in this examination, they mean the U.S. Patent and Trademark Office.

You may write anywhere on the examination booklet. However, do not remove any pages from the booklet. Only answers recorded in SECTION I of your Answer Sheet will be graded. Your combined score of both the morning and afternoon sessions must be at least 70 points to pass the registration examination.

1.   P, a registered patent practitioner, filed a reply to a first Office action which rejected all claims under 35 U.S.C. § 102(a) based on an earlier patent granted to Z. The Office Action was dated September 15, 1998 and set a three month shortened statutory period for reply. P's unsigned reply, filed February 3, 1999, did not include a petition for an extension of time and contained only the following paragraph:

> Applicant respectfully spits on the ludicrous position taken by the Examiner in rejecting all claims under 35 U.S.C. § 102(a) based on an invalid patent granted to Z. Applicant may be willing to overlook the Examiner's stupidity in making this rejection since it is possible that the Examiner was unaware that Z is a bum and a thief who stole Applicant's invention. Applicant has renumbered the claims and has attached a copy of Z's patent with notations made thereon. Applicant respectfully requests that the Examiner "WAKE UP" and take another look at Applicant's claims in light of these remarks. Please charge my deposit account number 99-1234 to cover the cost of any required fees.

P should not be surprised when the amendment is not entered because:

- (A)   The reply was not signed.
- (B)   An amendatory paper determined to contain objectionable remarks will be returned to the sender.
- (C)   P did not file a petition for an extension of time.
- (D)   (A) and (B) are correct.
- (E)   (A),(B), and (C) are correct.

2.   On August 20, 1998, you filed in the PTO a patent application which claims a new pharmaceutical compound and a method of using the pharmaceutical compound to treat obesity. On January 29, 1999, you received a restriction requirement from the examiner requiring election between the following groups of claims: group (I), directed to the product; and group (II), directed to the method of use. Which of the following statements, if any, is **not** a proper reply to the restriction requirement?

- (A)   You file a written reply provisionally electing the claims of group I, with traverse, and set forth the reasons why you believe the restriction requirement is improper.
- (B)   You file a written reply electing the claims of group I for prosecution on the merits, and an amendment canceling the method claims of group II.
- (C)   You file a written reply traversing the restriction requirement, and setting forth specific reasons why you believe the restriction requirement is improper.

(D)　You file a written reply electing the claims of group I for prosecution on the merits, without traverse of the restriction requirement.

(E)　None of the above.

3.　Which of the following statements regarding design patents are **not** true?

(A)　A design patent and a trademark may be obtained on the same subject matter.

(B)　A design patent claim for type fonts will be rejected for failure to comply with the "article of manufacture" requirement.

(C)　A computer-generated icon must be embodied in a computer screen, monitor, or other display panel to satisfy 35 U.S.C. § 171.

(D)　The claimed design is shown by solid lines in the drawing. It is not permissible to show any portion of the claimed design in broken lines.

(E)　Novelty and unobviousness of a design claim must generally be determined by a search in the pertinent design classes. It is mandatory that the search be extended to the mechanical classes encompassing inventions of the same general type.

4.　During a reexamination proceeding, the patent owner seeks to amend Claim 1 as follows:

1.(amended)　A [knife] cutting means having a handle portion and a serrated blade.

All changes in the claim are fully supported by the original patent disclosure. Should the claim, as amended, be rejected?

(A)　Yes, because the amendment broadens the scope of the claim of the patent.

(B)　No, because the claim is fully supported by the original patent disclosure.

(C)　No, because the amendment does not add new matter into the claim.

(D)　No, because the amendment narrows the scope of the patent.

(E)　Yes, because the claim has not been amended in accordance with PTO rules for amending patent claims.

5.   On February 13, 1998, practitioner Wally filed a complete nonprovisional application for patent, filing fee, and an executed oath under 37 CFR § 1.63 in the PTO identifying inventors A and B by their full names, and providing their residence, post office addresses, and citizenship. A and B have assigned their application to XYZ Corporation who Wally represents. Two weeks after the filing of the patent application, XYZ sends Wally a letter informing him that due to an oversight, a third inventor, C, should be added to the joint inventorship. Which of the following is the most proper procedure for correcting the inventorship of the patent application?

(A)   File a new oath signed by C, and file an amendment adding C as an inventor along with a statement of facts by C noting that the omission of him as an inventor was without deceptive intent and establishing when the error was discovered and how it occurred.

(B)   File a new oath signed by A, B, and C, and file an amendment adding C as an inventor along with a verified statement of facts by C noting that the omission of him as an inventor was without deceptive intent and establishing when the error was discovered and how it occurred.

(C)   File a new oath signed by A and B, and file an amendment adding C as an inventor along with the written consent of the assignee and a statement of facts verified by A and B noting that the omission of C as an inventor was without deceptive intent and establishing when the error was discovered and how it occurred along with payment of the petition fee.

(D)   File a new oath signed by A and B, and file an amendment adding C as an inventor along with the written consent of the assignee and a petition with the appropriate fee giving a verified statement of facts by A and B noting that the omission of C as an inventor was without deceptive intent and establishing when the error was discovered and whether they had reviewed and understood the contents of the specification including the claims as amended by any amendment specifically referred to in the oath or declaration and whether they had reviewed the oath or declaration prior to its execution and if so, how the error had occurred in view of such reviews.

(E)   File a new oath signed by A, B, and C, and file an amendment adding C as an inventor along with the written consent of the assignee, a petition, the appropriate fee, and a statement from C that the inventorship error occurred without deceptive intention.

6.   On January 7, 1998, your client published an article containing a complete and enabling disclosure of a new pharmaceutical compound she developed. On February 6, 1998, you prepared and filed in the PTO a provisional application for the client containing an enabling disclosure of the pharmaceutical compound disclosed in the publication. The provisional patent application was filed by depositing it directly with the United States Postal Service via "Express Mail Post Office to Addressee." On Saturday, February 6, 1999, you deposit a complete, nonprovisional U.S. patent application directly with the U.S. Postal Service via "Express Mail Post Office to Addressee." The nonprovisional application claims the new pharmaceutical compound and claims priority to the filing date of the provisional application under 35 U.S.C. § 119(e). The nonprovisional application is received in the PTO mailroom on Tuesday, February 9, 1999. The claims to the pharmaceutical compound are:

(A)   Patentable over your client's article. The effective filing date of the complete nonprovisional application is February 6, 1998.

(B)   Unpatentable. The effective filing date of the complete nonprovisional application is February 9, 1999, and thus the claims to the compound are barred by the publication of your client's article more than one year before the complete nonprovisional application's effective filing date.

(C)   Unpatentable over your client's article because the article is prior art under 35 U.S.C. § 102(a).

(D)   Patentable over your client's article. The effective filing date of the complete nonprovisional application is Monday, February 8, 1999. However, because the article was written by the inventor, the inventor can swear behind the article's publication date.

(E)   Unpatentable. The effective filing date of the complete nonprovisional application is February 9, 1999, and thus the claims to the compound are barred by the publication of your client's article more than one year before the complete application's effective filing date.

7.   A patent application claims a chemical composition and discloses in the application that the composition has a cleansing property in addition to being able to remove ink stains. The examiner rejected the claims in the application under 35 U.S.C. § 103 as being obvious over Parker in view of Cross. Each reference discloses chemical compositions which can be used to remove ink stains. The proposed combination of references includes all the limitations of the composition claimed in the application. However, neither reference shows nor suggests the cleansing property newly discovered by applicant. Does the combination of Parker and Cross support a *prima facie* case of obviousness?

    (A)   Yes, even though neither reference shows or suggests the newly discovered property of the claimed composition.

    (B)   Yes, because after reading applicant's specification, it would be obvious that both references can be combined to achieve the cleansing property claimed by applicant.

    (C)   No, unless in addition to structural similarity between the claimed and prior art compositions, the references contain a suggestion that the compositions will have the newly discovered cleansing property.

    (D)   No, because the discovery of a new property of a previously known composition imparts patentability to the known composition.

    (E)   No, because the burden of proof cannot be shifted to the applicant to show that the prior art compositions lacked the newly discovered property asserted for claimed composition unless one of the references discloses the property.

8.   An original application was prosecuted through final rejection. All of the claims in the original application were properly rejected by the examiner as being obvious over two patent references. The applicant allows the application to go abandoned without replying to the final rejection. Two years after the abandonment, the applicant files a substitute application in which all of the claims are identical to those in the original application. The examiner ____ make a final rejection in the substitute application in the first Office action on the merits _____.

    (A)   can ... provided any assignment in the original application has been applied to the substitute application

    (B)   can ... because the claims would have been properly finally rejected in the next Office action on the grounds of rejection and the same art of record in the original patent application

    (C)   can ... because the substitute application is entitled to the filing date of the original application

(D)   cannot ... because applicant is entitled to a new search and further consideration of the claims presented in the substitute application

(E)   cannot ... because the substitute application does not identify and make reference to the original application

9.   In a first Office action dated March 18, 1999, the examiner rejected Claim 1 under 35 U.S.C. § 103 and objected to Claim 2 as being dependent upon a rejected claim. The examiner stated that Claim 2 would be allowable if the subject matter of Claim 2 was rewritten in independent form to include all the limitations of Claim 1. On April 6, 1999, after consulting with your client, you filed an amendment canceling Claim 2 and incorporating the subject matter of Claim 2 into Claim 1. Two weeks later, your client has changed his mind and now desires to traverse the rejection of Claim 1 without incorporating the subject matter of Claim 2 into Claim 1. Which of the following would be the most appropriate procedure to take under the circumstances?

(A)   Advise your client that there is nothing you can do until a reply is due for the next Office action.

(B)   Immediately file a supplemental amendment traversing the rejection of Claim 1 and requesting that Claim 2 be reinstated.

(C)   Immediately file a supplemental amendment adding a claim identical to canceled Claim 2. The new claim should be underlined in its entirety with the parenthetical expression (amended) following the original claim number 2.

(D)   Immediately file a supplemental amendment adding a new Claim 3 which is identical to original Claim 2, amend Claim 1 to delete the subject matter added by the April 6, 1999, amendment, and traverse the rejection of Claim 1.

(E)   Immediately file a supplemental amendment adding a new Claim 3 which is identical to original Claim 2, adding a new Claim 4 which is identical to original Claim 1, cancel amended Claim 1, and traverse the rejection of Claim 1.

139

10. Your client informs you that he has filed an international application in the United States Receiving Office and timely elected and designated the United States. Your client now wishes you to file the necessary documents to enter the U.S. national stage prior to April 27, 1999, the 30 month deadline for entering the national stage. Which of the following actions should you take to obtain the benefit of the international filing date prior to April 27, 1999?

    (A)   File only the oath or declaration since that is all that is required for entry into the U.S. national stage.

    (B)   File a copy of the international application in the PTO if a copy has not been provided by the International Bureau, and a cover letter instructing that the U.S. national filing fee be deducted from your deposit account.

    (C)   File a request to enter the national stage with the PTO identifying the international application.

    (D)   File a paper with the PTO identifying the international application, and asking that the PTO send you a bill for the U.S. national filing fee.

    (E)   File a request that the International Bureau send all the necessary papers and the fee to the PTO, and send a new oath or declaration signed by your client.

11. Newly registered patent practitioner, Andy, is working at a large patent law firm. Supervising patent attorney, Pat, asks Andy to prepare a short memo which addresses the manner in which an issued patent may be corrected and/or amended. To fully respond to Pat's request, which of the subjects set forth below should Andy include in the following sentence: "An issued patent may be corrected by _____"

    (I)   filing for reissue
    (II)   filing a disclaimer
    (III)   filing a Continued Prosecution Application
    (IV)   filing a request for reexamination
    (V)   filing a certificate of correction

    (A)   (I), (II), (III), (IV), and (V)
    (B)   (I), (II), (III), and (V)
    (C)   (I) and (IV)
    (D)   (V) only
    (E)   (I), (II), (IV), and (V)

12.   Inventor X, a citizen of Germany, invented a new stapler in Germany on July 25, 1997. On January 22, 1998, X filed a patent application for the stapler in the German Patent Office. On January 22, 1999, you filed a complete U.S. patent application in the PTO claiming a stapler on behalf of X. The U.S. application was filed with a declaration under 37 CFR § 1.63 signed by X claiming foreign priority of the German patent application. In an Office action dated April 16, 1999, and setting a three month shortened statutory period for reply, the primary patent examiner properly rejected all the claims in the U.S. patent application as being anticipated under 35 U.S.C. § 102(a) by the disclosure in magazine articles describing how to make and use an identical stapler. The articles were published in the United States in February 1998, and in Great Britain in March 1998. Which of the following actions are in accord with proper PTO practice and procedure, and represent the most appropriate actions for overcoming the rejection?

(A)   File a petition to have the Commissioner exercise his supervisory authority and withdraw the rejection stating that the references cannot be properly used inasmuch as the declaration under 37 CFR § 1.63 makes clear that the application inventor X filed in the German Patent Office antedates the articles.

(B)   File a reply on or before July 16, 1999, which argues that the references cannot be used because the application inventor X filed in the German Patent Office antedates the articles.

(C)   On or before July 16, 1999, file a certified copy of the German application, an English translation of the German application, and point out that the references are no longer available as prior art.

(D)   File an affidavit under 37 CFR § 1.132 signed by you stating that the references cannot be used because the application which inventor X filed in the German Patent Office antedates the articles.

(E)   On or before July 16, 1999, file a certified copy of the German application, and an English translation of the German application.

13.   All of the following portions of an application can be used for interpreting the scope of the claims except the _____

(A)   description of the preferred embodiment.
(B)   abstract of the disclosure.
(C)   background of the invention.
(D)   drawings.
(E)   detailed description of the drawings.

The answer to each of Questions 14 and 15 is based upon the facts set forth in the paragraphs below. Answer each question independently of the other.

Smith discovered that a tungsten carbide insert for a metal cutting tool may be bonded (with a far superior bond strength over other known methods of attachment) to a steel tool holder. Smith filed a patent application on his invention which contained the following two claims:

> (1)   A method of bonding a carbide insert to a steel tool holder comprising the steps of providing a layer of polystick at the interface of the holder and insert, heating the holder, insert, and polystick to a temperature of 250°F. and thereafter cooling the holder, insert, and polystick at a rate of between 12 and 13°F. per hour until a temperature of 120°F. is reached.

> (2)   A carbide insert bonded to a steel holder by the method of Claim 1.

The examiner rejected Claim 1 under 35 U.S.C. § 103 as being unpatentable over a U.S. patent to Y in view of a British patent to Z. The examiner rejected Claim 2 under 35 U.S.C. § 102(b) as being anticipated by the patent to Y. The patent to Y teaches that a tungsten carbide insert is bonded to a steel tool holder by utilizing a layer of polystick at the interface of the insert and holder, but makes no mention of any particular temperatures. The patent to Z teaches that in a grinding tool, diamond chips may be "securely fastened" to a ceramic holder by applying a layer of polystick at the interface of the diamonds and holder, heating the holder, chips, and polystick to a temperature of 150°F. and thereafter "slowly" cooling the holder.

14.   Which of the following, if any, if submitted with the reply to the Office action, would most likely overcome the examiner's rejection of Claim 1?

> (A)   Evidence that a gear cutting machine which includes a carbide insert bonded to a steel tool holder by the method set forth in Claim 1 is outselling all other such machines by a two-to-one margin.
> (B)   An affidavit by Smith that, in his opinion, the patent to Y is inoperative.
> (C)   Evidence that heavy advertising resulted in increased sales of Smith's invention.
> (D)   An affidavit by Smith showing that the claimed method of bonding a carbide insert to a steel tool holder results in a bond which is 50 times greater than that of the invention disclosed in the patent to Y.
> (E)   None of the above.

15.   Which of the following, if any, if submitted with a reply to the Office action, would be most persuasive and most likely overcome the examiner's rejection of Claim 2?

(A)   Evidence that a gear cutting machine which includes a carbide insert bonded to a steel tool holder as set forth in Claim 1 is outselling all other such machines by a two-to-one margin.

(B)   An affidavit by Smith that, in his opinion, the patent to Z is inoperative.

(C)   Evidence that heavy advertising resulted in increased sales of Smith's invention.

(D)   An affidavit by Smith showing that there is a long felt need in the industry for Smith's carbide insert to a steel tool holder.

(E)   None of the above.

16.   Pete the patent practitioner is preparing a patent application for his client, Perry. The invention is disclosed in the specification as a pickle machine comprising A, B, and means C for performing a function. The specification discloses two specific embodiments for performing the function defined by means C, namely C' and C''. The specification also discloses that components D or E may be combined with A, B, and means C to form A, B, means C, and D, or to form A, B, means C and E. The specification further discloses that component G may be used with only means C', and then only if components D and E are not present.

The first three claims in the application are as follows:

1. A pickle machine comprising A, B and means C for performing a function.
2. A pickle machine as claimed in Claim 1, wherein means C is C'.
3. A pickle machine as claimed in Claim 1 or 2 further comprising D.

Which of the following would be a proper claim 4 and be supported by the specification?

(A)   A pickle machine consisting essentially of A, B, means C' for performing a function, D, and G.

(B)   A pickle machine as claimed in Claim 2, further comprising E.

(C)   A pickle machine as claimed in Claim 1, further comprising D.

(D)   A pickle machine as claimed in Claim 2 or 3, wherein means C is C'', and further comprising G.

(E)   A pickle machine as claimed in Claims 1, 2 or 3, further comprising G.

17.   You are a sole patent practitioner. You have just finished reading the opinion of the Court of Appeals for the Federal Circuit in *State Street Bank & Trust Co. v. Signature Financial Group, Inc.*, wherein the Federal Circuit held that patent claims directed to "a data processing system for managing a financial services configuration of a portfolio . . ." were directed to statutory subject matter under 35 U.S.C. § 101. Convinced that your background as a computer programmer and electrical engineer will now be more in demand as a result of the *State Street Bank* decision, you decide to place an advertisement in *PC Magazine*. Your advertisement reads as follows:

> **INVENTOR NEWSFLASH**!!! The highest patent court in the land has just ruled that computer programs can be patented. Don't miss this opportunity to make millions on your invention. To obtain a patent at a reasonable cost, call 1-888-**DO IT NOW**! Free initial consultation.

Would your advertisement violate the PTO Code of Professional Responsibility?

   (A)   Yes. Free consultations are not permitted.
   (B)   No. You have not given anything of value to *PC Magazine* for recommending your services.
   (C)   No. The PTO Code of Professional Responsibility permits advertising in magazines.
   (D)   Yes. The advertisement does not indicate that you are a registered patent agent.
   (E)   Yes. The advertisement does not include your name.

18.   Inventors Beavis and Barbara mailed their complete provisional patent application to the PTO via first class mail on Tuesday, January 13, 1998, with a certificate of mailing. The application was received in the PTO on Friday, January 16, 1998. In late December 1998, Beavis and Barbara acquired financing for their invention. Encouraged by their good fortune, Beavis and Barbara hire a patent attorney to file a patent application for them. It is Monday, January 4, 1999, and you are the patent attorney hired by Beavis and Barbara. What is the latest date that a nonprovisional patent application can be filed claiming the benefit of Beavis and Barbara's earlier filed provisional patent application?

   (A)   Saturday, January 16, 1999, via "Express Mail" date stamped as such in accordance with 37 CFR § 1.10.
   (B)   Tuesday, January 13, 1999, via "Express Mail" date stamped as such in accordance with 37 CFR § 1.10.
   (C)   Tuesday, January 13, 1999, via hand delivery to the PTO.
   (D)   Friday, January 15, 1999, via facsimile transmission.
   (E)   Friday, January 15, 1999, with a certificate of mailing.

19. Which of the following statements, if any, are *true* regarding representations to the Patent and Trademark Office under 37 CFR § 10.18 and 37 CFR § 1.4(d)(2)?

   (I) Practitioners are required to advise clients regarding the sanctions which apply for knowingly and willfully concealing a material fact in papers submitted to the PTO.

   (II) Every paper filed by a practitioner must be personally signed by the practitioner, except those required to be signed by the applicant or party.

   (III) Applicant has a duty to conduct a prior art search as a prerequisite to filing an application for patent.

   (A) I and II.
   (B) I only.
   (C) II only.
   (D) I, II, and III.
   (E) III only.

20. A parent application A was filed on September 9, 1988, and became abandoned on October 19, 1993. Application B was filed on October 21, 1993, and referred to application A as well as claimed the benefit of the filing date of application A. Application B issued as a patent on June 17, 1997. Application C was filed on October 29, 1993, and referred to application B as well as claimed the benefit of the filing date of application B. Application D was filed on December 20, 1996. Application D referred to application B and claimed the benefit of the filing date of application B. Both applications C and D were abandoned on July 22, 1998. Application E was filed on July 22, 1998 and is drawn to the same invention as claimed in applications C and D. Application E claims the benefit of the filing dates of applications A, B, C, and D, and makes reference to all preceding applications. The earliest effective filing date of application E with respect to any common subject matter in the prior applications is:

   (A) October 21, 1993
   (B) December 20, 1996
   (C) October 29, 1993
   (D) September 9, 1988
   (E) July 22, 1998

21.   Mike, an avid cyclist, has developed an invention relating to a bicycle having a "shaped handlebar" which provides improved aerodynamic properties for the bicycle. The invention is described in Mike's pending U.S. patent application. The "shaped handlebar" is disclosed as being "Y" shaped. The application as filed, however, contained only a single claim (Claim 1) to the bicycle having a "shaped handlebar". Claim 1 was properly rejected under 35 U.S.C. § 102(b) as anticipated by a U.S. patent to Lois which discloses a "V" shaped handlebar on a bicycle. Claim 1 was amended to add a bicycle wheel structure not disclosed or suggested by the Lois patent. Dependent Claims 2 and 3 were added to add further limitations to the invention. Claim 2 is dependent from Claim 1 and further defined the handlebar as being "Y" shaped. Claim 3 is also dependent from Claim 1 and further defined the handlebar as being "U" shaped. Which of the following statements is true?

(A)   Claim 3 would be unpatentable under the second paragraph of 35 U.S.C. § 112 as being indefinite.

(B)   Claim 2 would be unpatentable under the fourth paragraph of 35 U.S.C. § 112 because it does not further limit the subject matter of independent Claim 1.

(C)   Claim 3 would be unpatentable under the first paragraph of 35 U.S.C. § 112 since the description requirement is not satisfied.

(D)   Claim 2 would be unpatentable under 35 U.S.C. § 132 as being drawn to new matter.

(E)   Claims 2 and 3 would be unpatentable under 35 U.S.C. § 102(b) as being anticipated by the Lois patent.

22.   Which of the following does **not** have to be included as part of a request for reexamination of a patent filed by the patent owner?

(A)   The entire specification, claims, and drawings of the patent for which reexamination is requested in cut-up form.

(B)   Proposed amendments to the patent claims for which reexamination is requested.

(C)   A copy of every patent or printed publication relied upon as raising a substantial new question of patentability.

(D)   A statement pointing out each substantial new question of patentability based on prior patents and printed publications.

(E)   An identification of every claim for which reexamination is requested, and a detailed explanation of the pertinency and manner of applying the cited prior art to every claim for which reexamination is requested.

23.   Grish, Dersh, and you are registered practitioners and partners in a law firm. You prepared and filed in the PTO a patent application for Inahurry, your client. Inahurry has successfully marketed the claimed invention. Financial success of the invention is a real possibility. The application was filed with a combined Declaration and Power of Attorney signed by Inahurry appointing you, Grish, and Dersh as Inahurry's attorneys to prosecute the application. All of the claims in the application were rejected in the first Office action. After you filed a timely reply to the first Office action, the examiner issued a second Office action dated January 13, 1999, in which he made a final rejection of the claims, and set a three month shortened statutory period for reply. Promptly after receipt of the second Office action, you notified Inahurry of the action and possible replies. Inahurry, who is not well versed in patent practice and procedure, but who is dissatisfied with the course of prosecution with the application, sends you a letter dated April 5, 1999, discharging you, Grish, and Dersh. What are your ethical obligations as a result of Inahurry's letter?

(A)   You must file with the Commissioner by July 13, 1999, a request to withdraw signed by you on behalf of yourself, Grish, and Dersh; and take reasonable steps to avoid foreseeable prejudice to Inahurry's rights, including giving due notice to Inahurry of the request, the period for reply, the availability of extensions of time to reply and fees for the same, and delivery to Inahurry of all papers and property to which Inahurry is entitled, and refund any unearned fees.

(B)   You must obtain from the Commissioner approval to withdraw at least thirty days before the expiration of the statutory period for reply, give due notice to Inahurry of the request, and deliver to Inahurry all papers and property to which Inahurry is entitled, and refund any unearned fees.

(C)   You must continue to prosecute the application until Inahurry files a revocation of the power of attorney in the PTO and it is approved by the Commissioner.

(D)   You have an ethical obligation to talk to Inahurry and find out why he is dissatisfied with your firm and to persuade him to let your firm continue to represent him before the PTO.

(E)   You have an ethical obligation to continue to prosecute the application because Inahurry is not well versed in patent practice and procedure, and Inahurry's financial success will depend on securing a patent.

24. The first three claims in a pending patent application read as follows:

1. A widget comprising A, B, and C.
2. A widget as claimed in Claim 1, further comprising D.
3. A widget as claimed in Claims 1 or 2, further comprising E.

The application further discloses element G which can be combined with any combination of elements A, B, C, D, and E to form the widget. Which of the following claims would be a correct form for Claim 4?

(A) A widget as claimed in Claims 1, 2, and 3, further comprising G.
(B) A widget as claimed in Claim 2, further comprising D.
(C) A widget as claimed in Claim 3, further comprising D.
(D) A widget as claimed in Claims 1 or 2, further comprising G.
(E) A widget as claimed in Claims 1, 2, or 3, further comprising G.

25. Bert and Ernie are joint inventors of a widget that automatically adjusts television volume levels during commercial breaks. A nonprovisional patent application was filed on October 15, 1998, and a first Office action on the merits was mailed on January 11, 1999. A reply was filed on January 28, 1999, and a Notice of Allowance was mailed on February 26, 1999. The Issue Fee has not been paid. What is the **last day** that Bert and Ernie can file a properly drafted Information Disclosure Statement (IDS) **without** having to pay a fee and to ensure that the information submitted in the IDS would be considered by the examiner?

(A) Friday, January 15, 1999, via facsimile with a Certificate of Transmission
(B) Sunday, January 10, 1999, via facsimile with a Certificate of Transmission
(C) Thursday, January 28, 1999, via first class mail with no Certificate of Transmission
(D) Friday, January 15, 1999, via "Express Mail Post Office to Post Office" with a Certificate of Express Mailing
(E) Thursday, February 25, 1999, via facsimile with a Certificate of Transmission but without a statement that each item cited in the IDS was cited in a communication from a foreign patent office in a counterpart foreign application not more than three months prior to submission of the IDS

26.   A double patenting issue can be raised _____

        I.   between two or more pending applications.
        II.   in a reexamination proceeding.
        III.   between a pending international application
                   which has not yet entered the national stage
                   in the United States and a patent.
        IV.   between three pending applications and a patent.

(A)   I, II, III, and IV
(B)   I, III, and IV
(C)   I, II, and III
(D)   I, II, and IV
(E)   I and IV

27.   On April 3, 1997, Priscilla discovered a process for making a new composition by heating an aqueous mixture of a resin and a metal salt. Priscilla filed a patent application on July 28, 1997, which issued as a patent on January 19, 1999. The patent claims were directed only to the process for making the composition. Priscilla's patent discloses, but does not claim, the composition. On September 19, 1998, Bruce discovered that Priscilla's composition could be made by a different process comprising the steps of reacting a resin, a metal oxide, and an acid in a nitrogen atmosphere. On January 11, 1999, Bruce filed an application in the PTO which claims the composition and his method of making the composition. All work by Priscilla and Bruce was done in this country. Bruce's work is independent of and not derived from Priscilla. Bruce and Priscilla have never been employed by the same employer. The examiner rejected Bruce's composition claims over Priscilla's patent under 35 U.S.C. § 102. The rejection is:

(A)   improper because Priscilla discloses a process which is different from the process used by Bruce to make the composition.
(B)   proper because Priscilla's composition was known by others in this country before the invention thereof by Bruce.
(C)   improper because Bruce filed his application before Priscilla's patent issued.
(D)   proper because Priscilla discloses, but does not claim the composition, and has an earlier filing date than Bruce.
(E)   (B) and (D).

28.   Inventor Dan invented Y in the United States on February 5, 1998, and hired practitioner P to prepare and file a provisional application. On March 6, 1998, P filed a provisional patent application in the PTO. P received a Notice to File Missing Parts dated June 5, 1998, because the appropriate filing fee was not filed. The Notice set a period for reply which was two months from the date of the Notice. The filing fee and required surcharge were not filed in the PTO. The provisional patent application became abandoned. A Notice of Abandonment, dated August 10, 1998, was duly received by P's secretary in P's office, and P's secretary placed the notice in Dan's file. On March 3, 1999, Dan furnished P with a copy of a publication by Smith dated March 1, 1998, fully describing Y, and its method of manufacture. On March 4, 1999, P reviewed Dan's file and found the two notices. To properly protect Dan's patent rights, the most appropriate course of action for P to take is to _____

(A)   file in the PTO on Friday, March 5, 1999, a nonprovisional application claiming Y, and file a copy of the Smith publication, and an explanation of the relevance of the Smith publication.

(B)   deposit with the U.S. Postal Service as "Express Mail" in accordance with 37 CFR § 1.10, on Saturday, March 6, 1999, a nonprovisional application which claims Y, a copy of the Smith publication, and an explanation of the relevance of the Smith publication.

(C)   file in the PTO on Friday, March 5, 1999, another provisional application claiming the benefit of the filing date of the March 6, 1998, provisional application. For the March 6, 1998, provisional application, file the filing fee and surcharge, the appropriate petition and fee to revive the provisional application, a statement by P that the abandonment of the provisional application was unintentional, a copy of the Smith publication, and an explanation of the relevance of the Smith publication.

(D)   deposit in the U.S. Postal Service as "Express Mail" in accordance with 37 CFR § 1.10 on Saturday, March 6, 1999, a nonprovisional application claiming Y, and claiming the benefit of the filing date of the provisional application under 35 U.S.C § 119(e) along with a copy of the Smith publication, and an explanation of the relevance of the Smith publication. Also, in the provisional application, file the filing fee and surcharge for the provisional application along with the appropriate petition and fee to revive the provisional application as unintentionally abandoned, and a statement by P that the abandonment of the provisional application was unintentional.

(E) file in the PTO on Monday, March 8, 1999, a nonprovisional application claiming Y and claiming benefit of the filing date of the provisional application under 35 U.S.C § 119(e), and also file the filing fee and surcharge for the provisional application along with the appropriate petition and fee to revive the provisional application as unintentionally abandoned, a statement by P that the abandonment of the provisional application was unintentional, a copy of the Smith publication, and an explanation of the relevance of the Smith publication.

29. On April 1, 1999, Inventor Dave filed a patent application claiming a pancake flipper. To fully describe the pancake flipper, Dave refers to a February 1999 issue of a cooking magazine. The examiner objected to the specification on the ground that it improperly incorporated the material of the publication by reference. Which of the following actions would accord with proper PTO practice and procedure in overcoming the objection?

(A) Amend the specification to include the material incorporated by reference.

(B) File a declaration executed by Dave containing the essential material and stating that the material consists of the same material incorporated by reference.

(C) Abandon the application and file a new application incorporating by reference Dave's prior application.

(D) File an amendment which amends the specification to include the material incorporated by reference and file a petition to the Commissioner stating that the incorporation by reference was inadvertent with the proper fee.

(E) File an amendment to the specification to include the material incorporated by reference, and accompany it with an affidavit executed by Dave stating that the amendatory material consists of the same material incorporated by reference.

Answer Questions 30 and 31 independently of each other and based upon the following information. You have drafted and filed a patent application for JoJo Industries directed to a device for mechanically flushing food storage containers with gases which includes the following disclosure and drawings:

The gas flushing device of the present invention, illustrated generally at **10** in FIG. **1**, includes a main body **11** having a piston portion **12** with holes **14** that is securely attached to a piston rod **16**. The piston rod **16** is in communication with a source of a flushing gas such as carbon dioxide. The piston rod **16** conveys flushing gas to a chamber **17** in which the flushing gas under pressure exits through holes **14**.

In one preferred embodiment, the piston portion **12** of the gas flushing device **10** includes a bottom surface **18** that is substantially circular. The bottom surface **18** of the piston portion **12** is preferably made of a non-stick material such as nylon or teflon. The piston portion **12** also includes a cylindrical side surface **20** that meets the bottom surface **18** at the circumference of the bottom surface **18**. For a flat bottom surface **18**, the cylindrical surface **20** is substantially perpendicular to the bottom surface **18**.

The piston portion **12** also includes at least one hole **14**. In one embodiment, the hole **14** is positioned in the bottom surface **18** of the piston portion **12**. In another embodiment, the piston portion **12** includes a plurality of holes that are located on the bottom surface **18**. In another embodiment, the piston portion **12** includes a plurality of holes that are located on each of the bottom surface **18** and the cylindrical surface **20**. The piston portion **12** is securely attached to the hollow rod portion **16** by a threaded section **25** on the piston rod portion **16** that engages a threaded section **27** on the piston portion **12**. The piston rod portion **16** may be detached from the piston portion **12** by disengaging the threaded sections, thereby facilitating cleaning of the flushing device **10**.

The piston rod portion **16** of the main body **11** shown in FIG. **1** is a hollow rod. The piston rod portion **16** is threadibly attachable to and detachable to a source of flushing gas. In one embodiment, the piston rod portion **16** and piston portion **12** are parts of a single substantially hollow main body **11**.

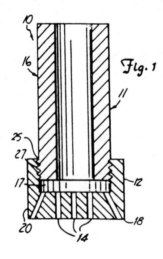

Fig. 1

The following independent claim is included in the application:

1. A gas flushing device for flushing a container enclosing food comprising a main body (11) that includes a piston portion (12) with at least one hole (14) providing direct contact between the gas and the food, a piston rod portion (16) which is threadibly attachable to and detachable to a source of flushing gas and which is securely attached to the piston portion (12), the piston portion (12) having a nonstick surface (18).

30. Which of the following claims, if any, comply with 35 U.S.C. § 112 based upon JoJo's disclosure and independent claim?

    (A) 2. The gas flushing device of Claim 1 wherein said piston portion (16) is attached to said piston rod portion (12) by a threaded section (25) on said piston rod portion (12) that engages a threaded section (27) on said piston rod portion (12).

    (B) 2. The gas flushing device according to Claim 1 wherein said piston portion is made of nylon.

    (C) 2. The gas flushing device of Claim 1 wherein the piston portion includes a bottom surface and a cylindrical side surface bounding the bottom surface.

    (D) 2. The gas flushing device of Claim 1 wherein said hole is positioned in said bottom surface of said piston portion.

    (E) None of the above.

31. Which of the following dependent claims, if any, cover the embodiment described in lines 15-16 of the disclosure?

    (A) 2. A gas flushing device as set forth in Claim 1 wherein the piston portion includes a plurality of holes located on each of said bottom surface and said cylindrical surface.

    (B) 3. A gas flushing device of Claim 2 wherein the piston portion includes a plurality of holes located on each of said bottom surface and said cylindrical surface.

    (C) 2. The gas flushing device of Claim 1 wherein the piston portion includes a cylindrical surface perpendicular to a bottom surface and said piston portion includes a plurality of holes located on each of said bottom surface and said cylindrical surface.

    (D) (A), (B), and (C).

    (E) (A) and (C).

32. XYZ Corporation has hired you to draft and file a patent application relating to a steel alloy. You diligently prepare the application and file it in the PTO on June 23, 1998, naming Baker as the inventor. On February 5, 1999, you receive a first Office action rejecting all the claims under 35 U.S.C. § 102(g)/103 over a patent assigned to XYZ Corporation. Able is the inventor named in the patent. The Able patent was granted on an application filed on June 25, 1996, and issued on January 13, 1998. You can overcome this rejection by _____

(A) filing an affidavit signed by an officer of the XYZ Corporation averring that both Able and Baker were subject to an obligation of assignment on the date the later invention was made, and stating facts which explain the officer's belief of ownership.

(B) filing an affidavit by Baker averring common ownership on the date of filing the Able patent application with the necessary fee.

(C) filing a terminal disclaimer so as not to extend the term of the Baker application beyond that of the Able patent if the Baker application matures into a patent.

(D) filing a request to suspend the prosecution of the Baker patent application, and petition the Commissioner for a corrected filing receipt dated January 13, 1998, because of common ownership.

(E) filing a request for reexamination of the Able patent based on prior art references not disclosed by Baker.

33. Inventor Cal files a provisional application in the PTO on June 5, 1997. On June 2, 1998, Cal asks you to prepare and file a nonprovisional utility patent application. On June 3, 1998, you file the nonprovisional utility application with a specific reference to Cal's June 5, 1997, provisional application. A Notice of Allowance is sent on February 3, 1999, and the Issue fee is timely paid on April 1, 1999. The patent will issue on June 1, 1999. When will Cal's patent term begin and end?

(A) The term will begin on June 1, 1999, and end on June 5, 2017.

(B) The term will begin on February 3, 1999, and will end on June 5, 2017.

(C) The term will begin on April 1, 1999, and will end May 1, 2018.

(D) The term will begin on June 1, 1999, and will end on June 3, 2018.

(E) The term will begin on February 3, 1999, and will end on June 3, 2018.

34.   A patent application is filed with the following original Claim 1:

A steam cooking device comprising:
    a steam generating chamber having a steam generator;
    a cooking chamber adjacent to said steam generating chamber for
        receiving steam from said steam; and
    a heat exchanger secured within said steam generator,
        said heat exchanger including at least one heating zone comprised
        of an inner having raised surface projections thereon, an outer
        panel having raised surface projections thereon, and a path between
        said raised surface projections whereby flue gases may pass for heating
        the walls of the heat exchanger.

Which of the following is in accord with proper PTO amendment practice and procedure?

    (A)   In Claim 1, line 4, after "steam" insert --generator--.
    (B)   In Claim 1, line 7, after "inner" insert --panel--.
    (C)   In Claim 1, line 6, delete [one], insert --two--, and amend
        "zone" to read --zones--.
    (D)   In Claim 1, lines 3-4, after "chamber" (second occurrence)
        delete [for receiving] and insert --to produce sufficient
        quantities of gas and--.
    (E)   In Claim 1, line 4, delete "secured within" and insert
        --attached to--.

35.   A Notice of Allowance is dated and mailed on September 25, 1998, to the applicant. In which of the following situations would the issue fee **not** be considered as timely paid?

    (A)   The issue fee is filed in the PTO on Monday, December 28,
        1998.
    (B)   The issue fee is filed in the PTO on Wednesday, November
        25, 1998.
    (C)   The issue fee is filed in the PTO on Thursday, March 25,
        1999, and is accompanied by a petition to the Commissioner
        for a three month extension of time, as well as the late
        payment fee.
    (D)   The issue fee is received in the PTO on December 29, 1998,
        and is accompanied with a certificate of mailing dated
        Monday, December 28, 1998.
    (E)   (A) and (D).

36.	Whenever a claim of a patent is held invalid:

(A)	the claim must be disclaimed by the patent owner to avoid invalidity of the remaining claims in the patent.
(B)	a portion of the claim can be disclaimed provided the remaining portion of the claim adequately defines the invention.
(C)	any disclaimer of the claim shall be in writing, but need not be recorded in the PTO.
(D)	and the invalid claim is to a composition of matter, the claims to a biotechnological process which result in that composition of matter will also be held invalid.
(E)	None of the above.

37.	Which of the following statements, if any, regarding amendments to claims in a reexamination proceeding are true?

(A)	If copies of the printed patent are used to amend the claims, additions to the claims are indicated by carets.
(B)	Brackets may not be used in amending claims if more than 5 words are being inserted into the claim.
(C)	Additions to amended claims are indicated by underlining, and new claims may be added, if and only if, an equal number of existing claims are canceled.
(D)	A patent claim should be canceled by a statement canceling the patent claim and renumbering any new claim to have the number of the canceled claim.
(E)	A previously proposed new claim should be canceled by a statement canceling the proposed new claim without presentation of the text of the previously proposed new claim.

38.	You are a registered patent agent representing a corporate client. An appeal is taken from the examiner's final rejection of Claims 1-8 of your client's nonprovisional patent application. Independent Claim 1 and its dependent Claims 2-4 stand rejected under 35 U.S.C. § 102(b) based on a U.S. patent to X. Independent Claim 5, independent Claim 6 and its dependent Claims 7-8 stand rejected under 35 U.S.C. § 103 based on a U.S. patent to Y in view of a U.S. patent to Z. None of the dependent claims are multiple dependent claims. The subject matter of Claims 1, 2, 3, 5, 6, and 8 is very important to your client and you consider each of these claims to be separately patentable over the art applied by the examiner in rejecting these claims. In your Appeal Brief, which of the following courses of action, if any, would be the most appropriate to follow on behalf of your client?

(A) Specify that dependent Claims 2-4 and 7-8 stand or fall together with their respective independent Claims 1 and 6, and present reasons as to why independent Claims 1, 5, and 6 are considered separately patentable.

(B) Point out the errors in the examiner's rejection of Claims 1-3 and how the specific limitations of Claims 1-3 are not shown in X's patent. Point out the errors in the examiner's rejection of Claims 5, 6, and 8 and how Y and Z, taken as a whole, do not suggest the claimed subject matter of Claims 5, 6, and 8.

(C) Point out that dependent Claims 4 and 7 stand or fall with their respective independent Claims 1 and 6, and present arguments as to the separate patentability of each of Claims 1, 2, 3, 5, 6, and 8.

(D) Argue the importance of each claim to your client, emphasizing the differences in what independent Claims 1, 5, and 6 cover, and state how the examiner erred in relying on X, Y, and Z's patents.

(E) All of the above.

39.   You are prosecuting a patent application in which there are two named inventors. You received a notice of allowance in the patent application. However, before the Issue fee became due, one of the named inventors died. Which of the following statements is *true* with respect to the application as a consequence of the death of the inventor?

(A) A new power of attorney must be submitted so that you can continue to represent the remaining inventor.

(B) The application is automatically abandoned upon the death of the inventor.

(C) A new application must be filed naming the heirs of the deceased inventor and the remaining inventor.

(D) The executor or administrator of the deceased inventor must intervene to prevent the application from being withdrawn from issue.

(E) The application matures to a patent after timely payment of the required fees.

40. You are a registered practitioner and you have filed a patent application in the PTO on behalf of your client, Wannaberich, on January 7, 1998. In the first Office action, the examiner made a restriction requirement. Although your client disagrees with the restriction, you have made a provisional election with traverse and vehemently argue the restriction requirement. In the next Office action, the restriction is made final and an action on the merits follows. The application is eventually allowed. The client now wants to pursue the non-elected invention. You file a divisional application directed to the non-elected invention before the parent application issues as a patent. In the first Office action in the divisional application, the examiner rejects the claims on the grounds of obviousness-type double patenting over the patent which issued from the parent application. What should be the most appropriate reply to the rejection?

(A) File a terminal disclaimer to obviate the double patenting rejection.
(B) Amend the claims in the pending application to overcome the rejection.
(C) File a 37 CFR § 1.132 antedating affidavit.
(D) Request reconsideration and point out that it is improper to use the parent patent in an obviousness-type double patenting rejection when a restriction requirement has been made by the examiner in the parent application.
(E) File a petition under 37 CFR § 1.183 to the Commissioner.

41. Petitions under 37 CFR § 1.48 are generally decided by the primary examiner except:

(A) When the application is involved in an interference.
(B) When the application is a national stage application filed under 35 U.S.C. § 371.
(C) When accompanied by a petition under 37 CFR § 1.183 requesting waiver of a requirement under 37 CFR § 1.48(a) or (c), e.g., waiver of the statement of lack of deceptive intent by an inventor to be added or deleted, or waiver of the reexecution of the declaration by all of the inventors.
(D) When a second conversion under 37 CFR § 1.48(a) is attempted.
(E) All of the above.

42. The examiner determined that amended Claim 1 contains new matter and rejected amended Claim 1. The claim was added by an amendment which was filed after the filing date of the application. Which of the following identifies the proper basis for the rejection of amended Claim 1 and the action which should be taken by the applicant to overcome the rejection?

(I) Claim 1 is rejected under 35 U.S.C. § 112, first paragraph. Applicant should amend the specification to include the new matter therein so as to provide antecedent support for the claim.

(II) Claim 1 is rejected under 35 U.S.C. § 132. Applicant should cancel the claim.

(III) Claim 1 is rejected under 35 U.S.C. § 112, first paragraph. Applicant should cancel the claim.

(IV) Claim 1 is rejected under 35 U.S.C. § 132. Applicant should file a declaration in accordance with 37 CFR § 1.63.

(A) (I)
(B) (II)
(C) (III)
(D) (IV)
(E) (III) and (IV)

43. Which of the following phrases, when appearing in a claim, would render the claim indefinite?

(A) A claim to a bicycle that recited "said front and rear wheels so spaced as to give a wheelbase that is between 58 percent and 75 percent of the height of the rider that the bicycle was designed for."

(B) A claim limitation specifying that a certain part of a pediatric wheelchair be "so dimensional as to be insertable through the space between the doorframe of an automobile and one of the seats."

(C) A claim limitation defining the stretch rate of a plastic as "exceeding about 10% per second."

(D) (A) and (B).

(E) (A), (B), and (C).

Both questions 44 and 45 are based on the following fact pattern:

B filed a patent application on March 31, 1997, for an ice cream machine. Discovering an added feature that improved productivity, B filed a CIP application on May 14, 1997. Thereafter, B abandoned the application filed on March 31, 1997. On June 30, 1998, a patent was granted to B for his invention in the CIP application. On March 1, 1999, B realizes that he is claiming less than he is entitled to in view of the added feature in the CIP application. B is worried that this will hurt his upcoming negotiations to assign his patent rights to Mega Corporation. B comes to you, a registered patent practitioner, on March 2, 1999, for advice regarding how to file an application for reissue.

44.   What is the latest date that B can file an application for reissue and be entitled to seek enlargement of the scope of the claims of the original patent?

    (A)   June 29, 2000
    (B)   May 14, 1999
    (C)   March 31, 1999
    (D)   June 30, 2000
    (E)   None of the above

45.   What documents must be filed as part of B's application for reissue in order to be granted a filing date?

        (I)   Reissue Oath or Declaration
        (II)   An offer to surrender
        (III)   Filing fee
        (IV)   Written Consent of Mega Corp.
        (V)   A specification, claims and
                 any required drawings.

    (A)   (I), (II), (III), (IV), and (V)
    (B)   (I), (II), (III), and (V)
    (C)   (I), (III), and (V)
    (D)   (V)
    (E)   (I), (II), (IV), and (V)

46.   The claims in an application filed on behalf of McTeal were rejected as being unpatentable under 35 U.S.C. § 103 over Gage in view of Nell. McTeal gave you, a registered practitioner, power of attorney to prosecute her application. Which one of the following items of information available to you would be relevant to overcoming the rejection of the claims without modifying or amending the claims?

(A)   Gage and Nell do not teach or suggest feature A of McTeal's invention which is set forth in each of the drawings and in the working examples in McTeal's application, but which is not recited in any of the rejected claims.

(B)   In the opinion of Billy, a noted expert in the field, McTeal's invention is patentable because it has revitalized the industry and Billy has nominated McTeal to receive the prestigious Phrog Foundation Award for Excellence.

(C)   McTeal's invention can be shown to possess unexpected superior properties over the prior art.

(D)   Gage was published 50 years before Nell and therefore contains no specific reference to Nell suggesting that his invention can be modified in the manner suggested by the Examiner.

(E)   The teachings of Gage and Nell, taken singularly or combined, would not be followed by one of ordinary skill in the art because it would be cost prohibitive to do so.

47.   Which of the following must be filed to obtain a filing date for a Continued Prosecution Application?

(I)   A copy of the originally filed specification, claims and drawings.

(II)   A newly executed oath or declaration signed by all the originally named inventors.

(III)   The filing fee.

(IV)   A request, on a separate paper, for an application under 37 CFR § 1.53(d) in compliance with that paragraph.

(A)   (I), (II), and (III)
(B)   (I)
(C)   (I), (II), (III), and (IV)
(D)   (IV)
(E)   (I) and (IV)

48.   Patent practitioner Luke filed a patent application in the PTO on behalf of his client Vader which contained three original claims directed to Vader's invention and which were fully supported by the specification. The three original claims read as follows:

1.   A widget comprising A, B, and C.
2.   A widget as claimed in Claim 1 wherein C further comprises D.
3.   A widget as claimed in Claim 1 and 2 wherein B is BB.

The examiner issued a rejection of Claim 3 under 35 U.S.C. § 112, second paragraph, citing the improper dependency of the claim. In the absence of issues of supporting disclosure, which of the following proposed amendments will overcome the rejection?

(A)   Cancel Claim 3 and substitute the following claim:
3.(Amended) A widget as claimed in claim 1 or 2 wherein B is BB.

(B)   3. (Amended) A widget as claimed in any one of Claims 1 and 2 wherein B is BB.

(C)   3. A widget as claimed in Claims 1 and 2 wherein B is BB.

(D)   Cancel Claim 3 and substitute the following Claim: 4. A widget as claimed in Claims 1 or 2 wherein B is BBB.

(E)   3. (Amended) A widget as claimed in Claim 1 [and 2] wherein B is BB.

49.   You are a registered practitioner and Henry has come to you to determine whether he has a patentable invention. He discloses to you that he has developed a composition that can be used as bait for a conventional mousetrap. He explains to you that his composition is so effective that one need only wait minutes to lure mice to the trap. You explain to Henry that you cannot give a patentability opinion until after a preliminary search has been made of the prior art. You have a search made and find that Henry's composition is a well known pork barrel lubricant that has been in public use for over 20 years. What should be your advice to Henry?

(A)   File a U.S. patent application claiming the composition as mouse bait.

(B)   File a U.S. patent application with claims directed to a method of using the composition as bait.

(C)   Explain that it would be impossible for any claims to the process of using the composition as mouse bait to be allowed under the current guidelines of the PTO.

(D) File a provisional patent application directed only to the composition in order to gain a competitive advantage for one year. Within one year of filing the provisional application, recommend that Henry file a nonprovisional application claiming the composition.

(E) None of the above.

50. Your client has invented a widget consisting essentially of an amplifier having a voltage of 100 to 300 amps, preferably 250 amps, and a woofer having a wattage of 400 to 450 watts, preferably 425 watts. You draft a patent application directed to your client's invention and satisfying the requirements of 35 U.S.C. § 112. You draft the following independent claim:

1. A widget consisting essentially of an amplifier having a voltage of 100 to 300 amps, and a woofer having a wattage of 400 to 450 watts.

Which of the following would **not** be a proper dependent claim if presented as an original claim in the application when the application is filed in the PTO?

(A) 2. The widget of Claim 1 wherein the amplifier has a voltage of up to 300 amps.

(B) 2. The widget of Claim 1 wherein the woofer has a wattage of 425 to 450 watts.

(C) 2. The widget of Claim 1 wherein the amplifier has a voltage of 300 amps and the woofer has a wattage between 430 and 450 watts.

(D) 2. A widget of Claim 1 further comprising an amplifier having a voltage of at least 250 amps and a woofer having a wattage of at least 425 amps.

(E) (A) and (D).

1.   ANSWER: (D) is the correct answer because (A) and (B) are both correct. 37 CFR § 1.3; MPEP §§ 714.19, items (E),(K); 714.25. (C) is not correct because 37 CFR § 1.136(a)(3) provides that "[a]n authorization to charge all required fees, fees under § 1.17, or all required extension of time fees will be treated as a constructive petition for an extension of time in any concurrent or future reply requiring a petition for an extension of time under this paragraph for its timely submission." Answer (E) is not correct because (C) is not correct.

2.   ANSWER: (C) is the correct answer. 37 CFR § 1.143; MPEP § 818.03(b). No invention is elected in (C). A provisional election must be made in response to a restriction requirement, even if the restriction requirement is traversed. MPEP § 818.03(b). (A), (B), and (D) are incorrect because they are all proper responses to a restriction requirement. MPEP § 818.03. (E) is incorrect because it includes (C) which is a correct answer.

3.   ANSWER: (B) is the correct answer because it contains a false statement regarding design patents. MPEP § 1504.01(a), subsection III. [p.1500-11] (A) is a true statement. MPEP § 1512, subsection III. [p.1500-38]. (C) is true. MPEP § 1504.01(a), subsection I.A.[p.1500-10] (D) is also a true statement. MPEP § 1503.03 [p. 1500-8]. (E) is true. MPEP § 1504.

4.   ANSWER: (A) is the correct answer. 35 U.S.C. § 305; 37 CFR § 1.530(d)(3); MPEP §§ 2250; 2258 subsection III. ("A broadened claim: A claim is broader than another claim if it is broader (greater in scope) 'in any respect,' even though it may be narrower in other respects. *In re Freeman*, 30 F.3d 1459, 1464, 32 USPQ2d 1444, 1447 (Fed. Cir. 1994).") The claim is broadened by changing "knife" to "cutting means," which is not limited to a knife, but may be a blade, scissors, etc.

5.   ANSWER: (E) is the correct answer. 37 CFR § 1.48; MPEP § 201.03. Under 37 CFR § 1.48(a), if the correct inventor or inventors are not named in an executed oath or declaration under 37 CFR § 1.63 in a nonprovisional application for patent, the application may be amended to name only the actual inventor or inventors so long as the error in the naming of the inventor or inventors occurred without any deceptive intention on the part of the person named as an inventor in error or on the part of the person who through error was not named as an inventor. 37 CFR § 1.48(a) requires that the amendment be accompanied by (1) a petition including a statement from each person being added that the error in inventorship occurred without deceptive intention on his or her part; (2) an oath or declaration by each actual inventor or inventors as required by 37 CFR § 1.63; (3) the fee set forth in 37 CFR § 1.17(i); and (4) the written consent of any existing assignee, if any of the originally named inventors has executed an assignment. (A), (C) and (D) are incorrect inasmuch as an oath or declaration under 37 CFR § 1.63 by each actual inventor has not

been presented. (B) is incorrect because it does not include the fee required and omits the written consent of the assignee. (E) is in accord with MPEP § 201.03 [p.200-6] which provides that "[t]he statement required from each inventor being added may simply state that the inventorship error occurred without deceptive intention. The statement need not be a verified statement."

6.   ANSWER: (A) is the correct answer. 35 U.S.C. § 102(b). The nonprovisional application deposited via Express Mail on Saturday, February 6, 1999, will be given a February 6, 1999, filing date. 37 CFR § 1.10; MPEP §§ 513; 201.04(b) [p. 200-14]. As such, the nonprovisional application was filed on the last day of pendency of the provisional application so as to claim an effective filing date of February 6, 1998. MPEP §§ 201.04(b); 706.02.

7.   ANSWER: (A) is the correct answer. 35 U.S.C. § 103, MPEP §§ 2112.01; 2144; 2145, paragraph II; *In re Dillon*, 919 F.2d 688, 16 USPQ2d 1897 (Fed. Cir. 1990) and *In re Spada*, 911 F.2d 705, 15 USPQ2d 1655 (Fed. Cir. 1990). The rationale to modify or combine the prior art does not have to be expressly stated in the prior art. MPEP § 2144. (B) is not correct because knowledge of applicant's disclosure cannot be relied upon to provide the motivation to combine the references relied upon. MPEP §§ 2142; 2144.04 [p.2100-120]. (C) is incorrect. It is not necessary that the prior art suggest the combination to achieve the same advantage or result discovered by applicant. MPEP § 2144. (D) is incorrect. The discovery of a new property or use of a previously known composition, even if unobvious from prior art, cannot impart patentability to a claimed composition. MPEP § 2112. (E) is incorrect. MPEP § 2112 [p. 2100-48].

8.   ANSWER: (B) is the correct answer. MPEP §§ 201.09; 706.07(b).

9.   ANSWER: (D) is the correct answer. 37 CFR § 1.121(a)(2)(ii); MPEP §§ 714.22; 714.24; 608.01(s).

10.   ANSWER: (B) is the correct answer. 37 CFR § 1.495(b); MPEP § 1893.01(b)(1).

11.   ANSWER: (E) is the correct answer. MPEP § 1400.1.[p. 1400-1] A Continued Prosecution Application is a request to expressly abandon a prior application. It cannot be used to correct an issued patent. MPEP § 201.06(d).

12.   ANSWER: (C) is the correct answer. 35 U.S.C. § 119(b); 37 CFR §§ 1.55 and 1.111(b); MPEP § 201.13.

13.   ANSWER: (B) is the correct answer. 37 CFR § 1.72(b); MPEP § 608.01(b).

14.   ANSWER: (D) is the correct answer. 37 CFR § 1.132; MPEP § 716. (A) is not the most likely action which would overcome the rejection because there is no nexus to show that the claimed method of bonding the carbide insert is responsible for the increased

sales of the gear cutting machine. MPEP § 716.01(b). (B) is not sufficient because it is not based on any factual evidence. MPEP § 716.01(c). (C) is not properly persuasive because it is an admission that the increased sales of Smith's invention were attributed to heavy advertising and not because of the claimed invention. (E) is not correct because (D) is the correct answer.

15. ANSWER: (E) is the correct answer. MPEP §§ 2131.04; 706.02(b). Claim 2 was rejected as being anticipated by the patent to Y. As set forth in MPEP § 706.02(b), a rejection based on 35 U.S.C. § 102(b) can be overcome by "(A) Persuasively arguing that the claims are patentably distinguishable from the prior art; or (B) Amending the claims to patentably distinguish over the prior art." Evidence of secondary considerations is irrelevant to § 102 rejections and thus cannot overcome a rejection so based. MPEP § 2131.04, citing *In re Wiggins*, 488 F.2d 538, 543; 179 USPQ 421, 425 (CCPA 1973).

16. ANSWER: (B) is the correct answer. 37 CFR §§ 1.75(b); 1.75(c). (A) is not supported by the specification. (C) is not correct because it does not differ substantially from Claim 3. MPEP § 706.03(k). (D) and (E) are not supported by the specification. Also, (D) and (E) are multiple dependent claims which are dependent on Claim 3, another multiple dependent claim.

17. ANSWER: (E) is the correct answer. 37 CFR § 10.32(c).

18. ANSWER: (A) is the correct answer. MPEP § 201.04(b). The filing date of Beavis and Barbara's provisional patent application is January 16, 1998, the date the complete provisional application was received in the PTO. 35 U.S.C. § 111(b)(4); MPEP § 201.04(b). Thus, in Beavis and Barbara's case, the last day of pendency is January 16, 1999, which is a Saturday. As set forth in MPEP § 201.04(b), "[s]ince a provisional application can be pending for no more than 12 months, if the last day of pendency is on a Saturday, Sunday, or Federal holiday, copendency would require that the later filed nonprovisional application be filed on or prior to the Saturday, Sunday, or Federal holiday. See 37 CFR 1.78(a)(3)." However, "if a new patent application is deposited in 'Express Mail' in accordance with 37 CFR 1.10 on a Saturday and the United States Postal Service gives it a date of deposit of Saturday, the Office will accord and stamp the correspondence with the Saturday date. 37 CFR 1.6(a)(2)." (A) is the correct answer because the PTO will accord and stamp the "Express Mail" date stamp of January 16, 1999. MPEP § 201.04(b). [p. 200-14]. Answers (B) and (C) are not correct because they are not the latest date that the nonprovisional application can be filed. The filing date of Beavis and Barbara's provisional application was not the day it was mailed, i.e. January 13, 1998, but the date it was received in the PTO, i.e. January 16, 1998. Answers (D) and (E) are incorrect because patent applications cannot be filed by facsimile, nor can a certificate of mailing be used. See 37 CFR §§ 1.6(d)(3); 1.8(a)(2)(i)(A).

19. ANSWER: (C) is the correct answer. 37 CFR § 10.18(a); MPEP § 402 (pp. 400-3). Statement (I) is not true because practitioners are not **required** to advise their clients regarding sanctions. MPEP § 410 (pp.400-30) Statement (III) is also not true. As

set forth in MPEP § 410, "an applicant has no duty to conduct a prior art search as a prerequisite to filing an application for patent." Accordingly, answers (A), (B), (D) and (E) are incorrect.

20.   ANSWER: (E) is the correct answer. There is no copendency between applications E and any prior application. MPEP § 201.11("If the first application is abandoned, the second application must be filed before the abandonment in order for it to be co-pending with the first."). See MPEP § 710.01(a), fourth paragraph.

21.   ANSWER: (C) is the correct answer. 35 U.S.C. § 112, first paragraph; MPEP § 2163. See *Gentry Gallery Inc. v. Berkline Corp.*, 45 USPQ2d 1498 (Fed. Cir. 1998); *In re Kaslow*, 217 USPQ 1089 (Fed. Cir. 1983). (A) is incorrect. It is inconsistent with the given facts. (B) is incorrect. Claim 2 further limits claim 1 by limiting the shape of the handlebar. (D) is incorrect. There is no new matter in claim 2 inasmuch as the shape of the handlebar was disclosed in the specification. (E) is incorrect. The Lois patent does not describe a "Y" or "U" shaped handlebar.

22.   ANSWER: (B) is the correct answer. 37 CFR § 1.510; MPEP §§ 2210; 2214. (A), (C), (D) and (E) are incorrect because they are required as specified in 37 CFR § 10.510(b)(1), (2), (3) and (4).

23.   ANSWER: (B) is the correct answer. 37 CFR §§ 1.36; 10.40(a); 10.40(b)(4); MPEP § 402.06. (A) is incorrect. The timing is inconsistent with MPEP § 402.06. (C) and (E) are incorrect. 37 CFR § 10.40(b)(4). (D) is incorrect. The PTO Disciplinary Rules do not impose the "obligation" to inquire.

24.   ANSWER: (D) is the correct answer. 37 CFR § 1.75(c); MPEP § 608.01(n). (A) is incorrect. The claim does not refer back in the alternative only. (B) and (C) are incorrect. They do not further limit the claims from which they depend, which already include D as an element. (E) is incorrect. Multiple dependent claim 3 serves as a basis for multiple dependent claim 4, which is not permitted. 37 CFR § 1.75(c), third sentence.

25.   ANSWER: (A) is the correct answer. 37 CFR § 1.97(b); MPEP § 609(B)(1) [p. 600-106]. (B) is not correct because it is not the latest date. (C) and (D) are incorrect. An Information Disclosure Statement (IDS) will be considered to have been filed on the day it was received in the Office, or on an earlier date of mailing if accompanied by a properly executed certificate of mailing or facsimile transmission. (C) did not include a certificate of mailing and (D) used an incorrect "Express Mail" service designation. 37 CFR § 1.10. (E) is incorrect because filing the IDS before the Notice of Allowance will require Bert and Ernie to pay the fee set forth in 37 CFR § 1.17(p) given that Bert and Ernie did not file a statement under 37 CFR § 1.97(e). An IDS filed pursuant to 37 CFR § 1.97(c) will be considered provided that the IDS is accompanied by either (1) a statement as specified in 37 CFR § 1.97(e); **or** (2) the fee set forth in 37 CFR § 1.17(p). MPEP § 609(B)(2)) [pp. 600-106-107].

26.   ANSWER: (D) is the correct answer. MPEP § 804, subsection I (Instances where Double Patenting Issue Can Be Raised) [p.800-15]. III is not correct because "[d]ouble patenting does not relate to international applications which have not yet entered the national stage in the United States." Id. (A), (B) and (C) are incorrect because they include III. (E) is not the most correct answer because it omits II, which is included in (D).

27.   ANSWER: (D) is the correct answer. 35 U.S.C. § 102(e). (B) is not correct because "known or used" implies knowledge that is publicly accessible. Priscilla's composition was not publicly known. "The statutory language 'known or used by others in this country' (35 U.S.C. § 102(a)), means knowledge or use which is accessible to the public." MPEP § 2132, subsection I. [p.2100-66] citing *Carella v. Starlight Archery*, 804 F.2d 135, 231 USPQ 644 (Fed. Cir. 1986). There are no given facts showing that Priscilla's patent application was accessible to the public, 35 U.S.C. § 122, or that she disclosed her invention to the public before her patent issued. (A) is incorrect. Inasmuch as Priscilla's patent is not being used to reject Bruce's claimed process, the difference in their processes does not show any impropriety in the rejection. (C) is incorrect. 35 U.S.C. § 102(e). (E) is incorrect because (B) is incorrect.

28.   ANSWER: (D) is the correct answer. 37 CFR §§ 1.131; 1.78(a)(3); 1.56; 1.53(c); MPEP §§ 201.11; 711.03(c), part III, subparts C.1 [p. 700-95] and I [p.700-108]. (A), (B), (C) and (D) are incorrect. The Smith publication would be a statutory bar under 35 U.S.C. § 102(b) to each nonprovisional application, each of which is filed more than one year after the Smith publication date. (E) is also incorrect because the nonprovisional application is filed later than 12 months after the date on which the provisional application was filed. MPEP § 201.11. Thus, petitioning to revive the abandoned provisional application, even if successful, would not prevent the Smith publication from being a statutory bar.

29.   ANSWER: (E) is in accord with MPEP § 608.01(p), "Improper Incorporation" [p. 600-73]. (A) is incorrect because it does not include the affidavit or declaration required by MPEP § 608.01(p). (B) is not correct because essential material may not be incorporated by reference to a magazine article and (B) does not state that an amendment has been filed to amend the specification to include the material incorporated by reference. MPEP § 608.01(p). (C) is incorrect because the new application would still contain the same objectionable material and be subject to the same objection. (D) is incorrect because the amendment still needs to be accompanied by an affidavit stating that the amendatory material was the same as that incorporated by reference as required by MPEP § 608.01. The petition and fee are superfluous.

30.   ANSWER: (C) is the correct answer. 37 CFR § 1.75(c). As set forth in the disclosure and in FIG. 1, "The piston portion **12** also includes a cylindrical side surface **20** that meets the bottom surface **18** at the circumference of the bottom surface **18**." (A) is not correct because it contains incorrect reference characters and is not supported by the disclosure. (B) is incorrect because the disclosure states that "The bottom surface **18** of the piston portion **12** is preferably made of a non-stick material such as nylon or teflon." It is

the bottom surface of the piston portion which is made of nylon and not the piston portion itself. (D) is not correct because "said bottom surface" has no antecedent basis in Claim 1. (E) is incorrect because (C) is the correct answer.

31.   ANSWER: (C) is the correct answer. (A) is not correct because there is no antecedent basis for "said bottom surface" and "said cylindrical surface." (B) is not correct because it is not known what is in Claim 2 and whether or not there is antecedent basis for "said bottom surface" and "said cylindrical surface." Questions 61 and 62 are independent of each other and the dependent Claim 2 set forth in Question 61 cannot properly be relied upon to respond to Question 62. (D) is not correct because (A) and (B) are not correct. (E) is not correct because (A) is not correct.

32.   ANSWER: (A) is the correct answer. MPEP § 706.02(l). (B) is incorrect. MPEP § 706.02(l), item II.B. (C), (D) and (E) are incorrect because no evidence of common ownership is presented. MPEP § 706.02(l). (D) and (E) are also incorrect because no response under 37 CFR § 1.111 has been filed.

33.   ANSWER: (D) is the correct answer. 35 U.S.C. § 154(a); MPEP §§ 1309; 1309.01. (A) and (B) are incorrect. MPEP § 1309.01 ("[P]riority under 35 U.S.C. 119(e) to one or more U.S. provisional applications is not considered in the calculation of the twenty year term.") (C) is incorrect. 35 U.S.C. § 154(a). (E) is incorrect. 35 U.S.C. § 154(a).

34.   ANSWER: (B) is the correct answer. 37 CFR § 1.121; MPEP § 714.22. The amendment in (B) specifies the exact matter to be inserted, the exact point where the insertion is to be made and is limited to five words or less. (A) is incorrect because there are two occurrences of "steam" appearing in line 4 and the exact point where the insertion is to be made has not been specified. (C) is incorrect because the amendment does not specify the exact point where the insertion of "two" is to occur. (D) is incorrect because the amendment would insert more than five words. (E) is incorrect because it fails to identify the correct point where the insertion is to be made.

35.   ANSWER: (C) is the correct answer. 35 U.S.C. § 151; 37 CFR § 1.8; MPEP §§ 505; 1306. (A) is incorrect. The procedure complies with 35 U.S.C. §§ 21(b) and 151. (B) is not correct. The procedure complies with 35 U.S.C. § 151. (D) is not correct. The procedure complies with 35 U.S.C. §§ 21(b); 151, and 37 CFR § 1.8. (E) is incorrect because (A) and (D) are incorrect.

36.   ANSWER: (E) is the correct answer. 35 U.S.C. §§ 253; 282.

37.   ANSWER: (E) is the correct answer. 37 CFR § 1.530(d)(2)(i)(A); MPEP § 2234. (A) is incorrect. Additions to claims are indicated by underlining. 37 CFR § 1.530(d)(2)(i)(C). (B) is incorrect. 37 CFR § 1.530(d)(i)(C). (C) is incorrect. There is no requirement that the number of new claims equal the number of cancelled claims. 37 CFR § 1.530(d). (D) is incorrect. 37 CFR § 1.530(d)(2)(i)(B).

38.   ANSWER: (C) is the correct answer. 37 CFR § 1.192(c)(7)-(8); MPEP § 1206 [pp.1200-8,9]. (A) is incorrect. The separate patentability of claims 2, 3 and 8 is neither pointed out or argued. (B) is incorrect. The separate patentability of the very important claims 1, 2, 3, 5, 6, and 8 is not pointed out and argued. (D) is incorrect. The separate patentability of the very important claims is not argued. (E) is incorrect because (A), (B) and (D) are incorrect.

39.   ANSWER: (E) is the correct answer. MPEP § 409.01 [p. 400-21]. A new power of attorney is needed only if the deceased inventor was the sole inventor, which he or she was not in the given facts. (A) is not correct because a new power of attorney is only necessary if the deceased inventor is the sole inventor or all the powers of attorney in the application have been terminated. MPEP §§ 409.01; 409.01(f). Likewise, (B), (C) and (D) are incorrect based on MPEP § 409.01(f).

40.   ANSWER: (D) is the correct answer. 35 U.S.C. § 121; MPEP § 804.01. (A), (B) and (C) are incorrect. The use of the patent as a reference against the divisional application is prohibited by 35 U.S.C. § 121. (E) is not the most correct answer because the petition does not stay the period or necessity to reply to the rejection. 37 CFR §§ 1.111; 1.181(f).

41.   ANSWER: (E) All of the above. See MPEP § 201.03 (pp. 200-3 - 200-4) As set forth in MPEP § 201.03, (A) is decided by the Board of Patent Appeals and Interferences; (B) is decided in the PCT Legal Office; (C) is decided in the Office of Petitions; and (D) is decided by the Group Director.

42.   ANSWER: (C) is the correct answer. MPEP § 2163.06. "If new matter is added to the claims, the examiner should reject the claims under 35 U.S.C. § 112, first paragraph - written description requirement. *In re Rasmussen*, 650 F.2d 1212, 211 USPQ 323 (CCPA 1981). (A) is incorrect because it adds new matter to the specification. (B), (D), and (E) are incorrect because they identify an incorrect basis, i.e. 35 U.S.C. § 132, for the rejection.

43.   ANSWER: (A) is the correct answer. MPEP § 2173.05(b) [p. 2100-166]. (B) is not a correct answer inasmuch as such limitation was held to be definite in *Orthokinetics, Inc. v. Safety Travel Chairs, Inc.*, 806 F.2d 1565, 1 USPQ 2d 1081 (Fed. Cir. 1986) cited in MPEP § 2173.05(b) [p. 2100-166]. The limitation recited in choice (C) was likewise found to be definite by the court in *W.L. Gore & Associates, Inc. v. Garlock, Inc.*, 721 F.2d 1540, 220 USPQ 303 (Fed. Cir. 1983) cited in *supra*. (D) is incorrect because it includes (B). (E) is incorrect because it includes (B) and (C).

44.   ANSWER: (D) is the correct answer. 35 U.S.C. § 251 ("No reissued patent shall be granted enlarging the scope of the claims of the original patent unless applied for within two years from the grant of the original patent."); MPEP § 1403 ("A reissue filed on the 2-year anniversary date is considered as filed within 2 years.")[p. 1400-3].

45.   ANSWER: (D) is the correct answer. 37 CFR §§ 1.53(b) and 1.171 ("An application for reissue must contain the same parts required for an application for an original patent, complying with all the rules relating thereto except as otherwise provided ...."). MPEP §§ 1403 ("A reissue application can be granted a filing date without an oath or declaration, or without the filing fee being present. See 37 CFR 1.53(f)."); 1410; 1410.01.

46.   ANSWER: (C) is the correct answer. 35 U.S.C. § 103; MPEP §§ 2145; 716.02(a). (A) is not correct because it is based upon arguing limitations which are not claimed. MPEP § 2145, VI. (B) is based upon the opinion of one person and is not supported by any factual evidence. MPEP § 716.01(c). (D) is incorrect. The age of the Gage reference, in and of itself is not persuasive of nonobviousness. MPEP § 2145, VIII [p. 2100-137]. (E) is not correct. MPEP § 2145, VII ("Arguing Economic Infeasibility").

47.   ANSWER: (D) is the correct answer. 37 CFR § 1.53(d)(2) ("The filing date of a continued prosecution application is the date on which a request on a separate paper for an application under this paragraph is filed."); MPEP §§ 201.06(d) [p.200-38]; 601.01 ("37 CFR 1.53(d) sets forth the filing date requirements for a continued prosecution application."). (A), (B), (C) and (E) are incorrect because the specification, claims, drawing , and declaration or oath of the previous application are utilized in a CPA. 37 CFR § 1.53(d)(2)(iv). The filing fee may be filed later. 37 CFR § 1.16(l).

48.   ANSWER: (E) is the correct answer. 37 CFR § 1.121(a)(2)(ii); MPEP § 608.01(n). (A) is incorrect because the claim number is underlined, as are all the words in the claim even though no matter is added. 37 CFR § 1.121(a)(2)(ii). (B) and (C) are incorrect because the claim does not refer back in the alternative only. MPEP § 608.01(n). (D) is incorrect because the claim number is changed and omitted words are not bracketed. 37 CFR § 1.121(a)(2)(ii).

49.   ANSWER: (B) is the correct answer. 35 U.S.C. § 102(b); MPEP § 2112.02 [p.2100-51]. (A) is incorrect because the claim is anticipated. 35 U.S.C § 102(b). (C) is incorrect because the process is not disclosed and current PTO guidelines support the claim. MPEP § 2112.02. (D) is incorrect because the process is anticipated. 35 U.S.C. § 102(b). (E) is incorrect because (B) is incorrect.

50.   ANSWER: (E) is the correct answer because it identifies both (A) and (D). (A) is not a proper dependent claim because "up to" 300 amps would include 0-300 amps which is outside of the 100-300 amp range disclosed in the specification. (D) is not a proper dependent claim because the phrase "at least" would encompass ranges outside those disclosed in the specification. MPEP § 2111.03. Use of the phrase "further comprising" adds an additional amplifier and woofer, which are not supported by the disclosure which describes only one amplifier and one woofer. (B) is a proper dependent claim because the wattage is within the wattage range limitation set out in claim 1. (C) is a proper dependent claim because the voltage and wattage are within the limitations for the same set forth in claim 1.

U. S. DEPARTMENT OF COMMERCE
UNITED STATES PATENT AND TRADEMARK OFFICE
REGISTRATION EXAMINATION
FOR PATENT ATTORNEYS AND AGENTS

APRIL 21, 1999

Afternoon Session (50 Points)   **Time: 3 Hours**

This session of the examination is an open book examination. You may use books, notes, or other written materials that you believe will be of help to you *except* you may not use prior registration examination questions and/or answers. Books, notes or other written materials containing prior registration examination questions and/or answers *cannot* be brought into or used in the room where this examination is being administered. If you have such materials, you must give them to the test administrator before this session of the examination begins.

All questions must be answered in SECTION I of the Answer Sheet which is provided to you by the test administrator. You must use a No. 2 pencil (or softer) lead pencil to record your answers on the Answer Sheet. Darken *completely* the circle corresponding to your answer. You must keep your mark within the circle. Erase *completely* all marks except your answer. Stray marks may be counted as answers. No points will be awarded for incorrect answers or unanswered questions. Questions answered by darkening more than one circle will be considered as being incorrectly answered.

This session of the examination consists of fifty (50) multiple choice questions, each worth one (1) point. Do not assume any additional facts not presented in the questions. When answering each question, unless otherwise stated, assume that you are a registered patent practitioner. Any reference to a practitioner is a reference to a registered patent practitioner. The most correct answer is the policy, practice, and procedure which must, shall, or should be followed in accordance with the U.S. patent statutes, the PTO rules of practice and procedure, the Manual of Patent Examining Procedure (MPEP), and the Patent Cooperation Treaty (PCT) articles and rules, unless modified by a subsequent court decision or a notice in the *Official Gazette*. There is only one most correct answer for each question. Where choices (A) through (D) are correct and choice (E) is "All of the above," the last choice (E) will be the most correct answer and the only answer which will be accepted. Where two or more choices are correct, the most correct answer is the answer which refers to each and every one of the correct choices. Where a question includes a statement with one or more blanks or ends with a colon, select the answer from the choices given to complete the statement which would make the statement *true*. Unless otherwise explicitly stated, all references to patents or applications are to be understood as being U.S. patents or regular (non-provisional) utility applications for utility inventions only, as opposed to plant or design applications for plant and design inventions. Where the terms "USPTO," "PTO," or "Office" are used in this examination, they mean the U.S. Patent and Trademark Office.

You may write anywhere on the examination booklet. However, do not remove any pages from the booklet. Only answers recorded in SECTION I of your Answer Sheet will be graded. Your combined score of both the morning and afternoon sessions must be at least 70 points to pass the registration examination.

Answer questions 1 and 2 based on the following facts:

Registered patent attorneys, Will, Able and Fleet, are partners in their own California law firm specializing in patent law. As luck would have it, a PTO filing deadline falls due for each partner on Friday, February 12, 1999. Having to forego their weekly Friday afternoon discussion of the MPEP, all three partners are scrambling to finish their papers. Will is drafting a Continued Prosecution Application (CPA) under 37 CFR § 1.53(d) which must be filed by Friday, February 12, 1999. Having just received the client's instructions that morning, Able is replying to a Final Office action dated August 12, 1998, which set a three month shortened statutory period for reply. Fleet, working hard to satisfy a forgetful, new client, is putting the finishing touches on a nonprovisional patent application based on a provisional application his new client had filed on February 12, 1998. Finishing their work at 8:30 p.m. Pacific time, all three partners head to the mailroom. There is only one facsimile machine. With their deadline fast approaching, Will and Able begin to argue about who should use the facsimile machine first to send their papers to the PTO. A complete transmission of Able's amendment would take fifteen minutes. A complete transmission of Will's CPA would take ten minutes. Thankful that they had been studying their MPEP, Will and Able come to an agreement. At exactly 8:40 p.m. Pacific time, a first facsimile transmission is sent to the PTO from Will and Able's firm.

1. Which one of the following choices outlines the best course of action taken by Will and Able so that both Will and Able's documents received a Friday, February 12, 1999, filing date?

    (A)   Will files his CPA via facsimile at 8:40 p.m. Pacific time with all the necessary papers including a Certificate of Transmission. The CPA is received in the PTO exactly ten minutes later. Able files his amendment via facsimile at 8:50 p.m. Pacific time with all the necessary papers including a Certificate of Transmission which states the date of transmission. Able's amendment is received in the PTO exactly fifteen minutes after he sent it.

    (B)   Able files his amendment via facsimile at 8:40 p.m. Pacific time with all the necessary papers including a Certificate of Transmission. The amendment is received in the PTO exactly fifteen minutes later. Will files his CPA via facsimile at 8:55 p.m. Pacific time with all the necessary papers including a Certificate of Transmission which states the date of transmission. Will's CPA is received in the PTO exactly ten minutes after he sent it.

(C) Will files his CPA via facsimile at 8:40 p.m. Pacific time with all the necessary papers including a Certificate of Transmission. The CPA is received in the PTO exactly ten minutes later. After a quick conference call with his client about the amendment, Able files the amendment via facsimile at 9:10 p.m. Pacific time with all the necessary papers but fails to include a Certificate of Transmission. Able's CPA is received in the PTO exactly fifteen minutes after he sent it.

(D) (A) and (B).

(E) None of the above.

2. At 8:45 p.m. Pacific time that same day, Fleet rushes to the nearest United States Post Office (USPS) down the street to send his nonprovisional patent application with all the necessary papers to the PTO. What is the best action for Fleet to take to receive a Friday, February 12, 1999, filing date?

(A) Send the application with a Certificate of Mailing via first class mail no later than 11:59 p.m. Pacific time on Friday.

(B) Deposit the application directly with an employee of the U.S. Postal Service by "Express Mail Post Office to Post Office" at 8:59 p.m. Pacific time.

(C) Deposit the application directly with an employee of the U.S. Postal Service by "Express Mail Post Office to Addressee" no later than 11:59 p.m. Pacific time.

(D) Send the application via "Federal Express" before 11:59 p.m. Pacific time.

(E) (B) and (C).

3. In addition to complying with 37 CFR § 1.4(d)(2), which of the following documents, if any, must also contain a separate verification statement?

(A) Small entity statements.

(B) An English translation of a non-English-language document.

(C) A claim for foreign priority.

(D) Petition to make an application special.

(E) None of the above.

4.   In early 1997, Goforgold, a company based in Australia, developed a widget with increased reflective properties. Goforgold filed a patent application in the Australian Patent Office on January 8, 1997, and filed a corresponding application in the USPTO on January 5, 1998. All research activities for the inventions disclosed and claimed in the U.S. and Australian applications took place in Australia. The U.S. patent application contains five claims:

1. A widget comprising elements A and B.
2. A widget according to Claim 1 wherein the widget further includes element D.
3. A widget comprising elements A and C.
4. A widget according to Claim 3 wherein the widget further includes element E.
5. A widget comprising elements A, B, and C.

The Australian application only supports claims 1, 2, and 5 of the U.S. application. During the course of prosecution of the U.S. application, the examiner properly rejected all of the claims under 35 U.S.C. § 102(e) as being anticipated by a U.S. patent assigned to Gotthesilver. The Gotthesilver patent was granted on October 6, 1998, on a U.S. application filed on June 15, 1997. The Gotthesilver patent specifically describes, but does not claim, the widget in claims 1-5 of the U.S. application filed by Goforgold. The subject matter of the Gotthesilver patent was reduced to practice in Flushing, New York as of February 12, 1997. Which of the following proposed arguments or actions would properly overcome the examiner's § 102(e) rejection with respect to all the claims?

(A)   File an affidavit under 37 CFR § 1.132 swearing behind the claims of the Gotthesilver patent by relying on the 1997 research activities of Goforgold in Australia.

(B)   File a claim for a right of priority based on the application filed in Australia along with a certified copy of the Australian patent application and canceling Claims 3 and 4.

(C)   File a claim for a right of priority based on the application filed in Australia along with a certified copy of the Australian patent application.

(D)   File an affidavit under 37 CFR § 1.132 swearing behind the February 12, 1997, reduction to practice date of the Gotthesilver patent.

(E)   File a terminal disclaimer.

5. In which of the following situations would a petition to make special **not** be granted?

    (A) The applicant files a petition with the petition fee requesting special status and stating that small entity status has been established; that the subject of the biotechnology patent application is a major asset of the small entity; and that the development of the technology will be significantly impaired if examination of the application is delayed, including an explanation of the basis for making the statement.

    (B) Applicant's invention materially enhances the quality of the environment. Applicant files a petition that the application be accorded special status and includes a statement explaining how the invention contributes to the restoration of a basic life-sustaining element. No fee is included.

    (C) Applicants have filed a request that their application which is directed to an invention for a superconductive material be accorded special status. Applicants' request is accompanied by a statement that the invention involves superconductivity. No fee is included.

    (D) Applicant's invention is directed to a system for detecting explosives. Applicant files a petition for special status which is accompanied by a statement explaining how the invention contributes to countering terrorism. No fee is included.

    (E) None of the above.

6. Which of the following fees are reduced for small entities?

    I.   Patent application filing fees
    II.   Petition for an extension of time fees
    III.   Petition to suspend the rules fees
    IV.   Patent Issue fees
    V.   Certificate of Correction fees

    (A) I, II, III, IV, and V.
    (B) I, IV, and V.
    (C) I, II, and IV.
    (D) I and IV.
    (E) None of the above.

The answer to each of questions 7-11 is based upon the facts set forth in the paragraph below. Answer each question independently of the others.

You are a registered patent agent with an office in Buffalo, New York. On January 13, 1998, Murphy, a resident of Canada, came to your office for purpose of obtaining a U.S. patent on her invention. She tells you that she first conceived her invention at her home in Ontario on December 18, 1996, and that she reduced it to practice on January 10, 1997, at her home. On January 13, 1998, Murphy provided you with a detailed written description fully disclosing her invention. You diligently proceeded to prepare the application. You filed the application in the PTO on February 12, 1998. Consider each of the situations presented in the questions below in light of the facts presented above and determine which paragraph of 35 U.S.C. § 102, if any, would prevent Murphy from obtaining a U.S. patent.

7.   Murphy's invention is described and claimed in a U.S. patent to O'Malley granted on February 9, 1999, on a national stage application filed in the United States on February 17, 1998, based on a PCT international application filed in France on November 13, 1997. O'Malley satisfied the requirements of 35 U.S.C. § 371(c)(1), (2), and (4) on February 17, 1998.

> (A)   35 U.S.C. § 102(b).
> (B)   35 U.S.C. § 102(c).
> (C)   35 U.S.C. § 102(e).
> (D)   35 U.S.C. § 102(f).
> (E)   None of the above.

8.   Murphy patented her invention in Canada on December 30, 1997 on a Canadian patent application filed on February 10, 1997.

> (A)   35 U.S.C. § 102(a).
> (B)   35 U.S.C. § 102(b).
> (C)   35 U.S.C. § 102(d).
> (D)   35 U.S.C. § 102(e).
> (E)   None of the above.

9.   In January of 1997, Murphy sold prototypes of her invention in Canada.

> (A)   35 U.S.C. § 102(a).
> (B)   35 U.S.C. § 102(b).
> (C)   35 U.S.C. § 102(f).
> (D)   35 U.S.C. § 102(g).
> (E)   None of the above.

10. After the application was filed in the U.S., Murphy admitted that in order to make the claimed invention operative, the mechanic who built the prototype of Murphy's invention added a novel feature without consulting Murphy which is included in all the claims of the application.

    (A)   35 U.S.C. § 102(a).
    (B)   35 U.S.C. § 102(b).
    (C)   35 U.S.C. § 102(f).
    (D)   35 U.S.C. § 102(g).
    (E)   None of the above.

11. Murphy's invention is described and claimed in a German Gebrauchsmuster petty patent granted on February 11, 1998, based on an application filed by Murphy on February 2, 1997. The German Gebrauchsmuster patent was published on February 14, 1998.

    (A)   35 U.S.C. § 102(b).
    (B)   35 U.S.C. § 102(c).
    (C)   35 U.S.C. § 102(d).
    (D)   35 U.S.C. § 102(e).
    (E)   None of the above.

12. Which of the following statements, if any, regarding Secrecy Orders are **false**?

    (A)   A Secrecy Order remains in effect for a period of one year from its date of issuance.
    (B)   If the Secrecy Order is applied to an international application, the application will not be forwarded to the International Bureau as long as the Secrecy Order remains in effect.
    (C)   If, prior to or after the issuance of the Secrecy Order, any significant part of the subject matter or material information relevant to the application has been or is revealed to any person in a foreign country, the principals must promptly inform such person of the Secrecy Order and the penalties for improper disclosure.
    (D)   Use of facsimile transmissions to file correspondence in a Secrecy Order case is permitted so long as it is transmitted to the Office in a manner that would preclude disclosure to unauthorized individuals and is properly addressed.
    (E)   (C) and (D).

13.   On January 19, 1999, inventor B filed a patent application in the PTO claiming invention X. Inventor B did not claim priority based on a foreign application filed by inventor B on April 3, 1998, in the Patent Office in Japan. In the foreign application, inventor B disclosed and claimed invention X, which inventor B had conceived on August 11, 1997, and reduced to practice on November 5, 1997, all in Japan. The U.S. patent examiner issued an Office action where all the claims in the patent application were properly rejected under 35 U.S.C. § 102(a) and (e) as being anticipated by a U.S. patent granted to inventor Z on September 1, 1998, on a patent application filed in the PTO on December 5, 1997. There is no common assignee between Z and B, and they are not obligated to assign their invention to a common assignee. Moreover, inventors Z and B, independently of each other, invented invention X, and did not derive anything from the other. The U.S. patent to Z discloses, but does not claim, invention X. Which of the following is/are appropriate reply(replies) which could overcome the rejections under §§ 102(a) and (e) when timely filed?

(A)   File an antedating affidavit or declaration under 37 CFR § 1.131 showing conception on August 11, 1997, and actual reduction to practice on November 5, 1997, all in Japan.

(B)   File a claim for the right and benefit of foreign priority wherein the Japanese application is correctly identified, file a certified copy of the original Japanese patent application, and argue that as a result of the benefit of foreign priority, the U.S patent is no longer available as a prior art reference against the claims.

(C)   Amend the claims to require particular limitations disclosed in inventor B's application, but not disclosed or suggested in inventor Z's patent, and argue that the limitations patentably distinguish the claimed invention over the prior art.

(D)   (A) and (C).

(E)   (B) and (C).

14.   A Certificate of Correction **cannot** be used to correct:

(A)   the failure to make reference to a prior copending application.

(B)   an incorrect reference to a prior copending application.

(C)   the omission of an inventor's name from an issued patent through error and without deceptive intent.

(D)   the omission of a preferred embodiment in the original disclosure overlooked by the inventor which would materially affect the scope of the patent.

(E)   (A), (B), and (D).

15.   In responding to a final rejection of Claims 1 to 5 as being obvious, applicant's patent agent argued that the references applied in the rejection neither taught nor suggested the claimed invention. The examiner issued a Notice of Allowance which included a statement of reasons for allowance. In the statement, the examiner explained her reasons for allowance of the claims. Upon receipt of the statement from the examiner, which of the following, if any, describes the most appropriate course of action the agent may take in reply to the examiner's reasons for allowance?

(A)   The agent may file a reply commenting on the examiner's statement, even though the failure to do so will not give rise to any implication that applicant agrees with or acquiesces in the examiner's reasoning.

(B)   The agent should object to the examiner's statement to avoid any implication that applicant agrees with or acquiesces in the examiner's reasoning.

(C)   Applicant may file comments on the reasons for allowance after payment of the issue fee upon submission of a petition for an extension of time.

(D)   Under current Office policy and procedure, the agent cannot reply to the examiner's statement.

(E)   The agent must file a timely reply to the examiner's statement to enable the examiner to reply to the comments submitted by applicant and to minimize processing delays.

16.   Which of the following statements regarding plant patent applications is (are) **true**?

(A)   Only one claim is necessary and only one claim is permitted.

(B)   The oath or declaration required of the applicant, in addition to the averments required by 37 CFR § 1.63, must state that he or she has asexually reproduced the plant.

(C)   A method claim in a plant patent application is improper.

(D)   Specimens of the plant variety, its flower or fruit, should not be submitted unless specifically called for by the examiner.

(E)   All of the above.

17.   The last day of a three month shortened statutory period to reply to a non-final rejection occurs today, April 21, 1999. Your client is overseas and sends you a facsimile asking you to cancel all of the current claims in the application. There is no deposit account. She further advises you that a new set of claims to replace the current claims will be sent to you no later than April 29, 1999. Which of the following would be the most appropriate course of action to take with regard to the outstanding Office action?

(A)   File a request for a one month extension of time today and pay the fee when you file the amendment.
(B)   File an amendment today canceling all claims in accordance with your client's instructions.
(C)   Await receipt of the new claims and then file the amendment and request for reconsideration with the appropriate fee for an extension of time, no more than 6 months from the date of the non-final rejection.
(D)   File a request for reconsideration today and state that a supplemental amendment will be forthcoming.
(E)   File a request for reconsideration today, stating that the rejection is in error because the claims define a patentable invention.

18.   Which of the following statements is **true** respecting product-by-process claims?

(A)   A lesser burden of proof may be required to make out a case of prima facie obviousness for product-by-process claims than is required to make out a prima facie case of obviousness when a product is claimed in the conventional fashion.
(B)   It is proper to use product-by-process claims only when the process is patentable.
(C)   It is proper to use product-by-process claims only when the product is incapable of description in the conventional fashion.
(D)   Product-by-process claims cannot vary in scope from each other.
(E)   Product-by-process claims may only be used in chemical cases.

19.   Patent applicant Smith claims "a rotary vane pump having impellers coated with ceramic X for the purpose of preventing cavitation of the impellers." The examiner rejected the claim under 35 U.S.C. § 103 as being unpatentable over a patent to John in view of a patent to Alex. John teaches a rotary vane pump having impellers coated with epoxy resin for the purpose of preventing corrosion of the impellers. Alex teaches a mixing device having agitator blades coated with ceramic X for the purpose of preventing corrosion of the blades. Alex also suggests that the ceramic X coating material "is useful on various types of pumps for the purpose of preventing corrosion." The examiner determined that (i) it would have been obvious to one having ordinary skill in the art to substitute the ceramic X coating material taught by Alex for the epoxy resin coating material in John and (ii) the resultant rotary vane pump would have coated impeller blades which would inherently prevent cavitation. The combination of John and Alex:

(A)   cannot support a *prima facie* case for obviousness unless the Alex reference contains a suggestion that ceramic X will cause cavitation.

(B)   cannot support a *prima facie* case for obviousness inasmuch as the discovery that ceramic X prevents cavitation imparts patentability to a known composition.

(C)   may support a *prima facie* case for obviousness even though the Alex reference does not disclose that ceramic X will prevent cavitation or can be used on the impellers of a rotary vane pump.

(D)   cannot shift the burden of proof to the applicant to show that the prior invention lacked the newly discovered property asserted for the claimed invention unless one of the references discloses the property.

(E)   can support a *prima facie* case for obviousness only if both references show or suggest that ceramic X can be used in a rotary vane pump.

20.   Claim 1 is independent. Claim 2 depends from Claim 1. Claim 3 depends from Claim 2. Claim 4 depends from Claims 2 or 3. Claim 5 depends from Claim 3. Claim 6 depends from Claims 2, 3 or 5. The application contains one independent claim. How many dependent claims are there for fee calculation purposes?

(A)   5
(B)   7
(C)   8
(D)   9
(E)   11

Answer questions 21 and 22 based on the following facts:

Registered patent practitioner P prepares and files a patent application for his Japanese client, XYZ Corp., on October 5, 1998. The application claims a banana peeler device. A Notice to File Missing Parts dated December 7, 1998, is received by P on December 10, 1998. P submits an executed oath, along with the surcharge, in order to fully reply to the Notice to File Missing Parts which is received by the PTO on December 23, 1998. In the first Office action dated January 6, 1999, the examiner rejects all of claims 1-5 as being anticipated by the disclosure of a U.S. patent to Apple. The Apple patent discloses, but does not claim, a banana peeler. The Apple patent issued October 7, 1997, and is based on an application filed on June 26, 1996. On January 20, 1999, P faxes a copy of the Office action and the Apple patent to his client in Japan. There is no common ownership between the prior art patent and XYZ's patent application. On March 20, 1999, XYZ faxed instructions to P which distinguish the claims from the Apple patent and includes a reference to a U.S. patent to Zucchini. XYZ discovered the Zucchini patent in February 1999. The Zucchini patent issued on January 12, 1993, and contradicts the teachings of the Apple patent.

21.   On March 20, 1999, XYZ instructs P to file an Information Disclosure Statement (IDS) which includes the Zucchini patent, ten Japanese patents, and a November 13, 1998, magazine article. The magazine article and the ten patents were received from the Japanese Patent Office in XYZ's counterpart foreign application on February 1, 1999. Which of the following actions, if any, taken by P would best comply with PTO practice and procedure?

(A)   File a properly drafted IDS via "Express Mail" in accord with 37 CFR § 1.10 on March 30, 1999, with the fee set forth in 37 CFR § 1.17(p).

(B)   File a properly drafted IDS via first class mail with a Certificate of Mailing dated March 30, 1999, with the required fee and a statement that each item of information was cited in a communication from a foreign patent office in a counterpart foreign application not more than three months prior to the filing of the IDS.

(C)   File a properly drafted IDS via facsimile with a Certificate of Transmission on March 23, 1999, along with a legible copy of each reference.

(D)   (B) and (C).

(E)   None of the above.

22.   Which of the following most correctly sets forth the sections of Title 35 U.S.C. under which XYZ **would not be entitled** to a U.S. patent based on the Apple patent?

    (A)   102(a)
    (B)   102(c)
    (C)   102(d)
    (D)   102(f)
    (E)   102(g)

23.   In a first action on the merits dated February 12, 1997, the examiner (1) rejected all of the claims under 35 U.S.C. § 112, second paragraph; (2) objected to new matter added to the specification by a preliminary amendment; and (3) required a substitute specification that includes a revised summary of invention, abstract, and an additional drawing showing the prior art. You, as a patent practitioner prosecuting the application, disagree with the propriety of the rejection, objection and requirement. Which of the following would be the most appropriate course of action to take to reply to the examiner's action?

    (A)   File a petition with the Group Director requesting withdrawal of the examiner's objection to the specification, and suspension of further action on the claims until three months after the petition has been decided.
    (B)   File a request for reconsideration and present arguments distinctly and specifically pointing out the supposed errors in the examiner's requirement, rejection, and objection, and otherwise fully reply to the rejection and objection.
    (C)   Appeal the objection and requirement of the examiner to the Board of Patent Appeals and Interferences, and request that the final rejection of the claims be suspended until the appeal is decided.
    (D)   Amend the claims to overcome the examiner's rejection under 35 U.S.C § 112, and file a motion to the Board of Patent Appeals and Interferences appealing the examiner's objection to the specification.
    (E)   Change the summary of invention to conform to the broadest claim, request reconsideration of the requirement for a substitute specification, request that the requirement for submission of the additional drawings be held in abeyance until after allowance of the application, and generally allege that the claims define a patentable invention.

24. Which of the following statements correctly sets forth the manner in which Inventor Ann, a U.S. citizen, may file documents regarding her international patent application with the United States Receiving Office?

- (A) Where the document is the PCT international application and Ann needs to receive an April 1, 1999, filing date, Ann should file her PCT international application via first class mail with the United States Post Office and include a Certificate of Mailing dated April 1, 1999.
- (B) Where the document is a Demand for international preliminary examination, two weeks before the deadline, Ann should file her Demand by facsimile transmission with a dated Certificate of Transmission.
- (C) Where the document is the PCT international application and Ann needs to receive an April 12, 1999, filing date, Ann should file a copy of her international application via facsimile transmission with a Certificate of Transmission dated April 12, 1999.
- (D) Where the documents are substituted drawing sheets due on April 15, 1999, Ann should file her substitute drawing sheets via facsimile on April 15, 1999.
- (E) All of the above.

25. A multiple dependent claim _____

- (A) may indirectly serve as a basis for another multiple dependent claim.
- (B) may directly serve as a basis for a multiple dependent claim.
- (C) shall be construed to incorporate by reference all the limitations of each of the particular claims to which it refers.
- (D) added by amendment should not be entered until the proper fee has been received by the PTO.
- (E) (C) and (D).

26. A design patent application was filed on July 5, 1995, which issued as a design patent on December 3, 1996. On December 16, 1996, a proper reissue design application was filed. The reissue patent was granted on September 2, 1997. When will the first maintenance fee be due?

- (A) December 2, 2000
- (B) December 16, 1999
- (C) December 3, 1999
- (D) March 3, 2000
- (E) None of the above

27.   After one of your client's claims has been allowed, another claim in the same application stands objected to as being a substantial duplicate of the allowed claim, i.e. they both cover the same thing. You and your client agree that the claim is a substantial duplicate. Which of the following could **NOT** overcome the objection?

(A)   Amending the claim objected to in a manner consistent with the specification to have a different scope.
(B)   Amending the allowed claim consistent with the specification to have a different scope.
(C)   Canceling the allowed claim to obviate the objection.
(D)   Filing a divisional application that includes the objected claim.
(E)   Canceling the claim objected to so as to permit issuance of the allowed claim.

28.   Which of the following statements regarding reissue applications is **false**?

(A)   If the file record is silent as to the existence of an assignee, it will be presumed that an assignee does exist.
(B)   An examination on the merits of a reissue application will not be made without an offer to surrender the original patent, the actual surrender, or an affidavit or declaration to the effect that the original is lost or inaccessible.
(C)   A broadened claim can be presented after two years from the grant in a broadening reissue which was filed within two years from the grant.
(D)   The filing of a continued prosecution application (CPA) under 37 CFR § 1.53(d) of a reissue application will not be announced in the *Official Gazette*.
(E)   When making amendments to the claims, patent claims must not be renumbered and the numbering of any claims added to the patent must follow the number of the highest numbered patent claim.

29.   Employees Larry and Curly work for Taylor, Inc., each with knowledge of the other's work, and with obligations to assign to Taylor inventions conceived while employed by Taylor. Larry invented a novel coating apparatus which utilized a spring released mechanism that worked well at temperatures of at least 32° F. Larry discussed his invention with Curly during work at Taylor. After their discussion, Curly conceived of an improvement and developed a piston activated mechanism for use in Larry's novel coating apparatus. Curly's piston activated mechanism worked extremely well at temperatures between 45 to 60° F. On April 8, 1997, Curly filed a patent application in the PTO disclosing the fact that Larry invented a novel coating apparatus and claiming an improved coating apparatus with a piston activated mechanism. Curly's specification disclosed the excellent results obtained when the piston activated mechanism was used at temperatures between 45 to 60° F. On August 14, 1997, Larry's application claiming the coating apparatus with the spring released mechanism for use at temperatures of at least 32° F. was filed in the PTO. On December 29, 1998, a patent was granted to Larry. In an Office action dated March 18, 1999, the examiner rejected the claims in Curly's application under 35 U.S.C. §§ 102(g)/103 over Larry's patent in view of a patent granted to Moe on August 25, 1992. Larry's patent claims the coating apparatus with the spring released mechanism for operation at temperatures of at least 32° F. The patent to Moe discloses a piston activated mechanism (substantially similar to Curly's piston activated mechanism) in combination with a different coating apparatus. The Moe patent also discloses that the piston activated mechanism would only operate at temperatures below 32° F. The examiner properly found that substitution of the piston activated mechanism of Moe for the spring released mechanism in Larry's coating apparatus would have been obvious. As a registered practitioner hired by Taylor to prosecute both the Larry and Curly applications, which of the following best describes the course of action you should take to provide Taylor with all the patent protection it is entitled to receive?

    (A)   Traverse the rejection by arguing that the rejection is improper, and in support thereof, submit an affidavit under 37 CFR § 1.132 signed by an officer of Taylor, Inc. attesting to the fact that at the time the inventions were made, Larry and Curly were obligated to assign their inventions to Taylor, Inc.

    (B)   Traverse the rejection by arguing that the rejection is improper and provide an affidavit signed by Larry stating that Curly derived his work from Larry and that both Curly and Larry were under an obligation to assign their inventions to Taylor.

    (C)   Traverse the rejection and submit an affidavit signed by Curly under 37 CFR § 1.131 stating that he made his invention in the United States before Larry filed his patent application and that both Larry and Curly were obligated to assign their inventions to Taylor, Inc. at the time the inventions were made.

(D) Amend the Curly application to claim only a piston activated mechanism which operates at temperatures between 45 - 60° F., and delete the coating apparatus from the claims.

(E) File a terminal disclaimer to have any patent granted on Curly's application expire on the same date the Larry patent expires.

Questions 30 and 31 are based on the following facts. Each question should be answered independently of the other.

Horatio invented a new widget for vacuum cleaners. You prepared and filed a patent application containing claims 1 through 10 directed to the widget. In a second Office action dated September 10, 1998, the examiner rejected claims 1 through 10 for the second time and on the same grounds and set a three month shortened statutory period for reply. You filed a reply to the second Office action on December 9, 1998. On January 8, 1999, the examiner sent another Office action containing a final rejection of claims 1 through 10 and set a three month shortened statutory period for reply.

30. Horatio asked you to file a Notice of Appeal. In which of the following situations, would the Notice of Appeal be considered **acceptable**?

(A) A Notice of Appeal signed by you, and the appropriate appeal fee are filed on April 8, 1999. The Notice does not identify the rejected claims appealed.

(B) A unsigned Notice of Appeal and the appropriate appeal fee is filed on April 8, 1999, and the Notice identifies the rejected claims appealed.

(C) A Notice of Appeal, signed by you, with the necessary fee for appeal and extension of time, are filed on July 8, 1999, without identifying the rejected claims appealed.

(D) (A) and (B).

(E) (A), (B), and (C).

31. An acceptable Notice of Appeal is timely filed in the PTO on March 23, 1999. Absent extraordinary circumstances, which of the following is the **last day** that an appeal brief can be filed if a proper petition and the necessary fees for the brief and extension of time are filed with the brief?

(A) April 8, 1999

(B) Monday, October 25, 1999

(C) August 23, 1999

(D) Monday, May 24, 1999

(E) September 23, 1999

32.　On a sunny January day in Minnesota, neighbors X and Y working together stumble across a novel means for melting snow with a device that X and Y have jointly invented. Being low on funds to market their invention, X and Y decide to save money and file their own patent application. X and Y decide to file a provisional patent application in order to have more time to market their invention. X and Y carefully prepare all the necessary papers for the filing of their provisional patent application and come up with the money to cover the filing fee. On Saturday, January 9, 1999, X and Y meet at their favorite coffee shop to take a final look at the specification and drawings they had prepared and to prepare a cover letter to accompany their application. In their eagerness to get to the Post Office after drinking two double mocha cappuccinos, the handwritten cover letter prepared by X and Y fails to identify X as an inventor. The cover letter only identifies the application as a provisional patent application; inventor Y's full name, residence and correspondence address; and the title of the invention. Unaware that X has not been identified as an inventor, X and Y make a copy of their application papers and mail the cover letter with the specification, drawings and the proper fee to the Patent and Trademark Office via first class mail that same morning. A huge winter storm is expected to hit Minnesota by dusk and X and Y hurry home to conduct further experiments with their snow melting invention. The papers are received in the Patent and Trademark Office on Monday, January 11, 1999.

Three weeks later, X and Y return to their favorite coffee shop to celebrate the outstanding success of their experiments with their snow melting device during the huge winter storm which hit Minnesota and to discuss the minor adjustment they made to their invention. In reviewing their application papers for the first time since they were mailed, X notices that the handwritten cover letter does not identify him as an inventor, and fails to include his residence and correspondence address. Which of the following is the best action to be taken by X and Y to correct these omissions from their handwritten cover letter in accordance with proper PTO practice and procedure?

      (A)　X and Y should timely file an amendment to the provisional patent application to add X as an inventor, accompanied by a petition stating that the error occurred without deceptive intent on the part of X and the appropriate fee.

      (B)　X and Y should file an amendment to their provisional patent application which describes the minor adjustment made to the snow melting device and sign the amendment naming X and Y as joint inventors.

      (C)　X and Y should file a request for a certificate of correction and with an explanation of how the error occurred without deceptive intent.

      (D)　X and Y should file a continuation application with a new declaration signed by X and Y.

      (E)　X and Y should timely file a new cover sheet during the pendency of their provisional application which identifies both X and Y as inventors, and provides the title of the invention, as well as the residences of X and Y and the correspondence address.

33. The claim, "An alloy consisting of 70.5 to 77.5% iron, 15.0 to 17.0% cobalt, 0.5 to 1.0% carbon, up to 2.5% chromium, and at least 7.0% tungsten" is anticipated by a reference disclosing an alloy having:

    (A)   76.0% iron, up to 15.0% cobalt, 0.5% carbon, and 8.5% tungsten.

    (B)   71% iron, 15% cobalt, 1.0% carbon, 1% chromium, 8% tungsten, and 4% nickel.

    (C)   71.3% iron, 15.2% cobalt, 0.9% carbon, 2.6% chromium, and 10% tungsten.

    (D)   76% iron, 15% cobalt, 1.0% carbon, at least 2.0% chromium, and 6% tungsten.

    (E)   72.0% iron, 16.5% cobalt, at least 2.0% carbon, 2.5% chromium, and up to 7.0% tungsten.

34. On January 6, 1999, Doe asked patent agent Bronson to prepare and file a patent application on an automobile jack which Doe had invented. Doe gave Bronson several sketches and a written description of the jack which described and showed the jack as utilizing only a scissors-type lifting mechanism. Bronson prepared a patent application disclosing the scissors-type lifting mechanism based on information provided by Doe. The claims of the patent application recited the lifting mechanism generically as "lifting means" since the specific type of lifting mechanism was not thought by Doe to be critical to the inventive feature of his jack. After Doe reviewed and signed the application, Bronson filed it in the PTO on February 3, 1999. On March 19, 1999, Doe discovered that his jack worked much better with a screw-type lifting mechanism as opposed to the scissors-type mechanism. The screw-type lifting mechanism is not disclosed in the application. Doe immediately informed Bronson of this fact. In reply to the first Office action, Bronson canceled all of the original claims and presented a new claim to the jack which included the provision of the screw-type lifting mechanism. Is the new claim proper at this stage of the prosecution?

    (A)   Yes, because the claim particularly points out and distinctly claims the subject matter which Doe regards as his invention or discovery.

    (B)   No, because the claim could be properly rejected under 35 U.S.C. § 112, first paragraph.

    (C)   Yes, because the claim sets forth the best mode contemplated by Doe for carrying out his invention.

    (D)   No, because the claim could be properly rejected under 35 U.S.C. § 132.

    (E)   No, because the claim could be properly rejected under 35 U.S.C. § 112, sixth paragraph.

35. On January 7, 1998, you filed a U.S. patent application containing Claims 1 through 8 on behalf of your client, Grumpy. In a first Office action, the examiner rejected Claims 1-8 under 35 U.S.C § 103 over a U.S. patent to Happy in view of a U.S. patent to Sleepy. The Happy patent issued on January 6, 1998, based on an application filed on June 11, 1996. The Sleepy patent issued in 1950. Which of the following responses would be the most persuasive in having the rejections withdrawn?

(A) Argue that the claimed invention is patentably distinguishable over the combination of the Happy and Sleepy patents, pointing out the specific language in the claims that is not shown by the combination of the references.

(B) Argue that the Sleepy patent is outdated and that its teachings are so obsolete that it would no longer be read by one of ordinary skill in the art.

(C) Argue that the claimed invention is patentably distinguishable from Sleepy, and point out the specific language in the claims that is not shown by Sleepy.

(D) Argue that the devices disclosed by Sleepy and Happy are not physically combinable.

(E) Argue that the Happy patent is not prior art because it was not granted more than one year before Grumpy filed his patent application.

36. The specification shall conclude with one or more claims and must set forth:

(A) the manner of making the invention, the theory of why the invention works, and at least one working example showing how the invention works.

(B) the manner and process of making and using the invention, a written description of the invention, and the best mode of carrying out the invention.

(C) a description of the invention, how the invention is distinguishable over the most relevant prior art, and the best mode of carrying out the invention.

(D) only a full, clear, and concise description of the invention.

(E) a complete description of the invention, and how to use the invention so that a person having ordinary skill in the art to which the invention pertains would be able to practice the invention.

37. Which of the following statements, if any, is true?

    (A) A claim for a "soap composition comprising a maximum of 0.2 parts by weight of X per part by weight of Y" is anticipated by a soap composition disclosed in a publication as having 5 parts by weight of X per part weight of Y.

    (B) A claim for "a laminate circuit material comprising a sheet of adhesive film, and a sheet of conductive material disposed on said sheet of adhesive film" is **not** anticipated by an article of manufacture consisting of an adhesive film disposed on one surface of a sheet of conductive material and a glass reinforced adhesive film disposed on the opposite surface of said sheet of conductive material."

    (C) An independent Claim 1 for an "article comprising a widget having a coating from 0.05 to 1 mm thickness," and a dependent Claim 2 for "an article according to Claim 1 wherein the coating is 0.3 mm thick," both are anticipated by "a widget having a coating of 0.5 mm thickness" described in a printed publication.

    (D) A claim for a "nickel alloy comprising nickel, chromium, iron and at least one member selected from the group consisting of copper, silver and tin" is anticipated by a printed publication which discloses "an alloy consisting of nickel, silver, chromium, iron, copper, and cobalt."

    (E) None of the above.

38. On Monday, April 5, 1999, an Office action was mailed to practitioner P. The Office action contained a rejection of all claims in the application and set a three month shortened statutory period for reply. The very last day for filing a reply without requesting an extension of time would be _____.

    (A) July 2, 1999
    (B) July 3, 1999
    (C) July 5, 1999
    (D) July 6, 1999
    (E) August 3, 1999

39.   Jones invented a widget. She disclosed to her patent agent that the widget can be any combination of colors, the most preferred embodiment being a widget having a blue, orange, yellow or purple color. The agent prepared a patent application which disclosed a widget having a blue, orange or purple color and which included the following claim: "1. A widget having a blue, orange or purple color." On January 8, 1999, Jones reviewed the application and signed the oath. Just after Jones left the agent's office, the agent remembered that Jones had also disclosed to him a yellow widget. The attorney immediately prepared a preliminary amendment which included instructions to amend the specification to also include a yellow widget and to rewrite Claim 1 as follows: "A widget having a blue, orange, yellow or purple color." The specification, oath, and the amendment were mailed to the PTO in the same envelope and were received in the PTO on January 12, 1999. Given these facts, which one of the following statements is true?

    (A)   Claim 1 cannot be properly rejected under 35 U.S.C. § 102(a) as being anticipated by a patent to Smith which was filed on March 2, 1997, and issued on August 13, 1998, and which discloses but does not claim, a widget having an orange color.

    (B)   Claim 1 can be considered to contain new matter even though the preliminary amendment was filed concurrently with the filing of the specification.

    (C)   Claim 1 can be properly rejected under 35 U.S.C. § 112, second paragraph, because the use of the word "or" renders the metes and bounds of the claim indeterminate.

    (D)   Claim 1 can be properly rejected on the ground of disclaimer.

    (E)   None of the above statements is true.

40.   In order to calculate when an appeal brief must be filed, which of the following documents should be used to establish the date that a Notice of Appeal was filed?

    (A)   A separate letter sent from the Patent and Trademark Office which acknowledges receipt of your Notice of Appeal.

    (B)   A self-addressed postcard included with the filing of your Notice of Appeal which was date stamped and returned to you.

    (C)   A copy of the Certificate of Mailing you signed which states the date you deposited the Notice of Appeal via first class mail.

    (D)   (A), (B), and (C).

    (E)   (B) and (C).

41.   Which of the following choices would be considered as independent grounds for filing a reissue application?

(I)   The claims are too narrow or too broad.
(II)   The disclosure contains inaccuracies.
(III)   Applicant failed to or incorrectly claimed foreign priority.
(IV)   The specification contains a plurality of obvious spelling and grammatical errors.
(V)   Applicant failed to make reference to or incorrectly made reference to prior copending applications.

(A)   (I),(II), and (IV)
(B)   (II), (III), and (V)
(C)   (I), (II), (III), (IV), and (V)
(D)   (I), (II), (III), and (V)
(E)   (I), (III), and (V)

42.   On April 19, 1999, Inventor Mary hires you for advice on a patent application. Mary informs you that she previously filed a provisional application for her invention on May 1, 1998. However, Mary has since made some improvements that were not described in her provisional application. To fully protect Mary's patent rights, what is the best course of action to recommend to Mary?

(A)   File an amendment in the provisional application on or before May 1, 1999, which describes the improvements made by Mary.
(B)   Immediately file a continued prosecution application based on the provisional application filed on May 1, 1998, and include a preliminary amendment which adds a description of the improvements made.
(C)   File a second provisional patent application which claims the benefit of the May 1, 1998, filing date of the first provisional patent application.
(D)   File a continuation-in-part application as soon as possible which adds a disclosure of the improvements made.
(E)   None of the above.

43. A U.S. patent application to AuGratin, a French national, was filed in the U.S. Patent and Trademark Office on August 10, 1997. The application disclosed and claimed an apparatus having a combination of elements A, B, and C. AuGratin filed a claim for priority in his U.S. application based upon an application which he filed in the French Patent Office on September 16, 1996. AuGratin's U.S. patent application as filed is an exact English translation of his French application. AuGratin's French application was issued and published as French Patent No. 1,234,567 on March 20, 1998. On April 12, 1999, AuGratin filed a continuation-in-part application (CIP) containing disclosure of new element D in the apparatus. The CIP application included new claims to an apparatus comprising a new combination of elements A, B, C, and D. The examiner properly rejected the new claims in the CIP application as being obvious over AuGratin's French Patent No. 1,234,567 in view of a U.S. patent to Baker which clearly suggests modifying AuGratin's apparatus by adding element D to the combination of elements A, B, and C. The rejection is a *prima facie* case of obviousness. Can AuGratin's French patent be removed as a reference?

  (A) Yes, because AuGratin can swear behind French Patent No. 1,234,567 since the publication date of AuGratin's French patent is less than one year prior to AuGratin's August 10, 1997, U.S. filing date.
  (B) Yes, because the claims in the parent application are supported in the CIP application.
  (C) No, because the new claims in the CIP are not entitled to the benefit of the filing date of the parent application since the combination of elements A, B, C, and D is not supported in the parent application.
  (D) Yes, because AuGratin's French patent cannot be used as prior art in view of the claim for priority in the parent application.
  (E) No, because the new claims are not supported in the CIP application.

44. A Customer Number in the USPTO may be used to do which of the following?

  (A) Designate the fee address of a patent.
  (B) Designate the correspondence address of a patent application.
  (C) Serve as the Deposit Account Number to pay an extension of time fee.
  (D) Submit a list of practitioners so that an applicant may in a Power of Attorney appoint those practitioners associated with the Customer Number.
  (E) (A), (B), and (D).

45. Where a flat board and parallel legs are separate elements which are intended to be included in a claim to the combination of the flat board and legs, the combination is properly set forth in which of the following claims?

(A) A table having a flat board and parallel legs secured to the flat board.

(B) A table having a flat board capable of being connected to parallel legs.

(C) A table having a flat board and means for securing parallel legs to the flat board.

(D) A table having a flat board with means whereby parallel legs can be secured to the flat board.

(E) A table having a flat board for receiving parallel legs.

46. Which of the following statements regarding design patent applications is (are) **false?**

(A) The use of trademarks in design patent application specifications is permitted under limited circumstances.

(B) It is improper to use a trademark alone or coupled with the word "type" in the title of a design patent.

(C) A design patent and a trademark may be obtained on the same subject matter.

(D) It is the policy of the Patent and Trademark Office to prohibit the inclusion of a copyright notice in a design patent application.

(E) (A) and (B).

47. Which of the following statements concerning the confidentiality of patent applications before the Patent and Trademark Office is **true?**

(A) All documents filed as part of the Disclosure Document Program are open to the public two years after filing.

(B) All reissue applications are open to the public.

(C) Copies of any document contained in the application file for which the United States acted as the International Preliminary Examining Authority will be furnished in accordance with Patent Cooperation Treaty (PCT) Rule 94.2 or 94.3 upon payment of the appropriate fee.

(D) (B) and (C).

(E) (A) and (B).

48.   Apple's claims have been properly rejected under 35 U.S.C. § 102(e) as being anticipated by Carrot. The rejection is based upon the disclosed, but unclaimed, subject matter in the Carrot patent. The Carrot patent issued six months after the filing date of Apple's application. The unclaimed subject matter in the Carrot patent was not invented by Carrot, but rather was disclosed to Carrot by Apple. Carrot's claimed invention is patentably distinct from Apple's claimed invention. The proper reply to obviate this rejection would be to:

- (A) Copy the claims in the Carrot patent to provoke an interference.
- (B) File an affidavit by Carrot establishing that Carrot derived his knowledge of the relevant subject matter from Apple.
- (C) Argue that the Carrot patent is not prior art because the patent did not issue before Apple filed his application.
- (D) File a terminal disclaimer signed by Apple.
- (E) File a terminal disclaimer signed by Carrot.

49.   In which of the following situations does the prohibition against double patenting rejections under 35 U.S.C. § 121 **not** apply?

- (A) The applicant voluntarily files two or more cases without a restriction requirement by the examiner.
- (B) The requirement for restriction was only made in an international application by the International Searching Authority or the International Preliminary Examining Authority.
- (C) The requirement for restriction was withdrawn by the examiner before the patent issues.
- (D) The claims of the second application are drawn to the "same invention" as the first application or patent.
- (E) All of the above.

50.   A patent application is filed with 10 claims. Claims 1, 2, and 3 are independent claims directed to a product. Claim 4 is an independent claim directed to a process for making the product.   Which of the following would be acceptable form for a dependent Claim 5?

(A)   A product as in claims 1-3, wherein …
(B)   A product as claimed in claims 1, 2, and 3, wherein …
(C)   A product as in claim 1, made by the process of claim 4.
(D)   A product as claimed in any one of claims 1, 2, or 3 wherein …
(E)   A product as claimed in claim 6 or claim 7, wherein …

1. ANSWER: (A) is the correct answer. The date of receipt accorded to any correspondence permitted to be sent by facsimile transmission, including a continued prosecution application (CPA) filed under 37 CFR § 1.53(d), is the date the complete transmission is received by an Office facsimile unit. A CPA may be transmitted to the Office by facsimile as specified in 37 CFR § 1.6(d)(3), but cannot receive the benefit of a certificate of transmission as specified in 37 CFR § 1.8(a)(2)(i)(A). (A) provides that Will's CPA was received in the PTO at 8:50 p.m. Pacific time or 11:50 p.m. Eastern time. i.e. by Friday, February 12, 1999. An amendment can receive the benefit of a certificate of transmission. 37 CFR §§ 1.6(d); 1.8(a). Able's amendment was sent at 8:50 p.m. Pacific time or 11:50 Eastern time, i.e. by Friday, February 12, 1999. Under 37 CFR § 1.8(a)(1), Able's amendment is considered timely, even though received by the PTO on Saturday. because transmission via facsimile began on February 12, 1999, prior to expiration of the set period of time via facsimile, and included a Certificate of Transmission stating the February 12, 1999, date of transmission. 37 CFR §§ 1.6(d); 1.8(a)(1)(i)(B); MPEP § 502.01. (B) is not correct because Will's CPA was not timely filed. Under 37 CFR § 1.8(a)(2), no benefit will be given to a Certificate of Mailing for a CPA and the actual date of receipt is used to determine if the correspondence has been timely filed. In (B), Will's CPA was received in the PTO at 9:05 p.m. Pacific time or 12:05 a.m. Eastern time on Saturday, and would therefore be accorded a receipt date of Tuesday, February 16, 1999 (Monday, February 15, 1999, is a Federal holiday - President's Day). MPEP § 502.01. (C) is not the correct answer because Able's amendment was not timely filed under 37 CFR § 1.8(a)(1). In this case, Able's amendment was received in the PTO at 9:25 p.m. Pacific time or 12:25 Eastern time on Saturday. "Correspondence for which transmission was completed on a Saturday . . . will be accorded a receipt date of the next succeeding day which is not a . . . Federal holiday within the District of Columbia." As such, Able's amendment would be accorded a receipt date of Tuesday, February 16, 1999. (D) is incorrect because (B) is incorrect. (E) is incorrect because (A) is correct.

2. ANSWER: (C) is the correct answer. MPEP § 513 [p. 500-46]. (A) is incorrect. 37 CFR § 1.8(a)(2)(i)(A). The filing date in (A) would be the day the application is received in the PTO. (B) is incorrect because "Express Mail" must be sent by "Express Mail Post Office to Addressee" and not "Express Mail Post Office to Post Office." MPEP § 502 ("Express Mail" Service at p. 500-7). (D) is incorrect. MPEP § 512 ("Office Procedure. A" at p. 500-43). (E) is incorrect because (B) is incorrect.

3. ANSWER: (E) "None of the above" is the correct answer. As noted in MPEP § 410, the first certification requirement set forth in 37 CFR § 10.18(b) "has permitted the PTO to eliminate the separate verification requirement previously contained in 37 CFR ... 1.27 [small entity statements], ... 1.52 [English translations of non-English documents], 1.55 [Claim for foreign priority], ... 1.102 [Petition to make an application special], ..."

4.   ANSWER: (B) is the most correct answer. MPEP §§ 706.02(b); 2136.05. (A) and (D) are incorrect because an affidavit under 37 CFR § 1.132 is inappropriate in this situation. MPEP § 715.01. (C) will not result in overcoming the rejection of claims 3 and 4 inasmuch as the disclosure of the Australian patent application only supported claims 1, 2, and 5. (E) is not correct because a terminal disclaimer will not overcome a 35 U.S.C. § 102(e) rejection. MPEP § 2136.05 [p. 2100-87].

5.   ANSWER: (D) is the correct answer because a fee is required, but is not included with the petition. 37 CFR § 1.102(c) and (d); MPEP § 708.02 [pp.700-72-73]. (A), (B), and (C) are incorrect because they conform to 37 CFR § 102. (E) is incorrect because (D) is correct.

6.   ANSWER: (C) is the correct answer. 35 U.S.C. § 41(h); 37 CFR §§ 1.17(h); 1.20(a); MPEP § 509.02. (A), (B), and (D) are incorrect because there is no reduced fee for small entities for III or IV. MPEP § 509.02. (E) is incorrect because (C) is correct.

7.   ANSWER: (E) is the correct answer. "Once a patent issues from a national stage application, the filing date for prior art purposes under 35 U.S.C. § 102(e) is not the international filing date, but is the date on which the requirements of 35 U.S.C. § 371(c)(1), (2) and (4) were met. . . . " MPEP §§ 1895.01, subsection E. [p.1800-130]; 2136.03, subsection II. The effective filing date of O'Malley's patent, therefore, is February 17, 1998 - which is **after** Murphy's U.S. filing date of February 12, 1998. The O'Malley patent is not prior art under 35 U.S.C. §102(e). (A), (B), (C) and (D) are incorrect. 35 U.S.C. §§ 102(b), (c), (e) and (f).

8.   ANSWER: (C) is the correct answer. The filing date in Canada is more than 12 months before the U.S. filing date for the same invention and the invention was patented in Canada before the U.S. filing date. MPEP § 2135; 2135.01. (A), (B), and (D) are incorrect. 35 U.S.C. §§ 102(a), (b) and (e). (E) is incorrect because (C) is correct.

9.   ANSWER: (E) "None of the above" is the correct answer. There is no statutory bar because the sales did not take place in the United States. MPEP § 2133.03(d). (A), (B), (C), and (D) are incorrect because the requirements of 35 U.S.C. §§ 102(a), (b), (f), and (g) were not satisfied.

10.   ANSWER: (C) is the correct answer. Murphy did not invent the subject matter sought to be patented. MPEP § 2137; 2137.01. (A), (B), and (D) are incorrect. 35 U.S.C. §§ 102(a), (b) and (g). (E) is incorrect because (C) is correct.

11.   ANSWER: (C) is the correct answer. A German Gebrauchmuster petty patent is usable in a 35 U.S.C. § 102(d) rejection. MPEP § 2135.01, subsection III. [p.2100-81]. The foreign patent was granted prior to Murphy's U.S. filing date. MPEP § 2135.01, subsection III, (E). Thus, Murphy's German application was filed more than 12 months prior to her U.S. filing date for the same invention and was granted before the U.S. filing

date. (A), (B), and (D) are incorrect. 35 U.S.C. §§ 102(b), (c), and (e). (E) is incorrect because (C) is correct.

12. ANSWER: (E) is the correct answer. Both (C) and (D) are false statements. MPEP § 120 [p. 100-15] states that "if such part of the subject matter was or is disclosed to any person in a foreign country . . . , the principals must not inform such person of the Secrecy Order, but instead must promptly furnish to the Assistant Commissioner . . . the following information . . . ." (D) is also a false statement. "Use of facsimile transmission is not permitted. 37 CFR 1.6(d)(6)" MPEP § 120 ("Correspondence"). (A) and (B) are true statements. MPEP §§ 120; 130.

13. ANSWER: (D) is the most correct answer because it includes both (A) and (C). Following the procedure in (A) is in accord with 37 CFR § 1.131 and MPEP § 715.07(c). By following the procedure in (C), the claims are no longer anticipated by Z's patent because particular limitations are now claimed in inventor B's application which are not disclosed or suggested by inventor Z's patent. 35 U.S.C. § 102 (a) and (e); MPEP § 2131. (B) is not correct. 37 CFR § 1.131; MPEP §§ 201.15; 715.07(c); 2132.01; 2136; and 2136.05.

14. ANSWER: (D) is the most correct answer because such a mistake could affect the scope and meaning of the patent and is not considered to be of the "minor" character required for the issuance of a Certificate of Correction. MPEP § 1481. (A) and (B) can be corrected by a Certificate of Correction. MPEP § 1481 [p.1400-47]. (C) can also be corrected by a Certificate of Correction. 37 CFR § 1.324; MPEP § 1481 [p.1400-44].

15. ANSWER: (A) is the correct answer. 37 CFR § 1.104(e); MPEP § 1302.14. (B) is incorrect. As set forth in 37 CFR § 1.104(e), "[f]ailure to file such a statement does not give rise to any implication that the applicant or patent owner agrees with or acquiesces in the reasoning of the examiner." (C) and (D) are incorrect. Comments are allowed and must be submitted no later than the payment of the issue fee. MPEP § 1302.14. (E) is incorrect. "[C]omments made by applicants on the examiner's statement of reasons for allowance will not be returned to the examiner after their entry in the file and will not be commented on by the examiner." MPEP § 1302.14 [p. 1300-11]

16. ANSWER: (E) is the correct answer. 37 CFR § 1.162; MPEP §§ 1604; 1605; and 1607.

17. ANSWER: (C) is the correct answer. 37 CFR § 1.111; MPEP § 714.02. (A) is incorrect because the fee must be paid when the request for an extension of time is made. 37 CFR § 1.136(a); MPEP § 710.02(e). (B) is not correct. MPEP §§ 714.19(A); 711.01. An amendment canceling all claims is non-responsive to the Office action. As set forth in 37 CFR § 1.111(b), "In order to be entitled to reconsideration . . ., the applicant . . . must reply to the Office action. The reply . . . must be reduced to a writing which distinctly and specifically points out the supposed errors in the examiner's action and must reply to every ground of objection and rejection in the prior Office action." MPEP §§ 714.19(A); 711.01.

(D) is not correct and does not comply with 37 CFR § 1.111(b). (E) is incorrect. As set forth in 37 CFR § 1.111(b), "A general allegation that the claims define a patentable invention without specifically pointing out how the language of the claims patentably distinguishes them from the references does not comply with the requirements of this section."

18.   ANSWER: (A) is the correct answer. MPEP § 2113 citing *In re Fessmann*, 489 F.2d 742, 744, 180 USPQ 324, 326 (CCPA 1974). (B) is incorrect inasmuch as "determination of patentability is based on the product itself. The patentability of a product does not depend on its method of production. If the product in the product-by-process claim is the same as or obvious from a product of the prior art, the claim is unpatentable even though the prior art product was made by a different process." MPEP § 2113 [p.2100-51] (C) and (D) are incorrect because "[t]he fact that it is necessary for an applicant to describe his product in product-by-process terms does not prevent him from presenting claims of varying scope." MPEP § 2173.05(p), item (I). (E) is incorrect. "A claim to a device, apparatus, manufacture, or composition of matter may contain a reference to the process in which it is intended to be used . . . so long as it is clear that the claim is directed to the product and not the process." MPEP § 2173.05(p), item (I)[p. 2100-174].

19.   ANSWER: (C) is the correct answer. 35 U.S.C. § 103; MPEP §§ 2143; 2144; 2145; *In re Dillon*, 919 F.2d 688, 16 USPQ2d 1897 (Fed. Cir. 1990). The motivation to modify the reference may suggest what the applicant has done, but for a different purpose. As discussed in MPEP § 2144 [p.2100-115], "[i]t is not necessary that the prior art suggest the combination to achieve the same advantage . . . .[citations omitted]" (A), (B), (D) and (E) are in correct because they are inconsistent with MPEP §§ 2143, 2144, and 2145, as well as *In re Dillon*, supra.

20.   ANSWER: (C) is the correct answer. 35 U.S.C. § 41(a). For fee calculation purposes, MPEP § 608.01(n), subsection G.2.(a) provides that "claims in proper multiple dependent form may not be considered as single dependent claims for the purpose of calculating fees. Thus, a multiple dependent claim is considered to be that number of dependent claims to which it refers. Any proper claim depending directly or indirectly from a multiple dependent claim is also considered as the number of dependent claims as referred to in the multiple dependent claim from which it depends."

21.   ANSWER: (A) is the correct answer. 37 CFR § 1.97(c); MPEP § 609. An IDS filed pursuant to 37 CFR § 1.97(c) will be considered provided that the IDS is accompanied by either (1) a statement as specified in 37 CFR § 1.97(e); **or** (2) the fee set forth in 37 CFR § 1.17(p). The filing date of the XYZ patent application is October 5, 1998. The omission of the oath from the XYZ application did not affect the filing date of the XYZ application. 37 CFR § 1.53(b); MPEP § 601.01(a). (B) is not correct because the Zucchini patent was not cited by the Japanese Patent Office. The Zucchini patent was discovered by XYZ. Also, under 37 CFR § 1.97(c), XYZ was **not** required to submit both a fee **and** a statement. (C) is not correct because it did not include either the statement **or**

fee required by 37 CFR § 1.97(c). (D) is not correct because (B) and (C) are incorrect. (E) is not correct because (A) is correct.

22. ANSWER: (A) is the correct answer. The invention was disclosed in a patent by Apple which issued on October 7, 1997, which is prior to the U.S. patent application by XYZ filed October 5, 1998. 35 U.S.C. § 102(a); MPEP § 2132.

23. ANSWER: (B) is the correct answer. 37 CFR §§ 1.111(b); 1.191(a); and 10.18; MPEP §§ 706.01; 714.02. (A), (C), (D), and (E) are incorrect because they do not constitute a reply and request for reconsideration in accordance with 37 CFR § 1.111.

24. ANSWER: (B) is the correct answer. MPEP §§ 1805; 1834.01. (A),(C), (D) and (E) are incorrect. MPEP § 1805. PCT international applications and papers relating to the applications are specifically excluded from the Certificate of Mailing or Transmission procedures of 37 CFR § 1.8. Also, facsimile may not be used to file applications or drawings for PCT applications. MPEP § 1805.

25. ANSWER: (E) is the correct answer because both (C) and (D) are correct. 37 CFR § 1.75(c); MPEP § 608.01(n) [pp.600-66-67]. (A) and (B) are not correct. MPEP § 608.01(n) ("[A] multiple dependent claim may not serve as a basis for any other multiple dependent claim, either directly or indirectly.").

26. ANSWER: (E) is the correct answer. There is no maintenance fee for a design patent. 35 U.S.C. § 41(b); 37 CFR §§ 1.362(b); 1.362(c)(4); and MPEP § 2504.

27. ANSWER: (D) is the correct answer. 35 U.S.C. § 121. MPEP § 706.03(k) reads "when two claims in an application are duplicates, or else are so close in content that they both cover the same thing, despite a slight difference in wording, it is proper after allowing one claim to object to the other claim under 37 CFR 1.75 as being a substantial duplicate of the allowed claim." 35 U.S.C. § 121 refers to an "independent and distinct" invention being in a divisional application. Including the objected claim in a divisional application is incorrect because it is not "independent and distinct." (A), (B), (C) and (E) are proper replies which could overcome the rejection.

28. ANSWER: (B) is the correct answer because it is a false statement. MPEP § 1416. (A) is a true statement. MPEP § 1410.01. (C) is true. MPEP § 1412.03 ("When a Broadened Claim Can Be Presented"). (D) is a true statement. MPEP § 1430. (E) is also true. 37 CFR § 1.121(b)(2)(i)(B).

29. ANSWER: (A) is the correct answer. MPEP §§ 2146; 706.02(l); 715.01; 715.01(b); and 716.10. (D) is not the best answer because it does not provide the assignee with the best patent protection. (B) and (C) are incorrect because they are both missing a statement from the assignee. The filing of a terminal disclaimer in (E) is inappropriate.

newgrounds.com.

30.   ANSWER: (E) is the correct answer. (A), (B), and (C) would all be considered acceptable. 37 CFR § 1.191; MPEP § 1205 ("the rules no longer require that the notice of appeal identify the rejected claim(s) appealed, or be signed . . .") (D) is incorrect because it does not include (C).

31.   ANSWER: (B) is the correct answer. (B) sets forth the latest date that an appeal brief can be filed based on a March 23, 1999, Notice of Appeal filing date. 37 CFR § 1.192; MPEP § 1206. The two month period from the date of the Notice of Appeal is not a statutory period and a proper extension of time can be obtained for an additional five months.

32.   ANSWER: (A) is the correct answer. 37 CFR § 1.48(d); MPEP § 201.03. [p.200-11]. Answer (B) is wrong because "[n]o amendment, other than to make the provisional application comply with the patent statute and all applicable regulations, may be made to the provisional application after the filing date of the provisional application." 37 CFR § 1.53(c); MPEP § 201.04(b). Answer (C) is wrong because a certificate of correction applies only after a patent issues. MPEP § 1481.   Answer (D) is not the best answer. MPEP § 201.03. There is no prior nonprovisional application from which a continuing application can be filed. (E) is incorrect because the filing of a new cover sheet is not sufficient to add X as an inventor when the earlier filed cover sheet identified only Y as the inventor and complied with 37 CFR § 1.51(c). MPEP § 201.04 [p.200-12].

33.   ANSWER: (A) is the correct answer. MPEP §§ 2131; 2131.03; 2173.05(c). The requirement for "up to 2.5% chromium" reads on an alloy containing no chromium since "up to" requires no minimum and includes zero as a lower limit. *In re Mochel*, 176 USPQ 194 (CCPA 1974). Each other element in the claim is disclosed in the reference, and the range amount of each element in the claim reads on the amount disclosed in the reference for each element. Choice (B) is incorrect because the term "consisting of" excludes the inclusion of nickel from the claimed alloy. Answer (C) is incorrect because "2.6% chromium" is not within the scope of "up to 2.5% chromium" recited in the claim. (D) is incorrect because "6% tungsten" is not within the scope of "at least 7% tungsten" recited in the claim. (E) is incorrect because "at least 2% carbon" is not within the claimed range of "0.5-1.0% carbon."

34.   ANSWER: (B) is the correct answer. The claim is rejected on the ground that it recites elements without support in the original disclosure under 35 U.S.C. § 112, first paragraph. MPEP §§ 706.03(o); 2163.06. "If new matter is added to the claims, the examiner should reject the claims under 35 U.S.C. § 112, first paragraph - written description requirement." MPEP 2163.06, citing *In re Rasmussen*, 650 F.2d 1212, 211 USPQ 323 (CCPA 1981) [p.2100-144]. (A) and (C) are incorrect. MPEP § 2165.01(IV).

35.   ANSWER: (A) is the correct answer. 35 U.S.C. § 103; MPEP §§ 2141 - 2143; § 2143.01; and § 2145. (B) is incorrect. MPEP § 2145(VIII). (C) is incorrect. MPEP § 2145(IV). (D) is incorrect. MPEP § 2145(III). (E) is incorrect. 35 U.S.C. §§ 102(a) and 103.

36.   ANSWER: (B) is the correct answer. 35 U.S.C. § 112, first paragraph; MPEP § 2161. (A) is incorrect. MPEP § 2138.05. (C), (D), and (E) are incorrect. MPEP § 2161.

37.   ANSWER: (D) is the correct answer. MPEP § 2111.03. The term "comprising" is inclusive or open ended and does not exclude additional, unrecited elements or method steps. (A) is incorrect because the amount of R in the prior art exceeds the limitation in the claim. (B) is incorrect because the claim does not exclude the glass reinforced adhesive film or its location. (C) is incorrect because the dependent claim is not anticipated by the prior art where the coating thickness is not 0.3mm thick. (E) is not correct because (D) is correct.

38.   ANSWER: (D) is the correct answer. MPEP § 710.01(a). ("[I]f the period ends on a Saturday, Sunday, or Federal holiday, the reply is timely if it is filed on the next succeeding business day.")   July 5, 1999, was a Federal holiday inasmuch as July 4, 1999, occurred on a Sunday.

39.   ANSWER: (B) is the correct answer. MPEP § 608.04(b). (A) is incorrect. 35 U.S.C. § 102(a). (C) is incorrect. 35 U.S.C. § 112, second paragraph; MPEP § 2173.05(h). (D) is incorrect. MPEP § 706.03(u). (E) is not correct because (B) is correct.

40.   ANSWER: (B) is the correct answer. 37 CFR §§ 1.8(a)(1); 1.8(b); MPEP §§ 1205; 1206. (A) is incorrect. MPEP § 1205 ("The Patent and Trademark Office does not acknowledge receipt of a Notice of Appeal by separate letter.") (C) is incorrect. MPEP § 1206 ("The Office date of receipt of the Notice of Appeal (and not the date indicated on any Certificate of Mailing under 37 CFR 1.8) is the date from which this 2 month time period is measured. See MPEP 512.") (D) is not correct because (A) and (C) are incorrect. (E) is not correct because (C) is not correct.

41.   ANSWER: (D) is the correct answer. MPEP § 1402. (IV) is not considered independent grounds for filing a reissue application. "[A]n error under 35 U.S.C. 251 *has not been presented* where the correction to the patent is one of spelling, or grammar, or a typographical, editorial or clerical error which does not cause the patent to be deemed wholly or partly inoperative or invalid for the reasons specified in 35 U.S.C 251." Id. [p.1400-2].

42.   ANSWER: (E) is the correct answer because none of the choices provided are in accord with proper PTO practice and procedure. (A) is not correct because no amendment, other than to make the provisional application comply with the patent statute and all applicable regulations, may be made to a provisional application after the filing date. 37 CFR § 1.53 (c). (B) is not correct because only a continuation or divisional application may be filed as a CPA. MPEP § 601.01 (p. 600-7). (C) is incorrect because a provisional application is not entitled to the benefit of the earlier filed provisional application. 35 U.S.C. § 111(b)(7); 37 CFR § 1.53(c). (D) is wrong because a continuation-in-part "is an

application filed during the lifetime of an earlier **nonprovisional** application." MPEP § 201.08 (emphasis added).

43.   ANSWER: (C) is the correct answer. 35 U.S.C. § 120; MPEP §§ 2133.01; 715; 2126; 2127. AuGratin's new claims to A, B, C **and D** is not supported by AuGratin's parent application. As such, the effective filing date of AuGratin's CIP application for the new claim is April 12, 1999. AuGratin's French Patent No. 1, 234, 567 has a critical reference date of more than one year before his April 12, 1999, effective filing date and cannot be removed as a reference. (A), (B) and (D) are incorrect because the CIP application does not get the benefit of the filing date of the parent application for the new claims. 35 U.S.C. § 120. (E) is incorrect because the new claims provide the supporting disclosure. MPEP § 2163.06.

44.   ANSWER: (E) is the correct answer because it includes (A), (B) and (D) which are identified in MPEP § 403 (pp.400-9). (C) is incorrect because a Deposit Account number is not the same as a Customer Number. When authorizing charges to a Deposit Account, it is extremely important that the authorization be clear and unambiguous. MPEP § 509.01.

45.   ANSWER: (A) is the correct answer. 35 U.S.C. § 112, first paragraph. (B) and (E) are incorrect because the only element of the table required by the claim is the flat board. (C) and (D) are incorrect because the claim requires only the flat board and securing means.

46.   ANSWER: (D) is the correct answer because it is a false statement. MPEP § 1512, II. Inclusion of Copyright Notice [p. 1500-37]. (A), (B), and (C) are true statements. See MPEP § 1512, III. Design Patent/Trademark Overlap and IV. Inclusion of Trademarks in Design Patent Applications [p. 1500-38]. (E) is incorrect because it includes (A) and (B) which are both true statements.

47.   ANSWER: (D) is the correct answer because both (B) and (C) are true statements. 37 CFR §§ 1.11(b); 1.14(g). (A) is false. MPEP § 1706. (E) is incorrect because it includes (A) which is a false statement.

48.   ANSWER: (B) is the correct answer. MPEP §§ 715.01(c); 716.10. (A) is incorrect because the facts are given that Apple invented that which Carrot claims. 35 U.S.C. § 102(g). (C) is incorrect. 35 U.S.C. § 102(g). (D) and (E) are incorrect. A terminal disclaimer does not overcome a 35 U.S.C. § 102(e) rejection. MPEP § 2136.05.

49.   ANSWER: (E) is the correct answer. MPEP § 804.01.

50.   ANSWER: (D) is the correct answer. 35 U.S.C. § 112; fifth paragraph; 37 CFR § 1.75(c); MPEP § 608.01 (n) [pp.600-65-66]. (A), (B) and (C) are incorrect because they are dependent on multiple claims in the conjunctive. (E) is incorrect because it depends on claims which follow, as opposed to precede, the claim. 37 CFR § 1.75(c).

The Best Test Preparation and Review Course

PATENT
BAR
EXAM

Patent Examination II

U. S. DEPARTMENT OF COMMERCE
UNITED STATES PATENT AND TRADEMARK OFFICE
REGISTRATION EXAMINATION
FOR PATENT ATTORNEYS AND AGENTS

NOVEMBER 3, 1999

Morning Session (50 Points)   **Time: 3 Hours**

This session of the examination is an open book examination. You may use books, notes, or other written materials that you believe will be of help to you *except* you may not use prior registration examination questions and/or answers. Books, notes or other written materials containing prior registration examination questions and/or answers *cannot* be brought into or used in the room where this examination is being administered. If you have such materials, you must give them to the test administrator before this session of the examination begins.

All questions must be answered in SECTION I of the Answer Sheet which is provided to you by the test administrator. You must use a No. 2 pencil (or softer) lead pencil to record your answers on the Answer Sheet. Darken *completely* the circle corresponding to your answer. You must keep your mark within the circle. Erase *completely* all marks except your answer. Stray marks may be counted as answers. No points will be awarded for incorrect answers or unanswered questions. Questions answered by darkening more than one circle will be considered as being incorrectly answered.

This session of the examination consists of fifty (50) multiple choice questions, each worth one (1) point. Do not assume any additional facts not presented in the questions. When answering each question, unless otherwise stated, assume that you are a registered patent practitioner. Any reference to a practitioner is a reference to a registered patent practitioner. The most correct answer is the policy, practice, and procedure which must, shall, or should be followed in accordance with the U.S. patent statutes, the PTO rules of practice and procedure, the Manual of Patent Examining Procedure (MPEP), and the Patent Cooperation Treaty (PCT) articles and rules, unless modified by a subsequent court decision or a notice in the *Official Gazette*. There is only one most correct answer for each question. Where choices (A) through (D) are correct and choice (E) is "All of the above," the last choice (E) will be the most correct answer and the only answer which will be accepted. Where two or more choices are correct, the most correct answer is the answer which refers to each and every one of the correct choices. Where a question includes a statement with one or more blanks or ends with a colon, select the answer from the choices given to complete the statement which would make the statement *true*. Unless otherwise explicitly stated, all references to patents or applications are to be understood as being U.S. patents or regular (non-provisional) utility applications for utility inventions only, as opposed to plant or design applications for plant and design inventions. Where the terms "USPTO," "PTO," or "Office" are used in this examination, they mean the U.S. Patent and Trademark Office.

You may write anywhere on the examination booklet. However, do not remove any pages from the booklet. Only answers recorded in SECTION I of your Answer Sheet will be graded. Your combined score of both the morning and afternoon sessions must be at least 70 points to pass the registration examination.

1.   Abigail has invented a novel watering mechanism for a flower pot. The flower pot also possesses a unique ornamental design. Abigail consults with patent practitioner P for advice on the differences between a design patent and a utility patent. Which of the following general statements regarding design and utility patents, if made by P, would be accurate?

   (A)   A "utility patent" protects the way an article is used and works, while a "design patent" protects the way an article looks.
   (B)   Unlike utility patent applications, a design patent application may not make a claim for priority of a provisional patent application.
   (C)   Maintenance fees are required for utility patents, while no maintenance fees are required for design patents.
   (D)   Both design and utility patents may be obtained on an article if the invention resides both in its utility and ornamental appearance.
   (E)   All of the above.

2.   A patent application filed in the PTO claims a nylon rope coated with element E for the purpose of preventing breakage of the rope. In the first Office action, the examiner rejects the claim as obvious over P in view of a trade journal publication, T. P teaches a nylon rope coated with resin for the purpose of making the rope waterproof. T teaches a nylon tent fabric coated with element E for the purpose of making the tent waterproof, and suggests the use of element E for making other nylon products waterproof. Following proper PTO practices and procedures, the combination of P and T:

   (A)   cannot support a prima facie case of obviousness because T lacks a suggestion to combine with P for the purpose of preventing breakage in nylon rope.
   (B)   cannot support a prima facie case of obviousness because P lacks a suggestion to combine with T for the purpose of preventing breakage in nylon rope.
   (C)   cannot support a prima facie case of obviousness because T only contains a suggestion to combine with P for the purpose of waterproofing nylon rope.
   (D)   can support a prima facie case of obviousness, even though T only contains a suggestion to combine with P for the purpose of waterproofing nylon rope.
   (E)   can support a prima facie case of obviousness because the applicant is always under an obligation to submit evidence of non-obviousness regardless of whether the examiner fully establishes a prima facie case of obviousness.

3.   What would **not** be permitted to be incorporated by reference in your client's U.S. utility patent application?

   (A)   Essential material from a U.S. patent.
   (B)   Essential material from a foreign application.
   (C)   Non-essential material from a prior filed, commonly owned U.S. application.
   (D)   Essential material from a magazine article.
   (E)   (B) and (D).

4.   Beverly is a research chemist. While cleaning a clogged shower drain she recovers several ounces of goop from the drain. She analyzes the ingredients and properties, and finds that the goop makes a highly effective industrial lubricant. She comes to you for help in preparing and filing an application. She informs you that the goop is formed from equal parts of chemicals W, X, Y and Z. She knows that chemical W comes from the soap she uses and that chemicals Y and Z are components of the conditioner she uses on her hair. Her soap uses the tradename "Acme SmellNice", and her shampoo and conditioner both use the tradename "A-1 Silky." Chemicals W, Y and Z are all readily available on the commercial market. Chemical X is also a common, readily available chemical, but she cannot determine how it got in the shower drain. She suspects it is the result of a reaction between A-1 Silky shampoo and Acme SmellNice soap that occurs when the two are mixed in the presence of hot water. You prepare an application describing a prophetic example setting forth one way to make the goop from commercially available chemicals and a working example describing (as well as the inventor can) how the goop is formed in the bathroom drain. The working example describes mixing of A-1 Silky shampoo and Acme SmellNice soap in the presence of water having a temperature of at least 100°F to form chemical X. Because you know that the ingredients for at least Acme SmellNice soap have recently changed, but the nature of the change is unknown, you list every ingredient of A-1 Silky shampoo, and Acme SmellNice soap in positive language so there will be no confusion as to what is meant. The application includes the following claims:

Claim 1.   An industrial lubricant consisting essentially of equal parts of chemical W, chemical X, chemical Y and chemical Z.

Claim 2.   The industrial lubricant of Claim 1, wherein said chemical X is formed by mixing A-1 Silky shampoo and Acme SmellNice soap in the presence of water having a temperature of at least 100°F.

Which of the following statements is/are correct?

(A)   Claim 1 cannot be supported by an enabling specification because Beverly does not fully understand the processes that occurred in the drain, and a prophetic example alone is never sufficient to enable a claim.

(B)   Claim 2 is not patentable because it sets forth an incorrect theory of formation of chemical X.

(C)   Claim 1 is not patentable because Beverly merely found the goop in her drain and did not formulate it herself.

(D)   Claim 2 is not patentable because it is indefinite.

(E)   (B) and (D).

5.   Jack, a registered patent agent, received a final rejection of all of the claims in an application directed to an article of manufacture. Jack is about to file a timely Notice of Appeal to the Board of Patent Appeals and Interferences. Before filing his notice of appeal, Jack would like to tie up some loose ends by amendment. Which of the following reply(replies) may he file without triggering the requirements of 37 CFR § 1.116(b)?

   (A)   A reply that presents his argument in a more defensible light and adds additional claims.
   (B)   A reply amending the claims into process claims.
   (C)   A reply amending all of the independent claims, accompanied by a declaration from the inventor.
   (D)   A reply complying with a requirement of form expressly set forth in the previous Office action.
   (E)   (A) and (D).

6.   You are preparing a patent application for filing in the PTO. The application contains the following partial claim:

   A walking device comprising:
   (i)   a vertical member having opposing top and bottom portions;
   (ii)   a handle connected to the top portion of the vertical member forming a 45E angle with the top portion of the vertical member;
   (iii)
   (iv)   a set of non-skid covers for the set of legs, said set of legs being aluminum.

Following proper PTO practices and procedures, which of the following claim limitations best completes the claim by providing the missing limitation (iii)?

   (A)   a horizontal member, substantially round in shape, having opposing sides connected along one of the opposing sides to the bottom side of the vertical member and along the other of the opposing sides to a set of legs; and
   (B)   a horizontal member, substantially round in shape, having first and second opposing sides connected along the first opposing side to the bottom side of the vertical member and along the second opposing side to a set of legs; and
   (C)   a horizontal member, substantially round in shape, connected to the bottom portion of the vertical member; and
   (D)   a horizontal member, substantially round in shape, having opposing top and bottom portions; the top portion of the horizontal member is connected to the bottom portion of the vertical member, and the bottom portion long the bottom portion of the vertical member is connected to a set of legs; and
   (E)   a horizontal member, substantially round in shape, having a top side connected to the bottom side of the vertical member and a bottom side connected to the set of legs; and

7. Which of the following statements, regarding amendments filed after final rejection in a timely manner, is correct?

   (A) Amendments touching upon the merits of the application presented after final rejection shall be entered upon payment of the proper fee and a showing of good and sufficient reasons why they are necessary and were not earlier presented.

   (B) An amendment filed after final rejection is entitled to entry if it amends only the claims that were finally rejected.

   (C) Amendments after final rejection may be made canceling claims or complying with any requirement of form expressly set forth in the final Office action.

   (D) An amendment after final rejections is entitled to entry if it cancels claims and adds new claims that clearly set forth a previously unclaimed embodiment of the invention.

   (E) Applicant cannot make any further amendments after final rejection, but may submit remarks and a notice of appeal.

8. In which of the following situations, considered independently of each other, is the original, new, or amended claim supported in the application as filed?

   (A) An amendment to the specification changing the definition of "holder" from "is a hook" to "is a hook, clasp, crimp, or tong" and no amendment is made of the claim, which uses the term "holder." The amendment is filed one month after the application was filed. There was no previous supporting disclosure in the specification of the holder being a clasp, crimp, or tong.

   (B) An amendment to the specification and claims changing the definition of "holder" from "is a hook" to "is a hook, clasp, crimp, or tong." The amendment is filed one month after the application was filed. There was no previous supporting disclosure in the specification of the holder being a clasp, crimp, or tong.

   (C) Original claim 1 in the application refers to "a holder," and original claim 2 depends from and refers to claim 1 stating, "said holder is a hook, clasp, crimp, or tong." There is no disclosure in the specification preceding the claims in the application as filed for the holder to be a clasp, crimp, or tong.

   (D) An amendment is filed presenting a claim to an electrical insulating device, copied from a patent for the purpose of provoking an interference. The claim refers to "nonconductive plastic holder." The application as filed contains a broad generic disclosure describing electrical insulating devices. The holder is described in the specification of the application as "conducting electricity." There is no disclosure in the specification of the holder being "nonconductive."

   (E) All of the above.

9. An application as originally filed contains the following Claim 1:

Claim 1. A doughnut making machine comprising:
(i)   an input conveyor that receives dough to be used in making said doughnuts;
(ii)   portioning means for portioning dough from said input conveyor into a plurality of dough balls, each of said plurality of balls containing dough sufficient to create a single doughnut;
(iii) forming means for forming each of said dough balls into a ring of dough;
(iv)   a deep fat fryer which receives rings of dough from said forming means and cooks said rings of dough;
(v)   applying means for selectively applying a flavored coating on cooked rings of dough to produce doughnuts; and
(vi)   placing means for placing a plurality of said doughnuts on a flat sheet.

The specification adequately describes the claimed subject matter. Two different "means for selectively applying" are described in the specification: a sprayer and a brush. Which of the following original claims is an improper dependent claim?

(A)   2. The doughnut making machine of Claim 1, wherein said placing means is a conveyor that extends from said applying means to said flat sheet.
(B)   3. The doughnut making machine of Claim 1, wherein said forming means includes a cutter that removes a center portion of each of said dough balls to form a ring of dough.
(C)   4. The doughnut making machine of Claim 1, wherein said applying means is omitted for making plain doughnuts.
(D)   5. The doughnut making machine of Claim 1, wherein said applying means includes a sprayer which receives a sugar based flavored coating, wherein said sugar based flavored coating is sprayed on said cooked rings of dough.
(E)   6. The doughnut making machine of Claim 1, wherein said applying means is a sprayer.

10. Which of the following dependent claims, each occurring in different patent applications, is in a proper claim format?

(A)   Claim 4. The process of claim 5, further characterized by…
(B)   Claim 2. The process of claim 1 or claim 5, further comprising…
(C)   Claim 6. The widget as in claims 1, 2 or 3, further including…
(D)   Claim 3. The widget as in the preceding claims, further containing…
(E)   Claim 5. The process as in claims 1-2 or 3, further comprising…

11.   In August 1999, a recently registered patent agent, who is not an attorney, asked a registered patent attorney to help the agent establish a practice. Considering the additional facts in the following choices separately, which choice best comports with the professional responsibilities of both the agent and the attorney?

(A)   The agent advertises as a registered practitioner authorized to practice before the Office in patent and trademark cases. The attorney supervises all the trademark work done by the agent.

(B)   The agent advertises on television and radio as a registered patent agent and accepts patent cases on a reasonable contingent fee.

(C)   The attorney has the agent prosecute trademark applications before the Office and the attorney signs all the papers submitted to the Office without reading the papers.

(D)   The attorney and agent enter into a partnership agreement that has no health or retirement benefits, but specifies that after termination of the partnership, the agent and the attorney will not practice in each other's neighborhoods or accept each other's established clients.

(E)   Without receiving anything of value from the agent, the attorney refers patent application clients to the agent, the agent informs the clients that the agent is a registered patent attorney, and the agent competently represents the clients in patent cases.

12.   On February 12, 1999, you filed a patent application containing two independent claims, Claims 1 and 2, directed to methods of forming an integrated circuit device. The applicant conceived the methods in Jacksonville, Florida on June 10, 1997. Commencing on June 10, 1997, the applicant exercised due diligence until she reduced the methods to practice on February 27, 1998. In an Office action dated August 18, 1999, the examiner rejected Claim 1 as being anticipated by Doppler under 35 U.S.C. § 102(b). Doppler is a French patent that was filed on July 18, 1996, and issued on January 13, 1998. The Doppler patent claims the method of the applicant's Claim 1 for forming integrated circuit devices. Claim 2 was rejected as being anticipated by Spot under 35 U.S.C. § 102(e). Spot is a U.S. patent that was filed on January 7, 1998, and discloses, but does not claim, the method of applicant's Claim 2 for forming an integrated circuit device. The Spot patent issued on May 5, 1999. Which of the following would be the most proper course of action to take to respond to the rejections?

(A)   File an antedating affidavit to overcome the rejection of Claim 1 and cancel Claim 2.

(B)   File an antedating affidavit to overcome both the rejections and request that an interference be declared with the Doppler patent.

(C)   File an antedating affidavit to overcome the rejection of Claim 2 and cancel Claim 1.

(D)   File a reply arguing that the rejections are improper because the Spot patent issued after the filing date of your client's application.

(E)   File an antedating affidavit to overcome both rejections.

13.   Able files a patent application in 1999 disclosing a barstool having a rectangular molded plastic seat portion supported by four adjacent vertical tubular steel legs connected to the underside of the seat portion. A set of four horizontal tubular steel support members connects adjacent tubular steel legs to brace the legs. The barstool further includes a plastic back member connected to the topside of the plastic seat portion. The application states that wood could be used in place of tubular steel for the legs and horizontal support members. No alternative to plastic is mentioned in the application for use in the seat portion, but it is well known in the art that plastic and wood are interchangeable. As originally filed, Baker's application included the following Claim 1:

Claim 1.   A barstool comprising:
    (i)   a rectangular seat portion having four vertical edges, an underside and a topside;
    (ii)   means for supporting said seat portion such that said underside is substantially horizontal; and
    (ii)   a back member connected to one of the vertical edges of said seat portion, said back member being substantially perpendicular to the topside of said seat portion.

The Examiner rejects the claim under 35 U.S.C. § 102 as being anticipated by a 1997 publication by Baker showing a three-legged wooden barstool with a rectangular seat, a back and arms. The Examiner cites, but does not apply against Claim 1, a 1996 patent to Charlie that discloses a four-legged wooden barstool with a round wooden seat. The Charlie patent states that in barstools the use of plastic and/or tubular steel is equivalent to the use of wood. Able responds to the rejection by amending his claim to require that the seat portion be formed of plastic, and by arguing that Baker does not disclose the recited "supporting means" because Baker utilizes only three legs, which is less stable than four legs. The examiner finds a 1980 Wilson patent that structurally equates three legged barstools to four-legged barstools. Which of the following is in accordance with proper PTO practices and procedures?

(A)   The anticipation rejection is withdrawn only because Baker does not disclose a plastic seat portion. An obviousness rejection is then made based on Baker in view of Charlie since Charlie suggests replacing a wood seat with a plastic seat. Able's argument concerning the recited "supporting means" of Claim 1 does not provide a basis for overcoming the anticipation rejection.

(B)   The anticipation rejection should be withdrawn because Baker does not disclose a plastic seat portion <u>and</u> because Baker does not disclose a four legged supporting means. An obviousness rejection is then made based on Baker in view of Charlie because Charlie suggests modifying Baker to utilize a plastic seat and four legs.

(C)   The anticipation rejection is maintained because one of ordinary skill in the art would understand that a plastic seat could readily replace a wood seat. Furthermore, Able's argument that the "supporting means" of Claim 1 is not disclosed because Baker utilizes only three legs is unsupported by any limitation in the Claim.

(D)   The anticipation rejection is withdrawn because Baker does not disclose a plastic seat. However, a rejection is made under 35 USC §112, paragraph 1 as being based upon an inadequate disclosure because the specification does not specify that the use of a plastic seat is critical to the invention.

(E)   (B) and (D).

14.   A patent application filed in the PTO contains the following original claim:

Claim 1.   A talbecloth for protecting the finish of a table comprising:
a layer of cotton;
a layer of vinyl affixed to the layer of cotton; and
a backing of felt.

Which of the following amendment(s) is/are not in accord with proper PTO amendment practices and procedures?

(A)   In claim 1, line 3, add -with an epoxy resin-.
(B)   In claim 1, line 2, after "cotton" add -woven to have 250 threads per inch-.
(C)   In claim 1, line 3, before "layer" add –thin-.
(D)   In claim 1, line 1, correct the spelling of "talbecloth" please.
(E)   All of the above.

15.   You draft a patent application disclosing and describing an electrical chronometer containing a resistor having a resistance of 20-90 ohms, preferably 40 ohms. You draft the following independent claim:

1.   An electrical chronometer comprising a resistor with a resistance of 20-90 ohms.

Which of the following would not be a proper dependent claim if presented as an original claim in the application when the application is filed in the PTO?

(A)   2. The electrical chronometer of Claim 1 wherein the resistor has a resistance of 40 ohms.
(B)   2. An electrical chronometer as in Claim 1 wherein the resistor has a resistance of 40-90 ohms.
(C)   2. An electrical chronometer as in Claim 1 wherein the resistor has a resistance of about 20 - 90 ohms.
(D)   2. The electrical chronometer of Claim 1 wherein the resistor has a resistance of between 50 and 90 ohms.
(E)   (C) and (D).

16.   When does jurisdiction over an application normally transfer from the examining group to the Board of Patent Appeals and Interferences?

    (A)   After the examiner has notified the appellant by written communication that the reply brief has been entered and considered, and that the application will be forwarded to the Board.
    (B)   After a supplemental examiner's answer, pursuant to a remand from the Board, has been mailed.
    (C)   After 2 months from the examiner's answer, plus mail room time, if no reply brief has been timely filed.
    (D)   (A), (B), or (C).
    (E)   (A) or (C).

17.   A request for reexamination of U.S. Patent X,XXX,XXX (the 'XXX patent) was filed by ABC Technology, Inc. (ABC) on the ground that a substantial new question of patentability exists. In the first Office Action during reexamination, all the claims, i.e., claims 1 through 4, were rejected as unpatentable under 35 U.S.C. § 103 over U.S. Patent Z,ZZZ,ZZZ (the 'ZZZ patent). Claims 1 through 4 are all independent and original claims, and are the only claims that were presented during prosecution of the application that matured into 'XXX patent. All the claims are directed to a hydrocyclone separator apparatus. The apparatus is used for separating material, including fibers suspended in a liquid suspension, into a light fraction containing the fibers, and a heavy fraction containing rejects. Assuming no issues under 35 U.S.C. §§ 102, 103, or 112 are raised, which of the following claims, if any, would be properly subject to rejection under 35 U.S.C. § 305?

    (A)   Claim 5. A hydrocyclone separator apparatus according to claim 4, wherein said blades are configured in the form of generally plane surfaces curved in one plane only.
    (B)   Claim 5. A hydrocyclone separator apparatus according to claim 4, wherein the outlet duct is in the form of two frustro-conical portions joined at their narrow ends.
    (C)   Claim 5. A method of separating material including fibers suspended in a liquid suspension comprising the steps of separating the material into a light fraction containing the fibers and a heavy fraction containing rejects, and converting the light fraction into a pulp and paper stock suspension.
    (D)   Claim 5. A hydrocyclone separator apparatus according to claim 4, wherein the separator chamber is conical in shape having at the narrow end an outlet for the heavy fraction and at its wide end an outlet for the light fraction.
    (E)   None of the above.

18.   A patent application filed in the PTO contains the following dependent claim:

2.   The method of Claim 1, further consisting of the step of cooling the mixture to a temperature of 32° F.

Following proper PTO practices and procedures, from which of the following claims does the dependent claim not properly depend?

(A)   1. A method of making liquid compound A consisting of the steps of mixing equal quantities of material C and material D in a beaker and heating the mixture to a temperature of 212° F.

(B)   1. A method of making liquid compound A comprising the steps of mixing equal quantities of material C and material D in a beaker and heating the mixture to a temperature of 212° F.

(C)   1. A method of making liquid compound A including the steps of mixing equal quantities of material C and material D in a beaker and heating the mixture to a temperature of 212° F.

(D)   1. A method of making liquid compound A characterized by the steps of mixing equal quantities of material C and material D in a beaker and heating the mixture to a temperature of 212° F.

(E)   (C) and (D).

19.   If a claim has been properly rejected under 35 U.S.C. § 103 as being rendered obvious over a combination of prior art references, then in accordance with proper PTO practice and procedure:

(A)   it is not necessary that the prior art suggests the combination to achieve the same advantage or result discovered by the applicant, if the combination provides motivation to make the claimed invention.

(B)   the rationale to modify or combine the prior art must be found expressly set forth in the prior art.

(C)   in considering the disclosure of prior art it is proper to take into account the specific teachings of the reference. It is not proper to take into account the inferences that one skilled in the art could reasonably draw from the specific teachings.

(D)   it is improper for a patent examiner to take official notice of facts outside the record which are capable of instant and unquestionable demonstration as being "well known."

(E)   it is proper to rely on equivalence in support of the rejection, the equivalence may be recognized in the prior art or in the applicant's disclosure.

20. An application is directed to novel and unobvious scissors for cutting hair having a pair of cutter blades and a pointer loop. The application includes the following partial independent Claim 1 and dependent Claims 2-5.

Claim 1.   An apparatus for cutting hair, said apparatus comprising:
(i)   a first cutting member having a first cutting edge at one end and the other end of said first cutting member terminating in a thumb loop;
(ii)   a second cutting member having a second cutting edge at one end and the other end terminating in a finger loop having an arcuate finger brace extending therefrom;
(iii)   _____
(iv)   said second cutting member additionally including a pointer loop between said finger loop and said mid-point, said finger loop having a finger loop center such that a plane through said finger loop center and said pointer loop center is generally parallel to said second cutting edge in order for the apparatus for cutting hair to be generally balanced when held by a user.

Claim 2.   The apparatus of claim 1, wherein said first cutting member includes a threaded aperture extending entirely therethrough between said thumb loop and said mid-point, and an adjusting screw that extends through said threaded aperture to engage a bearing surface below the pointer loop on said second cutting member.

Claim 3.   The apparatus of claim 2, wherein said connector is a rivet.

Without regard to prior art, and in view of partial Claim 1, which of the following best completes missing paragraph (iii) of Claim 1 while maintaining the broadest scope of protection and complying with proper PTO practice and procedure?

(A)   "said first cutting member having a mid-point between its ends and said second cutting member having a mid-point between its ends, and said first cutting member and said second cutting member are pivotally secured to each other at their respective mid-points by a connector; and"

(B)   "wherein said first cutting member and said second cutting member are formed entirely of metal and are pivotally secured to each other at respective mid-points; and"

(C)   "said first cutting member including a reservoir for dispensing disinfectant solution and having a mid-point between its ends; and"

(D)   "and said first cutting member and said second cutting member are pivotally secured to each other at their respective mid-points; and"

(E)   "said first cutting member and said second cutting member being pivotally secured to each other by a connector; and"

21.   Which of the following would be a proper rejection in a reexamination proceeding?

(A)   A rejection under 35 U.S.C. § 102(a) based on an affidavit that the invention was known or used by others before the invention thereof by the applicant for patent.

(B)   A rejection under 35 U.S.C. § 102(b) based on an affidavit that the invention was in the public use in this country more than one year prior to the date of the application for a patent in the United States.

(C)   A rejection under 35 U.S.C. § 102(e) that the invention was described in a patent by another filed in the United States before the invention thereof by the patent applicant.

(D)   A rejection under 35 U.S.C. § 102(f) that the applicant did not himself invent the subject matter sought to be patented.

(E)   A rejection under 35 U.S.C. § 102(b) that the invention was on sale in this country, more than one year prior to the date of the application for patent in the United States.

22.   Patentee P wishes to amend Claim 1 in the patent granted to P, and obtain the following amended Claim 1 either through reexamination or reissue:

1.   A <u>ball</u> valve comprising:
   i)   a housing;
   ii)   a valve [member] <u>ball</u> rotatably joined in the housing;
   iii)   a [flanged] seal engagable with surfaces of the [member] <u>ball</u>; and
   iv)   a <u>linear</u> spring [means] interposed between the housing and the seal and biasing the seal into engagement with the [member] <u>ball</u>.

The amended claim is supported by the original disclosure in the application, which matured into P's patent. In the absence of questions of recapture, novelty, obviousness, and utility which of the following statements is/are true?

(A)   A claim so amended is properly presented in a reissue application filed on October 14, 1999, and a reissue patent is grantable where reissuance is sought of a patent granted on September 9, 1997.

(B)   A claim so amended is properly presented in a reissue application filed on September 9, 1999, and a reissue patent is grantable where reissuance is sought of a patent granted on October 7, 1997.

(C)   A claim so amended is properly presented in a request for reexamination filed on October 14, 1999, and a certificate of reexamination is grantable where reexamination is sought of a patent granted on September 9, 1997.

(D)   A claim so amended is properly presented in a request for reexamination filed on September 9, 1999, and a certificate of reexamination is grantable where reexamination is sought of a patent granted on October 7, 1997.

(E)   (B) and (D).

23 and 24.   Answer Questions 23 and 24 based on the following facts.

Your client, Homer, invented a new system for laying underground pipes for in-ground sprinkler systems utilizing a tunneling tool he calls "the Mole." The Mole is placed in a small hole is dug in the ground at a starting location. A target is placed in the ground at the desired ending location. The Mole automatically tunnels through the ground to the target. The Mole has a clamp to pull flexible pipe behind it as it tunnels. A high-pressure air source is connected to the Mole to remove dirt as the Mole progresses toward the target. Homer informs you that he has continuously used this original system for three years in his commercial landscaping business, displayed the system to his numerous customers, and handsomely profited from his original system. In the original system, the Mole sensed and moved toward the target emitting electromagnetic signals. Recently, the Mole sometimes gets confused due to interference from ferromagnetic underground pipes and overhead power lines. Two months ago Homer modified the system to utilize ultrasonic signals emitted from the target. The ultrasonic signals are encoded with location information derived by the target from a Global Positioning System (GPS) satellite. The modified system decodes the location information and tunnels toward the specified location. The use of ultrasonic signals in the modified system is new and unobvious. Homer has reduced the modified system to actual practice, and kept it confidential. Homer prepared a draft patent application fully describing both the original system and the modified system. He wants you to review the draft application, make sure it meets all requirements, and revise it as necessary prior to filing. The draft application prepared by Homer includes the following draft claims:

Claim 1.   A system for laying underground flexible pipe in the ground, said system comprising:
    (i)   a target placed in the ground at a target location and including a transmitter which emits target signals;
    (ii)   a tunneling device including a clamp operable to connect one end of said flexible pipe to said tunneling device, said tunneling device further including a sensor which detects said target signals and steers said tunneling device to move toward said target; and
    (iii)   a source of high pressure air connected with said tunneling device for removing dirt as said tunneling device moves toward said target.

Claim 2.   The system of claim 1, wherein said transmitter emits electromagnetic signals.

Claim 3.   The system of claim 1, wherein said transmitter emits ultrasonic signals.

Claim 4.   The system of claim 3, wherein said ultrasonic signals include encoded position information that is decoded by the decoder portion of said tunneling device sensor.

Claim 5.   The system of claim 1, wherein said transmitter emits signals having encoded position information.

23. Which of the following would not be reasonable advice to Homer?

(A) Claim 5 is not indefinite even though it is not limited to ultrasonic target signals and the only disclosed embodiment that utilizes encoded position information utilizes ultrasonic target signals.

(B) Claim 1, as presently written, is statutorily barred, and the claimed invention should be limited to the modified system.

(C) Because the original system had a drawback in that it sometimes got confused by ferromagnetic underground pipes or power lines, and because Homer continued to develop the system to overcome these drawbacks, the original system was experimental and does not constitute prior art against the modified system.

(D) Claim 4 is indefinite.

(E) The language in Claim 1 reciting the "target" should be reworded to clarify that the ground is not part of the claimed combination, *e.g.*, by adding the words "adapted to be" before "placed".

24. Claims 1 and 2 are unpatentable under which of the following statutory provisions?

(A) 35 U.S.C. § 102(b).
(B) 35 U.S.C. § 102(c).
(C) 35 U.S.C. § 102(d).
(D) 35 U.S.C. § 102(e).
(E) None of the above.

25. Which of the following is not a PTO recommendation or requirement?

(A) Claims should be arranged in order of scope so that the first claim presented is the least restrictive.

(B) Product and process claims should be separately grouped.

(C) Every application should contain no more than three dependent claims.

(D) A claim which depends from a dependent claim should not be separated from that dependent claim by any claim which does not also depend from the dependent claim.

(E) Each claim should start with a capital letter and end with a period.

26. A patent was granted to inventor Munch on August 3, 1999, on a patent application filed in the PTO on March 5, 1997. In which of the following circumstances in a reexamination proceeding of the Munch patent, considered independently of each other, will the cited prior art reference(s) properly support a determination that there is substantial new question of patentability?

(A) In a reexamination proceeding, claims 7-15 in the Munch patent are rejected as being anticipated under 35 U.S.C. § 102(a) by the disclosure in the Leal patent. The Leal patent was granted on January 21, 1997. It is the only rejection in the reexamination proceeding. During the original prosecution of the Munch application, the Leal patent was used by the examiner as prior art to reject original claims 1-5 as being anticipated under 35 U.S.C. § 102(a).

(B) In a reexamination proceeding, newly added claims 16-20 in the Munch patent are rejected as being anticipated under 35 U.S.C. § 102(b) by the disclosure in the Zellot patent. The Zellot patent was granted in 1987. It is the only rejection in the reexamination proceeding. During the original prosecution of the Munch application the examiner cited the Zellot patent against claims 1-7 in the patent application Munch filed on March 5, 1997.

(C) In a reexamination proceeding, claims 1-15 in the Munch patent are rejected as being obvious under 35 U.S.C. § 103 over the Wills patent in view of the Note patent. The Wills patent was granted on December 3, 1996, and the Note patent was granted in 1994. It is the only rejection in the reexamination proceeding. During the original prosecution of the Munch application the examiner used the Wills patent as prior art to reject original claims 1 and 2 in the Munch application. The Note patent was never before the examiner during the original prosecution of the Munch application, is not cumulative with the prior art cited during the original prosecution, and is material to the question of obviousness.

(D) In a reexamination proceeding, claims 1-15 in the Munch patent are rejected as being anticipated under 35 U.S.C. § 102(a) by the disclosure in the Richards patent. The Richards patent was granted on January 14, 1997. It is the only rejection in the reexamination proceeding. During the original prosecution of the Munch application, the examiner used the Richards patent in combination with a patent to Smith, granted in 1923, to reject original claims 1-5 in the application as being obvious under 35 U.S.C. § 103.

(E) All of the above.

27.   Which of the following statements explains why Claim 1 below does recite subject matter eligible for protection under the Patent Statute?

    Claim 1.   A top soil for retaining water comprising:
                            about 10% of material X;
                            about 60% of material Y; and
                            balance of material Z.

    (A)   The subject matter is eligible if the top soil occurs in nature, and M was the first to find the topsoil on a remote tropical island.
    (B)   The subject matter is eligible if M developed the top soil through extensive research and experimentation with various materials, including materials X, Y, and Z.
    (C)   The subject matter is eligible because all inanimate objects are subject matter eligible for protection under the patent statute.
    (D)   The subject matter is eligible because the claim is sufficiently broadly written as not to exclude the inclusion of a living organism.
    (E)   (A) and (B).

28.   A patent application filed in the PTO contains the following three claims, including product by process Claim 3:

    Claim 1. A method for making an Ethernet cable comprising the steps of A, B and C.
    Claim 2. The method of claim 1, further characterized by the step of D.
    Claim 3. The Ethernet cable as in any one of the preceding claims.

In the first Office action, the examiner objects to Claim 3 as being an improper dependent claim and requires cancellation of the claim. Following proper PTO practices and procedures, which of the following replies best overcomes the examiner's objection and provides the client with the broadest patent protection?

    (A)   Amend Claim 3 to read: "The Ethernet cable as made by the process set forth in claims 1-2."
    (B)   Cancel Claim 3.
    (C)   Add Claim 4, which reads: "An Ethernet cable made by a process comprising the steps of A, B and C."
    (D)   Add Claim 5, which reads: "An Ethernet cable made by a process comprising the steps of A, B, C and D."
    (E)   (B), (C), and (D).

29.   Which of the following statements is in accordance with proper PTO practice and procedure?

    (A)   Unlike questions of public use, there is no requirement that "on sale" activity be "public."
    (B)   Sales to toy stores throughout the United States of a claimed rocking horse by an independent third party more than one year before the filing date of applicant's patent application without the applicant's consent will not bar applicant from obtaining a patent for the rocking horse.
    (C)   An offer for sale of a claimed invention, where the offer originates in the United States and is communicated to a potential buyer in Europe, more than one year before the filing date of applicant's patent application, cannot be sufficient activity to bar applicant from obtaining a patent for the invention.
    (D)   Delay alone in filing a patent application is sufficient to infer any required intent by the inventor to abandon the invention.
    (E)   "Patented" in 35 U.S.C. § 102(e) includes the publication of German applications as printed documents called Offenlegungsschrift.

30.   On September 14, 1999, you filed a patent application in the PTO on behalf of a large corporation together with an authorization to charge the filing fee to your deposit account. However, due to unforeseen circumstances, measures were not taken to cover the $760.00 filing fee against the amount in your deposit account, which has a $10.00 balance. Consequently, you received a notice from the PTO dated September 28, 1999, that your deposit account has insufficient funds. Which of the following steps avoids abandonment of the recently filed application?

    (A)   On September 29, 1999, replenish the deposit account with $800.00 in cash to encompass the filing fee, and the $10 fee required by 37 CFR § 1.21(b)(1).
    (B)   On September 29, 1999, open a new deposit account with $800.00 in cash, and file in the PTO correspondence authorizing the fee for filing the application be charged against your new deposit account.
    (C)   On September 29, 1999, file in the PTO a check for $760.00 for the filing fee, and file in the PTO correspondence authorizing the balance of the filing fee be paid from your deposit account.
    (D)   On September 29, 1999, replenish the deposit account with $890.00 in cash to cover the filing fee, and a surcharge fee for late payment of the filing fee, and file in the PTO correspondence authorizing the fees for the application be charged to your deposit account.
    (E)   (B) or (C).

31. The following claims are included in a newly filed patent application:

Claim No.
1. Independent
2. Dependent on claim 1
3. Dependent on claim 1
4. Dependent on claims 2 and 3
5. Independent
6. Dependent on claim 1, 2 or 5
7. Dependent on claim 6
8. Independent

Which of the following represents the proper number of total claims for fee calculation purposes?

    (A)   10
    (B)   13
    (C)   11
    (D)   12
    (E)   8

32. On August 23, 1999, you file a patent application in the PTO. Along with the application, you file an unexecuted declaration that refers to the application and a preliminary amendment that describes the best mode of carrying out the claimed invention. Subsequently, you file a signed declaration in reply to a Notice to File Missing Parts. The best mode is described only in the preliminary amendment. In the first Office action, the examiner objects to the preliminary amendment as adding new matter to the specification and requires cancellation of the new matter. Considering the following responses and the additional facts separately, the best way to respond to and overcome the objection, and obtain a patent is to:

    (A)   file a reply pointing out that the objection is improper because the declaration filed in reply to the Notice to File Missing Parts is a properly executed declaration that refers only to the amendment.

    (B)   file a reply pointing out that the objection is improper because the declaration filed in reply to the Notice to File Missing Parts is a properly executed declaration that refers only to the application and amendment.

    (C)   file a reply pointing out that the objection is improper because the declaration filed in reply to the Notice to File Missing Parts is a properly executed supplemental declaration that refers only to the amendment.

    (D)   file an appeal to the Board of Patent Appeals and Interference requesting review of the examiner's objection to the amendment as adding new matter.

    (E)   file a reply to the Office action canceling the new matter.

33. During a reexamination proceeding, you submit the following amendment less than two years from the date that a patent was granted with the claim:

1. (once amended) An application specific integrated circuit for calculating a correlation coefficient, comprising: a multiplication unit [having a plurality of sixty-four bit shift registers]; an integration unit coupled to said multiplication unit; and a digital filter unit coupled to <u>said integration unit and to said</u> multiplication unit.

The original disclosure in the patent application stated that a plurality of thirty-two bit shift registers could be used to form the multiplication unit. In accordance with PTO rules and procedure, which, if any, of the following statements, including any reasons given in support thereof, concerning the amendment is true?

(A) The form of the amendment is improper, since underlining and brackets are not proper in proceedings where only issues concerning substantial new questions of patentability may be raised.

(B) The claim as amended should be allowed if it overcomes the art of record in the application since the amendment was made less than two years from the date that a patent was granted.

(C) The claim as amended should be allowed if it overcomes the art of record in the application since the amendment, although broader in some respects than the claim of the patent, is narrower in other respects.

(D) The claim as amended should not be allowed since it broadens the scope of the claim of the patent.

(E) None of the above.

34. If a claim has been properly rejected under 35 U.S.C. § 103 as being rendered *prima facie* obvious over a combination of prior art references, then the rejection can be rebutted in accordance with proper PTO practice and procedure by:

(A) showing the criticality of the claimed range where the range in the claim overlaps the range disclosed in one or both prior art references.

(B) arguing that the client has recognized latent properties in the prior art which were not recognized by the prior art references.

(C) arguing that a combination would not be made by a businessman for economic reasons.

(D) contending that each of the prior art references, taken individually, does not teach or render obvious the claimed invention.

(E) (A), (B), and (C).

35.   Morris, a registered practitioner with a solo practice he operates out of his house, obtained a plant patent for a client on a commercial catnip hybrid. One morning, over four years later, as he was sorting through his cat's toys, he came across a letter from his client indicating the client's belief that a maintenance fee was due four years after issuance. By the time Morris found the letter, it was eight months after the four year anniversary of the plant patent's issuance. Morris should immediately:

(A)   Tender the maintenance fee and submit a petition (with the required fee) for acceptance of payment where the delay was unintentional.

(B)   Pay the maintenance fee plus the surcharge for filing a maintenance fee during the grace period.

(C)   Write the client that no maintenance fee is in fact owed, and apologize for the delay in responding to the client.

(D)   Do nothing because the patent is irrevocably lost due to failure to pay the maintenance fee within the grace period.

(E)   Tender the maintenance fee and submit a petition (with an affidavit blaming the cat and with the required fee) for acceptance of payment where the delay was unavoidable.

36.   Following proper PTO practices and procedures, which of the following reference(s) anticipates Claim 1:

1.   A composition consisting of:
        60-80% cellulose;
        16-18% nylon;
        up to 0.5% fiber; and
        at least 6% cotton;
        said composition being capable of absorbing water in the amount of not more than 45% by weight of the composition.

(A)   A reference disclosing a sponge having 69% cellulose, 16% nylon, 0.4% fiber, 7% cotton, and 7.6% silk.

(B)   A reference disclosing a sponge having 78% cellulose, 17% nylon, 0.2% fiber, 4.8% cotton, and a water content of 30% by weight.

(C)   A reference disclosing a sponge having 76% cellulose, 16% nylon, 8% cotton and containing no water.

(D)   A reference disclosing a sponge having 61% cellulose, 18% nylon, 0.6% fiber, 20.4% cotton, and a water content of 45% by weight.

(E)   (B) and (D).

37. A patent application includes the following partial Claim 1:

Claim 1.   A shaving implement comprising
    (i)   _____
    (ii)   a shaving head including a razor, said shaving head being connected to said handle at said first end;
    (iii) a collapsible tube of shaving cream positioned in and substantially filling said chamber, said tube including a neck having a dispensing opening;
    (iv) a tube squeezing slide positioned within said channel and said chamber, said slide including opposed slots thereon, said slots being in sliding engagement with said longitudinal sides of said channel; and
    (v)   a tube closure connected to said neck of said collapsible tube.

Which of the following, if included as paragraph (i) of Claim 1, best completes the claim while giving the client the broadest protection?

(A) a substantially rigid handle including a chamber and a channel formed in said handle, said channel being defined by longitudinal sides within said handle;

(B) a substantially rigid handle having a first end, said handle including a chamber and a channel formed in said handle, said channel being defined by longitudinal sides within said handle;

(C) a substantially rigid handle having a first end, said handle including a chamber and an elongated channel formed in said handle;

(D) a substantially rigid handle having a first end, said handle including a chamber and a channel formed in said handle;

(E) a substantially rigid handle having a first end, said handle including a channel formed in said handle, said channel being defined by longitudinal sides within said handle;

38. Which of the following must be included in a petition for a retroactive license to file a patent application in a foreign country?

(A) A verified statement containing an averment that the subject matter in question was not under a secrecy order at the time it was filed abroad, and that it is not currently under a secrecy order.

(B) A verified explanation of why the material was filed abroad through error and without deceptive intent without the required license first having been obtained.

(C) A listing of each of the foreign countries in which the unlicensed patent application was filed.

(D) (A) and (B).

(E) (A), (B) and (C).

39.   Applicant filed a patent application claiming a polyol. The application discloses that the claimed polyol is used to form rigid polyurethane foam having a structural formula. The examiner properly rejected the claimed polyol as unpatentable over prior art disclosing the claimed polyol and its use to form rigid polyurethane foam having the same structural formula. Given the fact that applicant's specification discloses that the polyol may be produced by a process comprising steps A, B, C, and D, and the process is novel and unobvious, which of the following claims, if introduced by amendment, would overcome the rejection?

(A)   A polyol having the property of forming rigid polyurethane foam having structural formula Z, the polyol being produced by the process comprising the steps A, B, C, and D.

(B)   A polyol produced by the process comprising the steps A, B, C, and D, said polyol having the property of forming rigid polyurethane foam having structural formula Z.

(C)   A polyol produced by the process comprising the steps A, B, C, and D.

(D)   A polyol comprising the resultant product of steps A, B, C, and D.

(E)   A polyol-producing process comprising steps A, B, C, and D, said process resulting in a polyol capable of forming rigid polyurethane foam having structural formula Z.

40.   In the course of prosecuting a patent application before the PTO, you receive a non-final Office action allowing Claim 1, and rejecting Claims 2 through 6, the remaining claims in the case. Claim 1 reads as follows:

1.   A ship propeller exhibiting excellent corrosion resistance, said ship propeller consisting essentially of a copper base alloy consisting of 2 to 10 percent tin, 0.1 to 0.9 percent zinc, and copper.

The specification of the application teaches that the copper base alloy made with the addition of 2 to 10 percent aluminum increases the alloy's wear resistance without detracting from its corrosion resistance. However, adding aluminum to the surface of the propeller does not increase wear resistance. Which of the following claims, if any, if added by amendment would accord with proper PTO practice and procedure?

(A)   7. A copper base alloy according to Claim 1 wherein said alloy includes 2 to 10 percent aluminum.

(B)   7. A ship propeller according to Claim 1 including the step of adding 2 to 10 percent aluminum to the copper base alloy.

(C)   7. A ship propeller according to Claim 1 including 2 to 10 percent aluminum.

(D)   7. A ship propeller according to Claim 1 wherein said alloy includes 2 to 10 percent aluminum.

(E)   None of the above.

233

41.   A claim limitation reads "a pH range between 7 and 12, preferably between 9 and 10." Which of the following is correct?

(A)   Since the limitation properly sets forth outer limits, it is definite.
(B)   As long as the limitation is supported in the written description, it is proper.
(C)   The limitation is indefinite.
(D)   Since the limitation sets forth a preferred range, it is definite.
(E)   An applicant is precluded from expanding the claim coverage beyond a pH range of 7-12 under the doctrine of equivalents.

42.   Patent practitioner Wally is hired to prepare a patent application directed to a method of making a particular composition. After consulting with his client, Wally believes that schematic drawings would be helpful, and that color drawings would be most helpful in disclosing the method. Wally diligently contacts a draftsperson to prepare the color drawings and proceeds to complete his draft patent application. The application contains only method claims. Upon completing the application, Wally forwards the draft application to his client for review. The application contains method claims, and does not include any reference to drawing figures. Before the color drawings are complete, Wally receives an urgent call from his client directing Wally to file the application by the close of business that day due to an unforeseen statutory bar date. Drawings are not required to understand the claimed method. A patent would be barred if the application is filed the following day. Which of the following combination of acts presents the **minimum** course of action to be taken by Wally in order to obtain a filing date that avoids the statutory bar?

(A)   File the application, oath and filing fee by the close of business without the drawings.
(B)   File the application by the close of business without the oath, filing fee or drawings.
(C)   File the application and filing fee without the drawings and later file a petition for accepting the color drawings along with the petition fee; three (3) sets of color drawings; and a proposed amendment to insert the following in the specification: "The file of this patent contains at least one drawing executed in color. Copies of this patent with color drawing(s) will be provided by the Patent and Trademark Office upon request and payment of the necessary fee."
(D)   File the application without the drawings by the close of business; file a preliminary amendment the next day that amends the specification to refer to drawing figures and which includes a set of black and white drawings.
(E)   None of the above.

234

43.   You received an Office action dated March 17, 1999, rejecting the claims of a pending patent application filed April 22, 1998. You prepared a timely reply that would overcome the examiner's rejections and place the application in condition for allowance. You put the reply in a correctly addressed envelope, with a metered mail stamp having a date of June 4, 1999. Your procedure is to give all outgoing mail to your staff assistant who keeps it locked in his desk drawer until he can mail it at the end of his work day. The reply fell inside the desk, behind the drawer, and was never mailed. Today, November 3, 1999, you receive a Notice of Abandonment of the patent application for which the reply was prepared. You searched and found the unopened and unmailed envelope. You know that the applicant, your mother, sold five items covered by all the claims of the now abandoned application over a year ago (but not before the original application was filed) and that her commercial survival depends on obtaining the claims in the abandoned application. A valid patent, including the claims in the abandoned application, can be obtained for your mother, if:

(A)   you submit a new reply to the patent examiner arguing the commercial success of the item as shown by the sales of the five items sold over a year ago with affidavits under 37 CFR § 1.132 traversing the holding of abandonment.

(B)   you mail the reply today in its original, sealed envelope which takes precedence over the Notice of Abandonment since the date stamped on the envelope is both before the due date for reply and before the Notice of Abandonment.

(C)   the applicant files a petition to revive an unintentionally abandoned application stating that the entire delay in filing the required reply was unintentional, files the reply that was prepared by you in June 1999, and submits the appropriate petition fee.

(D)   you provide the unopened envelope as evidence of the staff assistant's negligence and petition the Group Director to reopen prosecution of the application on the merits.

(E)   you file a petition to revive an unavoidably abandoned application stating that the entire delay in filing the reply was unavoidable, submitting the required reply prepared by you in June 1999, the proper petition fee, and a terminal disclaimer and fee dedicating to the public a terminal part of the term of any patent granted equivalent to the period of abandonment of the application.

44.   A practitioner should consider whether information presented during prosecution of an application may be used by the examiner as evidence against the applicant. What evidence may an examiner not use to demonstrate that a claim fails to correspond in scope with that which an applicant regards as his or her invention?

(A)   Arguments, containing admissions, advanced in a reply filed by the practitioner representing the applicant.

(B)   Admissions contained in a brief.

(C)   The lack of agreement between the claims and the specification.

(D)   Affidavits, containing admissions, filed under 37 CFR § 1.132.

(E)   All of the above.

45. Which of the following statements regarding a reissue patent application is *true*?

(A) Only one reissue patent application is permitted to be issued for distinct and separate parts of the thing patented.

(B) New matter may be properly added in a reissue application to correct an error made during the prosecution of the original patent application.

(C) A reissue will not be granted to "recapture" claimed subject matter deliberately canceled in an application to obtain a patent.

(D) To retain the benefit of priority under 35 U.S.C. § 119, it is not necessary to make a new claim for priority in the reissue patent application if a claim for priority was perfected in the application on which the original patent was made.

(E) (C) and (D).

46. You filed a patent application for Sam, who invented an apparatus for labeling and identifying baseballs. In the application, the apparatus is described as including means for marking baseballs; an ultraviolet light source; and a computer coupled to both the means for marking baseballs and the ultraviolet light source. The only means for marking baseballs set forth in the application was a commercially available invisible ink stamper, also known as a marker. The specification described the invention as being useful for identifying home run baseballs. The application was filed with one claim, which stated:

Claim 1.   An apparatus, comprising: an invisible ink stamper; an ultraviolet light source; and a computer coupled to said invisible ink stamper and to said ultraviolet light source.

Claim 1 was properly rejected under 35 U.S.C. §102(b) as being anticipated by a patent issued to McGoo, which disclosed an apparatus having only an invisible ink stamper, an ultraviolet light source, and a computer coupled to the invisible ink stamper and to the ultraviolet light source. The McGoo patent did not mention identifying baseballs, but described the invention as useful for labeling and identifying baseball bats. Which of the following amendments, if any, avoids anticipation of Claim 1 by the McGoo patent?

(A) 1. (amended once) An apparatus <u>intended to be used to identify home run baseballs</u>, comprising: an invisible ink stamper; an ultraviolet light source; and a computer coupled to said invisible ink stamper and to said ultraviolet light source.

(B) 1. (amended once) An apparatus, [comprising] consisting of: an invisible ink stamper, an ultraviolet light source, and a computer coupled to said invisible ink stamper and to said ultraviolet light source.

(C) 1. (amended once) An apparatus, comprising: [an invisible ink stamper] <u>a marker</u>; an ultraviolet light source, and a computer coupled to said means for marking baseballs and to said ultraviolet light source.

(D) (B) and (C).

(E) None of the above.

236

47. A patent application includes the following Claim 1:

Claim 1. A method of making an electrical device comprising the steps of:
  (i)   heating a base made of carbon to a first temperature in the range of 1800°C to 2000°C;
  (ii) passing a first gas over said heated base, said first gas comprising a mixture of hydrogen, $SiCl_4$, phosphorus, and methane, whereby said first gas decomposes over said heated base and thereby forms a first deposited layer of silicon, phosphorus and carbon on said heated base;
  (iii) heating said base having said deposited layer to a second temperature of approximately 1620°C; and
  (iv) passing a second gas over said base heated to said second temperature, said second gas consisting of a mixture of hydrogen, $SiCl_4$, $AlCl_3$, and methane, whereby said second gas decomposes over said heated base to form a second deposit layer adjacent said first layer, said second layer comprising silicon, aluminum and carbon.

Assuming proper support in the specification, which of the following claims, if presented in the same application, is a proper claim?

(A) Claim 2. The method of claim 1, wherein said first temperature is in the range of 1875°C to 1925°C, and preferably between 1895°C and 1905°C.

(B) Claim 3. The electrical device of claim 1, wherein said first gas further comprises an inert gas such as Argon.

(C) Claim 4. The method of claim 1, wherein said second gas further consists of Argon.

(D) Claim 5. The method of claim 1, wherein said first gas further comprises an inert gas such as Argon.

(E) Claim 6. The electrical device of claim 1, wherein said heated base has a first layer comprising silicon, phosphorus, and carbon.

48. An original claim in a patent application to a mechanical arts invention recites the limitation of "a clip," which is shown in an original application drawing as being one of several elements of the invention. The "clip" is well known in the mechanical arts. However, "a clip" does not appear in the original written description part of the application. Which of the following is correct?

(A) The written description may not be properly amended to include "a clip"
(B) The claim is indefinite with respect to "a clip."
(C) The application lacks an enabling disclosure as to "a clip."
(D) The claim is definite with respect to "a clip."
(E) The application fails to set forth the best mode for "a clip."

49.   A nonprovisional patent application has been filed for inventor Alton disclosing and claiming an alumino-silicate catalyst for oxidizing organic compounds. Which of the following statements, considered separately, about the best mode contemplated by Alton for the alumino-silicate catalyst is not true?

(A)   The best mode must be designated as the best mode in the application if the application contains several embodiments, one of which is the best mode.

(B)   The presence of one specific example in the specification is evidence that the best mode has been disclosed.

(C)   The best mode need not be updated if, between the time of filing the non-provisional patent application and a continuation application, Alton discovered a better catalyst than the best mode disclosed in the non-provisional application.

(D)   A failure to disclose the best mode in the application as filed cannot be cured by first introducing into the application by amendment a specific mode of practicing the invention.

(E)   There is no statutory requirement for the best mode being disclosed in the specification as a specific example.

50.   You are drafting a patent application disclosing and describing a door assembly wherein a door, a door frame, and a pair of hinges are separate elements which must be included in a claim to the assembled combination of a door secured to a door frame by a pair of hinges. The application discloses that it is essential to the invention that the door is secured to the doorframe in the described manner to permit the door to be readily opened and closed. The application further discloses that it is also essential to the invention for the assembly, in a closed relationship, to keep out exterior elements, while providing privacy and permitting quick egress in an emergency. Which of the following claims properly sets forth the combination?

(A)   An assembly having a door capable of being hingedly connected to a doorframe.

(B)   An assembly having a door and means for securing the door.

(C)   An assembly having a door and a pair of hinges for securing the door.

(D)   An assembly having a door, and a doorframe, said door being secured to said doorframe with a pair of hinges.

(E)   An assembly having a door adapted to be secured to a doorframe with a pair of hinges.

**Examination for Registration to Practice in Patent Cases
Before the U.S. Patent and Trademark Office
November 3, 1999**

Morning Session Answers

1. ANSWER: (E). MPEP §§ 1502.01, and 201.04(b) [p. 200-14].

2. ANSWER: (D). "It is not necessary in order to establish a <u>prima facie</u> case of obviousness…that there be a suggestion or expectation from <u>the prior art</u> that the claimed [invention] will have the same or a similar utility as <u>one newly discovered by the applicant.</u>" *In re Dillon*, 919 F.2d 688, 692, 16 USPQ2d 1897, 1900 (Fed. Cir. 1990) (emphasis in original). Thus, "[i]t is not necessary that the prior art suggest the combination to achieve the same advantage or result discovered by applicant." MPEP § 2144 ("Rationale Different from Applicant's is Permissible").

  Here, T suggests the combination with P to achieve a different advantage or result, i.e., waterproofing, from that discovered by applicant, i.e., reducing breakage. Answers (A) - (C) are incorrect because the suggestion to combine does not need to be for the same purpose as applicant discloses in the application. *Dillon*, 919 F.2d at 692, 16 USPQ2d at 1900; MPEP § 2144 ("Rationale Different from Applicant's is Permissible"). Answer (E) is incorrect because an applicant is under no obligation to submit evidence of non-obviousness unless the examiner meets his or her initial burden to fully establish a <u>prima facie</u> case of obviousness. MPEP § 2142.

3. ANSWER: (E). Both (B) and (D) cannot be incorporated into a U.S. utility application. MPEP § 608.01(p) [pp. 600-72-73].

4. ANSWER: (D) and (E). (D) is a correct statement because a claim that includes a tradename, whose definition is neither sufficiently precise nor definite, fails to comply with 35 U.S.C. § 112, paragraph 2. Claim 2 has two tradenames, "Acme SmellNice" and "A-1 Silky." The ingredient composition of "Acme SmellNice" has "recently changed," and the change is "unknown," and otherwise indefinite. MPEP §§ 608.01(v), and 706.03(d); and *Ex parte Simpson*, 218 USPQ 1020 (Bd. App. 1982). (E) is also correct to the extent (B) correctly points out that an incorrect theory of operation is incorporated into a claim, that claim is invalid under either 35 U.S.C. § 101 (utility) or 35 U.S.C. § 112 (enablement). *Raytheon Co. v. Roper Corp.*, 724 F2d 951, 220 USPQ 592, 596 (Fed. Cir. 1983). (B) alone is not accepted as a correct answer because no fact was given preceding the answer that claim 2 sets for an incorrect theory of formation of chemical X, whereas sufficient facts were given to recognize that (D) is a correct answer. (A) is incorrect at least because prophetic examples may well provide an enabling disclosure. MPEP 608.01(p), and 2164.02. Also, an inventor need not understand how an invention works. (C) is incorrect because naturally occurring compounds may be patented particularly when a new use (industrial lubricant) is part of the claim.

5. ANSWER: (D). 37 CFR § 1.116; MPEP § 714.13, Entry Not Matter of Right [p. 700-124]. The reply in (D) is directed to a reply authorized under 37 CFR § 1.116(a). (A), (B), and (C) are directed to the merits of the application, and are not in accord with 37 CFR § 1.116(a).

6.   ANSWER: All answers are accepted.

7.   ANSWER: (C) is the most correct answer. 37 CFR § 1.116; MPEP § 714.13.

8.   ANSWER (C). MPEP § 2163.03, item I. Original claims constitute their own description. *In re Koller*, 613 F.2d 819, 204 USPQ 702 (CCPA 1980). (A) and (B) are incorrect. As stated in MPEP § 2163.03, item I, "An amendment to the specification (e.g., a change in the definition of a term used both in the specification and claim) may indirectly affect a claim even though no actual amendment is made to the claim." There is no supporting disclosure in the original description of the invention for the holder to a clasp, crimp, or tong. (D) is incorrect. MPEP § 2163.03, item IV. A broad generic disclosure is not necessarily a sufficient written description of a specific embodiment, especially where the broad generic disclosure conflicts with the remainder of the disclosure. *Fields v. Conover*, 443 F.2d 1386, 170 USPQ 276 (CCPA 1970). (E) is not correct because (C) is correct.

9.   ANSWER: (C). Dependent Claim 4 must further limit Claim 1 from which it depends. 35 U.S.C. § 112, paragraph 4; 37 CFR § 1.75(c). The dependent claim 4 in (C) improperly seeks to broaden Claim 1 by omitting an element set forth in the parent claim.

10. ANSWER: (C). "A claim may be written in dependent or multiple dependent form." 35 U.S.C. § 112, paragraph 3. When written in dependent form, the claim "shall contain a reference to a claim previously set forth and then specify a further limitation of the subject matter claimed." 35 U.S.C. § 112, paragraph 4. When written in multiple dependent form, the claim "shall contain a reference, in the alternative only, to more than one claim previously set forth and then specify a further limitation of the subject matter claimed." 35 U.S.C. § 112, paragraph 5. See also 37 CFR § 1.75(c); MPEP § 608.01(n). Here, the claim is in proper multiple dependent form, referring back in the alternative to claims previously set forth, i.e., claims 1, 2 or 3. Answers (A) and (B) are incorrect because each claim does not refer back to a preceding claim. In Answer (A), claim 4 refers to claim 5. In Answer (B), claim 2 refers to claim 5. 35 U.S.C. § 112, paragraph 4; 37 CFR § 1.75(c); MPEP § 608.01(n) ("2. Claim Does Not Refer to a Preceding Claim"). Answers (D) and (E) are incorrect because each claim does not refer back in the alternative. In Answer (D), claim 3 refers to all the preceding claims, i.e., claims 1, 2 and 3. In Answer (E), claim 5 refers to claims 1 and 2, or claim 3. 35 U.S.C. § 112, paragraph 5; 37 CFR § 1.75(c); MPEP § 608.01(n) ("1. Claim Does Not Refer Back in the Alternative Only").

11. ANSWER: (B). The question is directed to the proper conduct by patent attorneys and agents. Practitioners, including registered patent agents, (37 CFR § 10.1(r)), may advertise on television and radio. 37 CFR § 10.32(a). Additionally, a registered patent agent may accept cases on a contingent fee basis. 37 CFR § 10.36(b)(8) (permits contingent and fixed fees that are not clearly excessive or illegal). (A) and (C) are incorrect. The patent agent is not authorized to practice in trademark cases. 37 CFR § 10.14(b). (D) is incorrect. Practitioners are proscribed

from entering into partnership agreements restricting their right to practice before the PTO. 37 CFR § 10.38(a). The agreement in choice (D) provides "that after termination of the partnership, the agent and the attorney will not practice in each other's neighborhoods or accept each other's established clients," which is contrary to §10.38(a). (E) is incorrect. A patent agent is proscribed from misrepresenting himself or herself as being a registered patent attorney. 37 CFR §§ 10.23(b)(4) and 10.34(b).

12. ANSWER: (C). 35 U.S.C. § 102(b) and (e); 37 CFR § 1.131(a). A reference under 35 U.S.C. § 102(b) cannot be antedated. Therefore, (A), (B) and (E) are incorrect. (D) is incorrect because it is non-responsive, and it does not matter when the Spot patent issued.

13 ANSWER: (A). 35 U.S.C. §§ 102, and 103. Anticipation requires that each and every limitation in the claim be shown in a single reference, either expressly or impliedly. MPEP §§ 706.02, and 2131. Here, Claim 1 has been amended to require that the seat portion be formed of plastic (see fifth and sixth lines following the claim). Baker does not disclose or imply a plastic seat. However, Baker does disclose the recited "supporting means" because under 35 U.S.C. § 112, paragraph 6, that claim language covers under its literal scope the disclosed structure (four legs) and equivalent structures (three legs), and Able's argument is therefore unconvincing. MPEP § 2181. An obviousness rejection over Baker/Charlie is appropriate because Charlie suggests replacing wooden seats with plastic seats. MPEP §§ 706.02, and 2143. (B) is not the most correct answer because the rationale that "Baker does not disclose a four legged supporting means" does not distinguish Baker from the claimed subject matter. Under 35 U.S.C. § 112, paragraph 6, the "means for supporting" in Claim 1 is equivalent to the supporting means disclosed in Baker inasmuch as the claimed means is not limited to four legs. The "three legged" supporting means in Baker is within the literal scope of the claim, and anticipation is not avoided on that basis. (C) is not the most correct answer because the issue of whether one of ordinary skill in the art would recognize that plastic could be substituted for wood goes to obviousness, not anticipation. Maintaining the anticipation rejection is improper because the claim has been amended to require that the seat portion be formed of plastic (see fifth and sixth lines following the claim), a limitation not disclosed by Baker. (D) is incorrect because there is an adequate written description of the plastic seat in the application, and applicants commonly (and properly) limit claims to a preferred embodiment during prosecution. MPEP § 2172 (III. SHIFT IN CLAIMS PERMITTED). (E) is incorrect because (B) and (D) are both incorrect.

14. ANSWER: (E). A claim may be amended by specifying the exact matter to be deleted or added, and the precise point where the deletion or addition is to be made. 37 CFR § 1.121(a)(2)(i). The amendments are limited to additions of no more than 5 words per claim or deletions. 37 CFR §§ 1.121(a)(2)(i)(A) and 1.121(a)(2)(i)(B). Here, Answer (A) is improper because the amendment does not specify the precise point where the addition is to be made. Answer (B) is improper because the amendment adds more than 5 words to the claim. Answer (C) is improper because line 3 contains the word "layer" twice and the amendment does not specify whether the word "thin" is added before the first occurrence, second occurrence, or

all occurrences of the word "layer." Answer (D) is improper because the amendment gives no direction for how to correctly spell "talbecloth."

15. ANSWER: (C). 37 CFR § 1.75(c). A dependent claim must further limit the claim from which it depends. The claim in (C) is an improper dependent claim because it includes resistance outside the scope of Claim 1. In the claim in (C), the term "about" allows for a range slightly above 90 ohms or below 10 ohms, which is "outside" the scope of Claim 1. See MPEP § 2144.05. (A), (B), and (D) are proper dependent claims because they further limit Claim 1 by limiting the resistance to amounts within the scope of Claim 1. (E) is incorrect because (D) is a proper dependent claim.

16. ANSWER: (D). MPEP § 1210.

17. ANSWER: (C). 35 U.S.C. § 305 recites, *inter alia*, "No proposed amended or new claim enlarging the scope of a claim of the patent will be permitted in a reexamination proceeding under this chapter." MPEP §§ 2254, and 2258, item III. Since no claims drawn to a method were ever presented during prosecution of the 'XXX patent, (claims 1-4 "are the only claims that were presented during prosecution of the application that matured into 'XXX patent"), the claim recited in (C) is not directed to "the invention as claimed." Moreover, such claim is regarded as enlarging the scope of the claims in the 'XXX patent. *Ex parte Wikdahl*, 10 USPQ2d 1546, 1549 (Bd. Pat. App. & Int. 1989). (A), (B), and (C) are all incorrect because each of their claims are directed to a hydrocyclone separator apparatus, i.e., "the invention as claimed," and they do not enlarge the scope of the claims in the 'XXX patent. (E) is an incorrect answer because (C) is the correct answer.

18. ANSWER: (A). The phrase "consisting of" excludes any step not specified in the claim. MPEP § 2111.03. Thus, a claim that depends from a claim which "consists of" the recited steps cannot add a step. Id. Here, the dependent claim adds the step of cooling. Answer (B) is incorrect because the transitional term "comprising" is inclusive or open-ended and does not exclude additional, unrecited steps. MPEP § 2111.03. Answers (C) and (D) are incorrect because the terms "including" and "characterized by" are synonymous with the term "comprising." MPEP § 2111.03. Answer (E) is incorrect because Answer (C) and Answer (D) are incorrect.

19. ANSWER: (A). MPEP § 2144. *In re Linter*, 458 F.2d 1013, 173 USPQ 560 (CCPA 1972); *In re Dillon*, 919 F.2d 688, 16 USPQ2d 1897 (Fed. Cir. 1990), cert. denied, 500 U.S. 904 (1991). (B) is incorrect. MPEP § 2144. The rationale to modify or combine the prior art does not have to be expressly stated in the prior art; the rationale may be expressly or impliedly contained in the prior art or it may be reasoned from knowledge generally available to one of ordinary skill in the art, established scientific principles, or legal precedent established by prior case law. *In re Fine*, 837 F.2d 1071, 5 USPQ2d 1596 (Fed. Cir. 1988); *In re Jones*, 958 F.2d 347, 21 USPQ2d 1941 (Fed. Cir. 1992). (C) is incorrect. MPEP § 2144.01. *In re Preda*,

401 F.2d 825, 159 USPQ 342, 344 (CCPA 1968) ("[I]n considering the disclosure of a reference, it is proper to take into account not only specific teachings of the reference but also the inferences which one skilled in the art would reasonably be expected to draw therefrom."). (D) is incorrect. *In re Ahlert*, 424 F.2d 1088, 1091, 165 USPQ 418, 420 (CCPA 1970) (Board properly took judicial notice that "it is common practice to postheat a weld after the welding operation is completed" and that "it is old to adjust the intensity of a flame in accordance with the heat requirement"); and MPEP § 2144.03. (E) is incorrect. MPEP § 2144.06 (Substituting Equivalents Known For The Same Purpose). To rely on equivalence as a rationale supporting an obviousness rejection, the equivalency must be recognized in the prior art, and cannot be based on applicant's disclosure. *In re Ruff*, 256 F.2d 590, 118 USPQ 340 (CCPA 1958).

20. ANSWER: (A). (A) provides proper antecedent basis for "said mid-point" in part (iv) of Claim 1 and in Claim 2, and "said connector" in Claim 3. (B) is incorrect at least because it includes the unnecessary limitation that the cutting members are formed of metal and because it does not provide antecedent basis for "said connector" in Claim 3. (C) is incorrect because it includes the unnecessary limitation of a reservoir, and it does not provide antecedent basis for "said connector" in Claim 3. (D) is incorrect because it does not provide antecedent basis for "said mid-point" in part (iv) of Claim 1 and Claim 2, and for "said connector" in Claim 3. (E) is incorrect because it does not provide proper antecedent basis for "said mid-point" in part (iv) of Claim 1 and in Claim 2.

21. ANSWER: (C). 35 U.S.C. § 301; 37 CFR § 1.552; and MPEP § 2258. (A), (B), (D) and (E) are incorrect because reexamination is limited to substantially new questions of patentability based on patents and publications.

22. ANSWER: (B). The scope of Claim 1 is enlarged, or broadened by the deletion of "flanged" as a modifier of "seal." Inasmuch as the reissue application is filed less than two years after the original patent was granted, and the application seeks to enlarge the scope of Claim 1, a reissue patent may be properly granted containing the claim. 35 U.S.C. § 251. (A) is incorrect. Inasmuch as the scope of Claim 1 is enlarged by the amendment and the reissue application was filed more than two years from the grant of the original patent, no reissue patent shall be granted. 35 U.S.C. § 251. (C) and (D) are incorrect inasmuch as the scope of Claim 1 is enlarged, or broadened as discussed above, and claims cannot be enlarged or broadened in a reexamination application regardless of when the application is filed. 35 U.S.C. § 305; 37 CFR § 1.552(b). (E) is incorrect since (D) is incorrect.

23. ANSWER: (C). Under the stated facts, Homer's commercial use is a bar under 35 U.S.C. § 102(b) because it was not experimental, so (C) would be unreasonable advice. MPEP § 2133.03. For the same reason, and because the modified system is new and unobvious, (B) would be reasonable advice. (A) would be reasonable advice because whether the claim is limited to ultrasonic signals is a question of breadth, not definiteness. MPEP § 2173.04. (D) is reasonable advice because there is no antecedent basis for "the decoder portion of said tunneling device

sensor". (E) is reasonable advice because an argument could be made that the claim, as originally drafted, could not be infringed until the target is actually placed in the ground. Thus, a sale of the system, with the target in a box, technically might not be a literal infringement of that claim.

24. ANSWER: (A). 35 U.S.C. § 102(b). The claimed invention is unpatentable inasmuch as the invention was in public use and on sale more than one before Homer files a patent application. (B) - (D) are incorrect because the given facts do not meet the conditions negating patentability set forth in 35 U.S.C. § 102(c), (d), or (e). (E) is incorrect because (A) is correct.

25. ANSWER: (C). The PTO does not require or recommend a minimum or maximum number of dependent claims. 37 CFR § 1.75(c). (A) is a PTO recommendation. See MPEP § 608.01(m) ("Claims should preferably be arranged in order of scope so that the first claim presented is the least restrictive."). (B) is a PTO recommendation. See MPEP § 608.01(m) ("Similarly, product and process claims should be separately grouped."). (D) is a PTO requirement. See MPEP § 608.01(n), at 600-63 (Claim Form and Arrangement). (E) is a PTO requirement. See MPEP § 608.01(m) ("Each claim begins with a capital letter and ends with a period.").

26. ANSWER: (C). The combination of references presents a substantial new question of patentability. MPEP § 2244. *In re Hiniker Co.*, 150 F.3d 1362, 47 USPQ2d 1523 (Fed Cir. 1998) (where the prior art references are applied in combination, and one reference served as a rejection in the prosecution of the original patent while the other reference "was never before the examiner during the original prosecution and is thus new art[, and t]here is no indication that the [new art] was not material to the question of obviousness vel non or that it was cumulative with any old art" the decisions rejecting the claims "were based on a substantial new question of patentability." Answers (A) and (D) are incorrect because a "prior art reference that served as a rejection in the prosecution of the original patent could not support a substantial new question of patentability that would permit the institution of a reexamination proceeding." *In re Recreative Technologies*, 83 F.3d 1394, 38 USPQ 1776 (Fed. Cir. 1996). Answer (B) is incorrect because "prior art that was before the original examiner could not support a reexamination proceeding despite the fact that it was not the basis of a rejection in the original prosecution; as long as the art was before the original examiner, it would be considered 'old art'." *In re Portola Packaging, Inc.*, 110 F.3d 786, 42 USPQ2d 1295 (Fed. Cir. 1997). Answer (E) is incorrect because answers (A), (B) and (D) are incorrect.

27. ANSWER: (B). "Whoever invents or discovers any new and useful...manufacture, or composition of matter...may obtain a patent therefor, subject to the conditions and requirements of this title." 35 U.S.C. § 101. However, "laws of nature, physical phenomena, and abstract ideas" are not subject matter eligible for protection under the patent statute. Diamond v. Chakrabarty, 447 U.S. 303, 309, 206 USPQ 193, 198 (1980). But, a "nonnaturally occurring manufacture or composition of matter—a product of human ingenuity—having a distinctive name, character, [and] use" is subject matter eligible for protection under the patent statute. Id.

See also MPEP § 2105. Thus, Answer (B) is correct because the top soil is a product of M's ingenuity. Answer (A) is incorrect because the top soil is a physical phenomenon, i.e., naturally occurring manufacture or composition of matter, M was merely the first to locate. Chakrabarty, 447 U.S. at 309, 206 USPQ at 198; MPEP § 2105. Answer (C) is incorrect because only non-naturally occurring inanimate objects, i.e., products of human ingenuity, are subject matter eligible for protection under the patent statute. Chakrabarty, 447 U.S. at 309, 206 USPQ at 198; MPEP § 2105.

28. ANSWER: (E). The cancellation of Claim 3 overcomes the examiners objection. The addition of Claim 4 and 5 provide the client with patent protection in product by process format for the cable by both methods of manufacture. Thus, if Claim 4 is invalid, Claim 5 may remain valid. Answer (A) is incorrect because it is an improper multiple dependent claim. 35 U.S.C. § 112, paragraph 5; 37 CFR § 1.75(c); MPEP § 608.01(n) ("1. Claim Does Not Refer Back in the Alternative Only"). Answer (B) alone is incorrect because, even though canceling the claim will overcome the rejection, it will also leave the application without a claim to the Ethernet cable made using the processes set forth in either claim 1 or claim 2.

29. ANSWER: (A). MPEP § 2133.03(b), item III (A). "Public" as used in 35 U.S.C. 102(b) modifies "use" only. "Public" does not modify "sale." Hobbs v. United States, 451 F.2d 849, 171 USPQ 713, 720 (5th Cir. 1971). (B) is incorrect. MPEP § 2133.03(b), item IV (A). Sale or offer for sale of the invention by an independent third party more than 1 year before the filing date of applicant's patent will bar applicant from obtaining a patent. Although "an exception to this rule exists where a patented method is kept secret and remains secret after a sale of the unpatented product of the method. Such a sale prior to the critical date is a bar if engaged in by the patentee or patent applicant, but not if engaged in by another." In re Caveney, 761 F.2d 671, 675-76, 226 USPQ 1, 3-4 (Fed. Cir. 1985). (C) is incorrect. MPEP § 2133.03(d). An offer for sale, made or originating in this country, may be sufficient prefatory activity to bring the offer within the terms of the statute, even though sale and delivery take place in a foreign country. The same rationale applies to an offer by a foreign manufacturer, which is communicated to a prospective purchaser in the United States prior to the critical date. C.T.S. Corp. v. Piher Int'l Corp., 593 F.2d 777201 USPQ 649 (7th Cir. 1979). (D) is incorrect. MPEP § 2134. Delay alone is not sufficient to infer the requisite intent to abandon. Moore v. U.S., 194 USPQ 423, 428 (Ct. Cl. 1977) (The drafting and retention in his own files of two patent applications by inventor indicates an intent to retain his invention; delay in filing the applications was not sufficient to establish abandonment). (E) is incorrect. MPEP § 2135.01, item III (B). Ex parte Links, 184 USPQ 429 (Bd. App. 1974) (German applications, which have not yet been published for opposition, are published in the form of printed documents called Offenlegungsschriften 18 months after filing. These applications are unexamined or in the process of being examined at the time of publication. The Board held that an Offenlegungsschriften is not a patent under 35 U.S.C. § 102(d) even though some provisional rights are granted. The court explained that the provisional rights are minimal and do not come into force if the application is withdrawn or refused.).

30. ANSWER: (D). 37 CFR § 1.16(a) and (e); and MPEP § 509.01, which states, "For applications filed after February 27, 1983, if there is an authorization to charge the filing fee to a deposit account which is overdrawn or has insufficient funds, a surcharge (37 CFR § 1.16(e)) is required in addition to payment of the filing fee. Failure to timely pay the filing fee and surcharge will result in abandonment of the application."

31. ANSWER: (D). 37 CFR § 1.75(c); MPEP § 608.01(n).

32. ANSWER: (B). When an amendment accompanies a non-provisional patent application filed without a signed declaration, the amendment is considered part of the original disclosure, provided that the subsequently filed declaration refers to both the patent application and the amendment. MPEP §§ 608.04(b), and 714.09. Here, the application was filed with an unexecuted declaration, i.e., an unsigned declaration. Thus, the best way to overcome the rejection is to file an executed declaration that refers to both the application and amendment.
Answer (A) is incorrect because the declaration must refer to both the application and amendment. MPEP §§ 608.04(b), and 714.09. Answer (C) is incorrect because, even if the original declaration had been signed, the original disclosure of an application cannot be altered by filing a supplemental declaration that refers to paper different from those referred to in the original declaration. 37 CFR § 1.67(b) (no new matter may be introduced into a non-provisional patent application after its filing date even if a supplemental declaration is filed). See also MPEP § 608.04(b). Answer (D) is incorrect because an examiner's objection to an amendment as adding new matter to the specification is a matter petitionable to the Commissioner, pursuant to 37 CFR § 1.181(a)(1). See also MPEP § 608.04(c). Answer (E) is incorrect because, while canceling the new matter will overcome the examiner's objection, it is not the best way to overcome the rejection because, after cancellation, the application will fail to set forth the best mode contemplated by the inventor of carrying the claimed invention. 35 U.S.C. § 112.

33. ANSWER: (D). MPEP § 2258, item III. (A) is incorrect because it is nonsensical and the form of the amendment is proper. MPEP § 2250. (B) is incorrect because the amendment broadens the scope of the claim of the patent, which is never allowed in a reexamination proceeding. MPEP § 2258, item III (C) is incorrect because a claim is broader than another claim if it is broader in any respect, even though it may be narrower in other respects. MPEP § 2258, item III. (E) is incorrect because (D) is correct.

34. ANSWER: (A). MPEP § 2144.05, item III states, "Applicant can rebut a *prima facie* case of obviousness based on overlapping ranges by showing the criticality of the claimed range," citing *In re Woodruff*, 919 F.2d 1575, 16 USPQ2d 1934 (Fed. Cir. 1990). (B) is incorrect. MPEP § 2145, item II. Mere recognition of latent properties contained in the prior art does not render nonobvious an otherwise known invention. The court, in *In re Wiseman*, 596 F.2d 1019, 201 USPQ 658 (CCPA 1979), points out that granting a patent on the discovery of latent or unknown, but inherent property would remove from the public that which is in the public domain

by virtue of the property's inclusion in, or obviousness from, the prior art. (C) is incorrect. MPEP § 2145, item VII. The fact that a combination would not be made by a businessman for economic reasons does not mean that a person of ordinary skill in the art would not make the combination because of some technological incompatibility. *In re Farrenkopf*, 713 F.2d 714. 219 USPQ 1 (Fed. Cir. 1983). (D) is incorrect. MPEP § 2145, item IV. Nonobviousness cannot be shown by attacking references individually where the rejection is based on a combination of references. *In re Keller*, 642 F.2d 413, 208 USPQ 871 (CCPA 1981). (E) is incorrect (B) and (C) are incorrect.

35. ANSWER: (C). 35 U.S.C. § 41(b); 37 CFR § 1.20(e). There is no maintenance fee for a plant patent. Thus, all of the other answers, which assume that a maintenance fee is owed, are wrong.

36. ANSWER: (C). A claim is anticipated only if each and every element as set forth in the claim is found, either expressly or inherently described, in a single prior art reference. Verdegaal Bros. v. Union Oil Co. of Cal., 814 F.2d 628, 631, 2 USPQ2d 1051, 1053 (Fed. Cir. 1987). See also MPEP § 2131. Further, the use of the phrase "up to" includes zero as a limit, and the use of the phrase "a water content of not more than" includes no water, i.e., dry, as a limit. MPEP § 2173.05(c) ("II. Open-Ended Numerical Ranges"). Here, Answer (C) shows 76% cellulose, 16% nylon, 0% fiber, 8% cotton ("balance cotton") and no water content. Thus, the reference sets forth all the claim limitations. Answer (A) is incorrect because the phrase "consisting of" excludes the inclusion of silk in the claimed sponge. See MPEP § 2111.03. Answer (B) is incorrect because "balance cotton" equals 4.8% cotton, a limit outside the range of "at least 6% cotton" recited in the claim. Answer (D) is incorrect because "0.6% fiber" is outside the limit outside the range of "up to 0.5% fiber" recited in the claim. Answer (E) is incorrect because Answer (B) and Answer (D) are incorrect.

37. ANSWER: (B). (A) fails to provide proper antecedent basis for "said first end" in part (ii) of the claim. (C) and (D) fail to provide proper antecedent basis for "said longitudinal sides of said channel" in part (iv) of the claim. (E) fails to provide proper antecedent basis for "said chamber" in part (i) and subsequent parts of the claim.

38. ANSWER: (E). 35 U.S.C. § 184; 37 CFR § 5.25(a); MPEP § 140.

39. ANSWER: (E). 35 U.S.C. §§ 102 and 103; *Ex parte Edwards*, 231 USPQ 981 (Bd. Pat. App. & Int. 1986); *In re Thorpe*, 777 F.2d 695, 697, 227 USPQ 964, 966 (Fed. Cir. 1985), and MPEP §§ 2113 and 2173.05(p). (A) - (D) are wrong because they are product-by-process claims, and the novelty is only in the process.

40. ANSWER: (E). "None of the above" is correct because (A), (B), (C), and (D) are wrong. (A) is wrong because Claim 1 is directed to a ship propeller, whereas (A) recites a claim which purports to be dependent upon Claim 1 but involves a *non sequitur*, i.e., it is directed to a copper

base alloy rather than a ship propeller. Therefore, the dependent claim is indefinite and violates 35 U.S.C. § 112, paragraph 2. (B) is wrong because Claim 1 is directed to a product. i.e.. a ship propeller, whereas (B) recites a claim that purports to be dependent upon Claim 1, but involves a process step. Therefore, the claim is directed to more than one statutory class of invention and violates 35 U.S.C. § 112, paragraph 2. While a claim to a product may be permissible when defining the claimed product in terms of the process by which it is made or in terms of the process by which it is intended to be used (MPEP § 2173.05(p)), the situation presented here is different and not permissible. In this regard, the term "consisting of" in Claim 1 excludes any element, step, or ingredient not specified in the claim. Thus, as stated in MPEP § 2111.03, "A claim which depends from a claim which 'consists of' the recited elements or steps cannot add an element or step." (B) recites a claim that also violates this caveat. (C) is wrong because it recites a dependent claim that attempts to add "2 to 10 percent aluminum" to the propeller of Claim 1. Since the specification teaches the addition of aluminum to the copper base alloy and not the propeller of Claim 1, the dependent claim introduces new matter. Thus, the claim may be subject to a rejection under the first paragraph of 35 U.S.C. § 112. MPEP § 608.04. It is not clear from the language of the claim that the addition of aluminum is to the alloy. (E) is wrong because it recites a dependent claim which is directed to a ship propeller according to Claim 1 including 2 to 10 percent of aluminum, which has been excluded by the term "consisting of" in Claim 1. Thus, as stated in MPEP § 2111.03, "A claim which depends from a claim which 'consists of' the recited elements or steps cannot add an element or step." (D) recites a claim that violates this caveat.

41. ANSWER: (C). MPEP § 2173.05(c), part (a) indicates that a preferred narrower range set forth within a broader range is an indefinite claim limitation. (A), (B), and (D) are not correct because MPEP § 2173.05(c), part (a) indicates that a preferred narrower range set forth within a broader range may render the claim indefinite. (E) is wrong because the doctrine of equivalents operates to expand claim coverage beyond the literal scope of the claim language.

42. ANSWER: (B) is the most correct answer. MPEP § 601.01(f). "It has been PTO practice to treat an application that contains at least one process or method claim as an application for which a drawing is not necessary for an understanding of the invention under 35 U.S.C. § 113 (first sentence)." As such, the application will be processed for examination. (A) is not the minimum that must be submitted to obtain a filing date given that the filing fee and oath may be submitted after the specification and drawing are submitted. 35 U.S.C. § 111(a)(3). (C) is not the correct answer because the filing of a petition may be deferred until the examiner requires acceptable formal drawings. MPEP § 608.02 [p. 600-86]. Also, the filing fee may be filed after the specification is submitted. 35 U.S.C. § 111(a)(3). (D) is not correct because it does not represent the minimum, which must be submitted to obtain a filing date before the statutory bar. (E) is not correct because (B) is correct.

43. ANSWER: (C). 37 CFR § 1.137(b).

44. ANSWER (C). Applicant's own disclosure in the specification and claims may not be used against the applicant. The content of the applicant's specification may not be used as evidence that the scope of the claims is inconsistent with the subject matter that applicant regards as his invention. Claiming that which applicant regards as his invention is a matter of compliance with 35 U.S.C. § 112, second paragraph. As noted in *In re Ehrreich,* 590 F.2d 902, 200 USPQ 504 (CCPA 1979), the lack of agreement between the claims and specification is properly considered only with respect to 35 U.S.C. § 112, first paragraph; MPEP § 2172, item II. (A), (B) and (D) are incorrect. Evidence demonstrating that a claim does not correspond in scope with that which an applicant regards as his invention can be found in the admissions in arguments or briefs, *In re Prater*, 415 F.2d 1393, 162 USPQ 541 (CCPA 1969), or in affidavits filed under 37 CFR § 1.132. *In re Cormany*, 476 F.2d 998, 177 USPQ 450 (CCPA 1973); MPEP § 2172, item II. (E) is incorrect because (C) is correct.

45. ANSWER: (C). 35 U.S.C. § 251; and MPEP §§ 1411, 1411.02, and 1412.02. (D) is not a correct answer. MPEP § 1417. (A) is incorrect. 35 U.S.C. § 251, paragraph 2. (B) is incorrect. 35 U.S.C. § 251, paragraph 1.

46. ANSWER: (E). (A) is incorrect because a preamble is generally not accorded patentable weight where it merely recites the intended use of a structure. MPEP § 2111.02. (B) is incorrect because the facts set forth that the McGoo invention is described as limited to the elements recited in (B). MPEP § 2111.03. (C) is incorrect because the structure corresponding to means for marking baseballs and equivalents thereof, includes an invisible ink stamper. (D) is incorrect since (B) and (C) are both incorrect.

47. ANSWER: All answers are accepted.

48. ANSWER: (D). MPEP § 2173.05(e) indicates that as long as a claim phrase has a reasonable degree of clarity, such as reciting something well known in the mechanical arts, e.g., "a clip," the claim phrase is definite despite the lack of antecedent basis in the written description. (A) is not correct because MPEP § 2163.06, paragraph (c) demonstrates that an original written description may be amended to include originally claimed subject matter. (B) is not correct because MPEP § 2173.05(e) shows that a claim phrase, which has no antecedent basis in the written description, is not necessarily indefinite because it may have a reasonable degree of clarity to those skilled in the art. (C) is not correct because MPEP § 2164.05(b) demonstrates that ordinary skill in the mechanical arts is presumed when considering the question of enablement. (E) is not correct because MPEP § 2165.03 indicates that absent evidence to the contrary, it is assumed that the best mode is present. In the present case, "a clip" is disclosed in the drawing in the original application. The fact that the screw is not recited in the original description does not detract from the disclosure of the best mode.

49. ANSWERS: (A) and (B). (A) is correct. MPEP § 2165.01, item III. There is no requirement in the statute for applicants to point out which of the disclosed embodiments they

consider to be the best mode. *Ernsthausen v. Nakayam*, 1 USPQ 2d 1539 (Bd. Pat. App. & Inter. 1985). (B) is correct. MPEP §2165.01, item II. The presence of only one specific example in the application is not evidence that the best mode has been disclosed. (C) is incorrect. *Transco Products, Inc. v. Performance Contracting Inc.*, 38 F.3d 551, 32 USPQ2d 1077 (Fed. Cir. 1994); MPEP § 2165.01, item IV. (D) is incorrect. New matter cannot cure the defect. 35 U.S.C. § 132; *In re Hay*, 534 F.2d 917, 189 USPQ 790 (CCPA 1976), MPEP § 2165.01, item V. (E) is incorrect. The statement is a correct statement of the law. 35 U.S.C. § 112, first paragraph; *In re Gay*, 309 F.2d 768, 135 USPQ 311 (CCPA 1962); MPEP § 2165.01, item II.

50. ANSWER: (D). 35 U.S.C. § 112, first paragraph; *In re Mayhew*, 527 F.2d 1229, 188 USPQ 356 (CCPA 1976); MPEP §§ 2164.08(c), and 2173.05(l). (D) describes the combination. (A) through (C), and (E) do not describe the combination of the door secured to the doorframe by two hinges. (A) through (C), and (E) do not describe the necessary structural relationship because they describe a door and door frame which are not yet secured together. In (A), "capable of being hingedly connected" describes an intended use, as opposed to a currently existing structural connection. In (B), "having...means for securing the door" describes the existence of a means for securing a door, but not a door currently secured to a frame. In (C), "hinges for securing the door" describes the existence of the hinges for securing a door, but does not require a door be secured by hinges to a frame. In (E), a "door adapted to be secured to a door frame" describes an intended use, but does not describe a door currently secured to a doorframe. Moreover, the enablement disclosure does not describe a door assembly having a door frame without a door secured to it by a pair of hinges which is capable of keeping out the elements and provides privacy.

Test Number 456
Test Series 299

Name _____

U. S. DEPARTMENT OF COMMERCE
UNITED STATES PATENT AND TRADEMARK OFFICE
REGISTRATION EXAMINATION
FOR PATENT ATTORNEYS AND AGENTS

NOVEMBER 3, 1999

Afternoon Session (50 Points)   **Time: 3 Hours**

This session of the examination is an open book examination. You may use books, notes, or other written materials that you believe will be of help to you *except* you may not use prior registration examination questions and/or answers. Books, notes or other written materials containing prior registration examination questions and/or answers *cannot* be brought into or used in the room where this examination is being administered. If you have such materials, you must give them to the test administrator before this session of the examination begins.

All questions must be answered in SECTION I of the Answer Sheet which is provided to you by the test administrator. You must use a No. 2 pencil (or softer) lead pencil to record your answers on the Answer Sheet. Darken *completely* the circle corresponding to your answer. You must keep your mark within the circle. Erase *completely* all marks except your answer. Stray marks may be counted as answers. No points will be awarded for incorrect answers or unanswered questions. Questions answered by darkening more than one circle will be considered as being incorrectly answered.

This session of the examination consists of fifty (50) multiple choice questions, each worth one (1) point. Do not assume any additional facts not presented in the questions. When answering each question, unless otherwise stated, assume that you are a registered patent practitioner. Any reference to a practitioner is a reference to a registered patent practitioner. The most correct answer is the policy, practice, and procedure which must, shall, or should be followed in accordance with the U.S. patent statutes, the PTO rules of practice and procedure, the Manual of Patent Examining Procedure (MPEP), and the Patent Cooperation Treaty (PCT) articles and rules, unless modified by a subsequent court decision or a notice in the *Official Gazette*. There is only one most correct answer for each question. Where choices (A) through (D) are correct and choice (E) is "All of the above," the last choice (E) will be the most correct answer and the only answer which will be accepted. Where two or more choices are correct, the most correct answer is the answer which refers to each and every one of the correct choices. Where a question includes a statement with one or more blanks or ends with a colon, select the answer from the choices given to complete the statement which would make the statement *true*. Unless otherwise explicitly stated, all references to patents or applications are to be understood as being U.S. patents or regular (non-provisional) utility applications for utility inventions only, as opposed to plant or design applications for plant and design inventions. Where the terms "USPTO," "PTO," or "Office" are used in this examination, they mean the U.S. Patent and Trademark Office.

You may write anywhere on the examination booklet. However, do not remove any pages from the booklet. Only answers recorded in SECTION I of your Answer Sheet will be graded. Your combined score of both the morning and afternoon sessions must be at least 70 points to pass the registration examination.

1.   Your client, Smith, invents a composition for adhering metal to glass. You prepare a patent application including a specification and several claims of varying scope. Your specification includes a detailed description of Smith's invention, which sets forth the following: the composition is made from, among other things, a combination of A, B, and C; the composition is at least 20% A but can be up to 30% A; the composition works best if it is 24% to 26% A; and the composition contains substantially equal portions of B and C. Your specification also includes guidelines for determining what would constitute substantially equal portions of B and C in the composition. Furthermore, your specification includes a detailed explanation of why it is preferable to use 24% to 26% A. Among the following claims drawn to Smith's invention, which is the broadest claim that is unlikely to be properly rejected under 35 U.S.C. 112, second paragraph?

(A)   A composition comprising 20 to 30% A, and substantially equal portions of B and C.
(B)   A composition comprising 20 to 30% A, preferably 24% to 26%A.
(C)   A composition comprising 20 to 30% A, 30% B, and 30% C.
(D)   A composition comprising 24% A, and substantially equal portions of B and C.
(E)   A composition comprising 20 to 30% A, and equal portions of B and C.

2.   On August 17, 1999, you filed a reissue application to enlarge the scope of the claims directed to an electrical device in a patent granted to your client on January 20, 1998. In the patent, as well as the patent application on which the patent was granted, the broadest disclosure (including the specification and the original claim) regarding the resistance of the device is that "the device's resistance is .02 to 1.5 ohms." The examiner issued a non-final first Office action containing a rejection of several claims in the reissue application. Your reply to the first Office action includes presentation of an amendment to the specification adding the following disclosure: "The device can have a resistance of 3.0 to 4.5 ohms." No petition and fee requesting entry of the amendment was filed. In accordance with PTO practice and procedure,

(A)   the amendment will be entered, and if the examiner objects to the amendment to the specification as being new matter, you should traverse the objection on the grounds that the patent owner is entitled to enlarge the scope of the content of the patent.
(B)   the amendment will not be entered because the amendment to the specification does not enlarge the scope of the claim.
(C)   the amendment will not be entered because a petition and necessary fee requesting entry of the amendment was not filed.
(D)   the amendment will be entered, and if the examiner objects to the amendment to the specification as being new matter, you should file another amendment canceling "The device can have a resistance of 3.0 to 4.5 ohms."
(E)   the amendment will be entered because is does not introduce new matter.

3.   Smith received a second Office action in his pending application finally rejecting pending claims 1-20 on prior art grounds. Claims 1 and 11 are presented in independent form, claims 2-10 depend from claim 1, and claims 12-20 depend from claim 11. To continue prosecution, Smith submitted an Amendment After Final Rejection narrowing the scope of independent claims 1 and 11. Smith believed the Amendment placed the application in condition for allowance and, accordingly, requested entry of the Amendment and allowance of the application. However, the Examiner denied entry on the ground that the Amendment presented new issues requiring further consideration or search. Rather than appeal the rejection, Smith filed a request for a Continuing Prosecution Application (CPA), and asked that the Amendment After Final be entered as a Preliminary Amendment. The Examiner issued a first Office action in the CPA allowing claims 1-10 and finally rejecting claims 11-20 on substantially the same grounds that these claims had been rejected in the parent application. Which of the following statements regarding the first Office action in the CPA is correct?

   (A)   The Examiner cannot properly allow claims 1-10 because a determination was made in the parent application that the Amendment After Final Rejection presented new issues requiring further consideration or search.

   (B)   The Examiner is precluded from rejecting claims 11-20 on substantially the same grounds that these claims had been rejected in the parent application because a determination was made in the parent case that the Amendment After Final Rejection presented new issues requiring further consideration or search.

   (C)   The Amendment After Final Rejection cannot be entered as a Preliminary Amendment in the CPA application.

   (D)   The finality of the rejection of claims 11-20 is improper.

   (E)   (B) and (D).

4.   After filing a proper appeal brief for an application you are prosecuting, you begin to have doubts as to how convincing your arguments would be to the Board of Patent Appeals and Interferences ("Board"). After further consideration, you agree to the examiner's suggestions. You file an amendment incorporating all of the examiner's suggestions after you filed the appeal brief and before an examiner's answer is mailed in this patent application. In accordance with PTO practice and procedure, the amendment _____

   (A)   may be entered if the amendment obviously places the application in condition for allowance and there is a showing of good and sufficient reasons why it was not earlier presented.

   (B)   will not be entered as it was not sent prior to or with the appeal brief.

   (C)   will not be entered because it was not in the form of a petition.

   (D)   will be entered and appended to the appeal brief for the Board's consideration.

   (E)   will not be entered because a petition should have accompanied it since it was filed after the appeal brief.

5.   On March 1, 1995, applicant filed a nonprovisional patent application for a stool. The original disclosure set forth that a base member of the stool was generally elliptical and, in particular, could be circular (a special kind of ellipse). It also stated that all leg members must be parallel to each other. The only claim included in the application stated as follows:

> 1.   A stool for sitting on, comprising a circular shaped base member having a top surface and a bottom surface; said bottom surface having a center portion and three circular holes equally spaced about said center portion; and three leg members connected to said bottom surface, each hole having a leg member protruding therefrom.

In a first Office action rejection, the examiner rejected claim 1 under 35 U.S.C. § 102(e) as unpatentable over a U.S. Patent to Pigeon. The Pigeon patent specified that each of the leg members formed a thirty degree angle with each of the other leg members. Applicant filed a timely response to the Office action, amending the specification to state that the leg members could be substantially parallel and including guidelines for determining what would be considered "substantially parallel." Applicant also amended claim 1 as follows:

> 1.   (once amended) A stool for sitting on, comprising a circular shaped base member having a top surface and a bottom surface; said bottom surface having a center portion and three circular holes equally spaced about said center portion; and three leg members connected to said bottom surface, each hole having a leg member protruding therefrom, wherein the leg members are parallel to each other.

The examiner allowed Claim 1 as amended and a patent was granted to applicant on January 5, 1997. On January 5, 1999, applicant filed a reissue application, including a proper declaration pursuant to 37 CFR § 1.175. Assume that there is no other relevant prior art. In accordance with PTO rules and procedure, which of the following statements concerning the reissue application is true?

(A)   Any amendment to claim 1 so as to broaden its scope will likely be considered untimely.

(B)   If applicant amends claim 1 to replace "a circular shaped member" with "an elliptical shaped member," then the amendment should be considered untimely since the amendment would broaden the scope of the claim.

(C)   If applicant amends claim 1 to delete "wherein the leg members are parallel to each other," then the amended claim should be allowed.

(D)   If applicant amends claim 1 to replace "parallel" with "substantially parallel," then the amended claim will likely be allowed.

(E)   None of the above.

6.   If each of the following claims is in a different utility patent application, and each claim is fully supported by the disclosure in preceding claims or in the application in which the claim appears, which claim properly presents a process claim?

(A)   A process of utilizing a filter comprising electrical components, placing a plurality of electrodes on the human body, receiving electrical signals from the electrodes, and passing the signals through the filter which comprises electrical components.

(B)   A process of polymerizing an organic compound by combining in a reaction vessel a catalyst and reactants dissolved in a solvent, heating the mixture in the vessel to a high temperature to start the reaction, separating an upper organic layer from the remaining materials, and evaporating the solvent.

(C)   The use of a water repellant paint as a sealant for wooden patio furniture.

(D)   (A) and (B).

(E)   (A), (B), and (C).

7.   You were drafting a patent application claiming a widget invented by your client Able. While drafting the application, you looked through a recent *Official Gazette* and noticed a patent, No. 888,888,888, directed to a widget that appears to be the same as the widget you are claiming. You obtained a copy of the patent and discovered that the patent was granted on May 4, 1999, to your client's strongest competitor, QED Incorporated. Claim 5 in the QED patent is the same widget Able invented. Claim 6 in the QED patent is an improvement to Able's widget. The QED patent was granted on a patent application filed on December 22, 1997. You have evidence that Able invented his widget before December 22, 1997. You copied, as claim 9 in Able's application, QED claim 5. Today, November 3, 1999, you are about to file, in the PTO, Able's nonprovisional patent application containing claim 9, and an information disclosure statement (IDS) listing several patents, including the OED patent, and publications. Which of the following would be the most proper course of action to take to comply with your duties to your client and the PTO?

(A)   In the IDS, state and explain why the identified patents may be relevant, and state that the burden has shifted to the examiner to find and disclose other pertinent or relevant prior art.

(B)   Identify the QED patent in bold in the list in the IDS, and include the following explanation about the QED patent: "QED discloses a relevant type of widget."

(C)   In the IDS, state, "The QED patent discloses a relevant type of widget," and provide a copy of the patent.

(D)   In the IDS, state, "Claim 9 in this application has been copied from claim 5 in the QED patent," and provide a copy of the patent.

(E)   In the IDS, state, "Claim 9 in this application has been copied from a claim in a QED patent," and argue that "Claim 6 in the QED patent is an obvious improvement to the instant invention," and provide a copy of a QED patent.

8.	Jones' patent application was filed in the PTO in January 1999, claiming an invention Jones conceived and reduced to practice in the United States. Claim 1 in the application was rejected under 35 U.S.C. § 102 as being unpatentable over a U.S. patent to Smith. Smith did not derive anything from Jones, or visa versa. Smith and Jones were never obligated to assign their inventions to the same employer. In which of the following situations should a declaration by Jones under 37 CFR § 1.131 overcome the rejection in accordance with proper PTO practice and procedure?

(A)	The rejected claim is drawn to a genus. The Smith patent issued in March 1998, on an application filed in June 1994. The patent discloses, but does not claim, a single species of the genus claimed by Jones. The declaration shows completion in April 1994, of the same species disclosed by Smith.

(B)	The rejected claim is drawn to a species. The Smith patent issued in March 1998 on an application filed in June 1994. The patent discloses, but does not claim, the species claimed by Jones. The declaration shows completion in April 1994, of a different species.

(C)	The rejected claim is drawn to a genus. The Smith patent issued in March 1998, on an application filed in June 1994. The patent discloses, but does not claim, several species within the genus claimed by Jones. The declaration shows completion in April 1994, of a species different from the reference's species and the species within the scope of the claimed genus.

(D)	The rejected claim is drawn to a genus. The Smith patent issued in March 1997, on an application filed in June 1994. The patent discloses, but does not claim, several species within the genus claimed by Jones. The declaration shows completion in April 1994, of one or more of the species disclosed in the patent.

(E)	The rejected claim is drawn to a genus. The Smith patent issued in November 1998, on an application filed in June 1994, and the patent discloses and claims several species within the genus claimed by Jones. The declaration shows completion in April 1994, of each species claimed in the Smith patent.

9.	A personal interview with an examiner to discuss the merits of the claims **may not** be properly conducted by:

(A)	the inventor, even though the attorney of record is present at the interview.

(B)	a registered practitioner who does not have power of attorney in the application, but who is known to the examiner to be the local representative of the attorney of record in the case.

(C)	an unregistered attorney who is the applicant in the application.

(D)	an unregistered attorney who has been given the associate power of attorney in the particular application.

(E)	a registered practitioner who is not an attorney of record in the application, but who brings a copy of the application file to the interview.

10.	Which of the following claim phrases may be used in accordance with proper PTO practice and procedure?

(A)	R is selected from the group consisting of A, B, C, or D.
(B)	R is selected from the group consisting of A, B, C, and D.
(C)	R is selected from the group comprising A, B, C, and D.
(D)	R is selected from the group comprising A, B, C, or D.
(E)	R is A, B, C, and D.

11.	A final rejection, with a mailing date of Thursday, February 4, 1999, was received Saturday, February 6, 1999. The examiner set a three month shortened statutory period for reply. Which of the following will be considered as being timely filed?

(A)	A reply, mailed using the U.S. Postal Service, first class mail, on Friday, August 6, 1999, and received by the PTO on Monday, August 9, 1999 accompanied by a petition and appropriate fee for a three-month extension of time, and a certificate of mailing stating, "I hereby certify that this correspondence is being deposited with the United States Postal Service with sufficient postage as first class mail in an envelope addressed to: Assistant Commissioner for Patents, Washington, D.C. 20231, on August 6, 1999." The certificate of mailing was signed by and contained the printed name of one who reasonably expected the response to be mailed in the normal course of business by another no later than August 6, 1999.

(B)	A reply, mailed using the U.S. Postal Service, on Tuesday, May 4, 1999 and received by the PTO on Thursday, May 6, 1999 accompanied by a copy of a U.S. Postal Service certificate of mailing, which states "One piece of ordinary mail addressed to: Assistant Commissioner for Patents, Washington, D.C. 20231." The certificate of mailing contained an official U.S. Postal Service date stamp of May 4, 1999, and the printed name of one who reasonably expected the response to be mailed in the normal course of business no later than May 4, 1999.

(C)	A reply, mailed using the U.S. Postal Service, first class mail, on Wednesday, August 4, 1999, and received by the PTO on Monday, August 9, 1999, accompanied by a petition and the appropriate fee for a three-month extension of time, and a certificate of mailing stating, "I hereby certify that this correspondence is being deposited with the United States Postal Service with sufficient postage as first class mail in an envelope addressed to: Assistant Commissioner for Patents, Washington, D.C. 20231, on August 6, 1999." The certificate of mailing was signed by and contained the printed name of one who reasonably expected the response to be mailed in the normal course of business by another no later than August 4, 1999.

(D)	(A) and (C).
(E)	None of the above.

12.   Which of the following statements is true concerning terms of degree (relative terms, e.g., such as, "hotter") used in claim language?

(A)   Definiteness of claim language using terms of degree should not be analyzed using a claim interpretation that would be given by one possessing the ordinary level of skill in the art, and only the specification should be used to interpret the claim.

(B)   A claim may be rendered indefinite even if the specification uses the same term of degree as the claim language, if the term of degree is not understandable by one of ordinary skill in the art when the term of degree is read in light of the specification.

(C)   If the specification includes guidelines which would enable one of ordinary skill in the art to determine the scope of a claim having a term of degree, then the language of the guidelines must be included in the claim in order to render the claim definite.

(D)   If the original disclosure does not include guidelines which would enable one of ordinary skill in the art to determine the scope of a claim having a term of degree, then as long as the term of degree in the claim was part of the original disclosure, the claim will be properly rendered definite by amending the specification to provide guidelines concerning the term of degree which would enable one of ordinary skill in the art to determine the scope of the claim.

(E)   None of the above.

13.   You are a registered patent agent prosecuting a patent application filed on behalf of Harry. You received an Office action having a mailing date of August 13, 1999, in which the examiner set a three month shortened statutory period for reply and rejected all of the claims in the application under 35 U.S.C § 112 for failing to particularly point out and distinctly claim the invention. After receiving the Office action, you discovered a recently issued U.S. patent that you believe discloses and claims your client's invention. On September 28, 1999, you filed an amendment copying some of the claims from the patent for the purpose of provoking an interference and notify the examiner that you have copied specific claims from the patent. In a second Office action dated October 13, 1999, the examiner rejected the copied claims under 35 U.S.C. § 112 as being based on a non-enabling disclosure and set a three month shortened statutory period for reply. If no requests for an extension of time are filed, the last day(s) for filing replies to the first and second Office actions, is(are):

(A)   Monday, November 15, 1999.
(B)   Monday, November 15, 1999, and Thursday, January 13, 2000, respectively.
(C)   Monday, November 29, 1999, and Wednesday, January 12, 2000 respectively.
(D)   Tuesday, December 28, 1999.
(E)   Thursday, January 13, 2000.

14. Claim 1 in a patent application states the following:

1. A modular telephone plug crimping tool comprising:
   (i) a pair of body parts comprising first and second body parts, each having a fixed length;
   (ii) a flexible member connecting an end of the first body part to an end of the second body part;
   (iii) a hand lever;
   (iv) a pivot pin connecting the hand lever to the first body part;
   (v) an interchangeable crimping punch removably seated in the first body part and guided relative to an interchangeable crimping anvil removably seated in the second body part;
   (vi) a roller mounted on the pivot pin for engaging the crimping punch; and
   (vii) a guide pin being fixed in said second body part and extending in aligned bores in said pair of body parts.

Which, if any, of the following claims, if presented in the application, is a proper dependent claim in accordance with PTO rules and procedure.

   (A) 2. The modular telephone according to claim 1, wherein said crimping punch comprises integral contact and strain relief punch portions.
   (B) 2. The modular telephone plug crimping tool according to claim 1, wherein said second body part has an adjustable length.
   (C) 2. A process for using the modular telephone plug crimping tool of claim 1 to connect a telephone to a telephone line.
   (D) 2. The modular telephone plug crimping tool according to claim 1, further comprising: a free end on each of said first and second body parts; first and second stripping blades adjustably and detachably provided at said free ends of said first and second body parts, respectively; and at least one severing blade held in cooperating relationship with a severing anvil, said severing blade and severing anvil being provided on said first and second body parts, respectively.
   (E) None of the above.

15. You are prosecuting an application for inventor Smith that receives a rejection under 35 U.S.C. § 102(b) based on a U.S. patent to Jones that discloses and claims the same invention. Which of the following, if any, will overcome the rejection?

   (A) An affidavit or declaration showing that Jones is not the true inventor.
   (B) An affidavit or declaration showing commercial success of the Smith invention.
   (C) An affidavit or declaration containing an argument that the invention claimed in the Smith application provides synergistic results.
   (D) An affidavit or declaration swearing back of the Jones patent.
   (E) None of the above.

Questions 16 and 17 are based on the following facts. Answer each question independently of the other.

A patent application contains a single independent claim:

1. A process for manufacturing water soluble crayons which comprises (i) preparing one or more water soluble alkoxylation products by contacting an organic compound selected from the group consisting of alcohols and carboxylic acids, with an alkylene oxide in the presence of an effective amount of a catalyst under alkoxylation conditions; (ii) preparing a water soluble crayon composition by adding a coloring agent to the one or more water soluble alkoxylation products; (iii) pouring said water soluble crayon composition into a mold; and (iv) solidifying said water soluble crayon composition by cooling.

The coloring agents disclosed in the specification include pigments selected from the group consisting of titanium dioxide, red iron oxide and carbon black. These pigments are used in an amount of about 1 to 30 weight percent or greater, preferably about 4 to about 25 weight percent, of the total weight of the crayon composition. As disclosed in the specification, preferred organic compounds useful in the process of this invention also include alcohols, carboxylic acids, and amines. The specification also discloses that the water soluble crayon compositions harden readily upon cooling, i.e. when exposed to a temperature of from about 10°C. to 15°C.

16.   Which of the following choices would be a proper dependent claim which could be added to the application by amendment and be supported by the specification?

(A)   2. A process according to Claim 1 wherein said water soluble crayon composition is exposed to a temperature of at least 10°C.

(B)   2. A process as set forth in Claim 1 wherein said coloring agent is titanium dioxide.

(C)   2. A process for manufacturing water soluble crayons as set forth in Claim 1 wherein said coloring agent is 1 to 30 weight percent of the total weight of the crayon composition.

(D)   2. A process as set forth in Claim 1 wherein said organic compound further comprises amines.

(E)   (B) and (C).

17.   Which of the following amendments to Claim 1 are in accordance with PTO policy and procedure and are supported by specification?

(A)   In Claim 1, line 3, before "alcohols" delete "monohydric".
(B)   In Claim 1, line 4, after "alcohols" insert "amines".
(C)   In Claim 1, line 6, delete "a coloring agent" and insert "titanium dioxide".
(D)   In Claim 1, line 7, after "cooling" insert "to a temperature of 13°C."
(E)   (B) and (C).

18.   Bill wishes to amend the sole, original Claim 1 of the patent granted to him and obtain the following amended Claim 1. The amended Claim 1 set forth below is fully supported by the original disclosure in the application:

1.   A computer processor comprising:
    a.   a plurality of registers divided into a global port subset and a local pool subset;
    b.   means for distinguishing a successful [unconditional] interruptable jump operation;
    c.   means for receiving interrupts or exceptions; and
    d.   an interrupt or exception handler for handling the interrupts or exceptions in   response to distinguishing the [unconditional] interruptable jump operation [from the local pool subset].

In the absence of questions of recapture, novelty, obviousness, and utility, which of the following statements, if any, is true?

(A)   A claim so amended is properly presented during a reexamination proceeding where a request for reexamination was filed on September 9, 1999, and a certificate of reexamination may be issued where reexamination is sought of a patent granted on July 15, 1997.
(B)   A claim so amended is properly presented in a reissue application filed on September 9, 1999, and a reissue patent is grantable where reissuance is sought of a patent granted on July 15, 1997.
(C)   A claim so amended is properly presented in a reissue application filed on September 9, 1999, and a reissue patent is grantable where reissuance is sought of a patent granted on November 18, 1997.
(D)   A claim so amended is properly presented in a request for reexamination filed on September 9, 1999, and a certificate of reexamination may be issuedwhere reexamination is sought of a patent granted on November 18, 1997.
(E)   A claim so amended is properly presented in a reissue application filed any time before expiration of the term of the patent inasmuch as the scope of Claim 1 in the original patent is narrowed by replacing the word "unconditional" with the word "interruptable."

19.   Which of the following requirements of 35 U.S.C. § 112 does not apply to design patent claims?

    (A)   The written description requirement of the first paragraph.
    (B)   The best mode requirement of the first paragraph.
    (C)   The requirement in the second paragraph to distinctly claim the subject matter which the applicant regards as his invention.
    (D)   The requirement in the third paragraph for an independent claim.
    (E)   None of the above.

20.   Inventors Moe and Jeff originally gave attorney Curly a power of attorney to prosecute their application before the PTO. At this time, inventor Jeff has decided that he no longer wants attorney Curly to represent him. Instead, inventor Jeff wants you to represent him. Thus, Jeff wants the power of attorney to Curly revoked. Moe does not agree and wants Curly to continue. How, if at all, should the revocation and appointment of a new power of attorney be properly handled?

    (A)   Papers revoking Curly's power of attorney with regard to Jeff, and giving you a new power of attorney need to be signed by Jeff and must include a statement from Moe indicating that Moe wishes to retain Curly.
    (B)   Papers revoking Curly's power of attorney with regard to Jeff, and giving you a new power of attorney cannot be accepted without concurrence by Curly.
    (C)   Papers revoking Curly's power of attorney with regard to Jeff, and giving you a new power of attorney signed only by you should be accompanied by a petition giving good and sufficient reasons as to why such papers should be accepted upon being filed together with an appropriate fee.
    (D)   Papers revoking Curly's power of attorney with regard to Jeff, and giving you a new power of attorney signed only by Jeff should be accompanied by a petition giving good and sufficient reasons for acceptance should be filed together with an appropriate fee.
    (E)   Papers revoking Curly's power of attorney with regard to Jeff, and giving you a new power of attorney cannot be accepted without concurrence of Moe and Curly.

21.   Which of the following files is ordinarily **not open** to the public?

    (A)   A substitute application.
    (B)   An interference proceeding file involving a U.S. patent.
    (C)   A reissue application.
    (D)   A reexamination proceeding file.
    (E)   All of the above.

22. You are preparing a patent application for filing in the PTO. The application describes a microcomputer having several components. You have drafted the following independent claim:

1. A micro-computer comprising:
   (i) a central processing unit for processing information;
   (ii) a memory unit for storing information;
   (iii) an input device for entering information characterized by a keyboard;
   (iv) an output device for viewing information consisting of a video monitor; and
   (v) a bus for interconnecting the central processing unit to the memory unit, the input device and the output device.

In the absence of issues of supporting disclosure, and following proper PTO practices and procedures, which of the following dependent claim(s) is (are) an improper dependent claim?

Claim 2. The micro-computer of Claim 1, wherein the memory unit contains random access memory.

Claim 3. The micro-computer of Claim 1 or 2, wherein the input device includes a light pen.

Claim 4. The micro-computer in any one of the preceding claims, wherein the output device is a printer or a video monitor.

Claim 5. The micro-computer of Claim 4, wherein the memory unit contains read-only memory.

(A) Claim 2.
(B) Claim 2 and Claim 3.
(C) Claim 3.
(D) Claim 5.
(E) Claim 4 and Claim 5.

23. To avoid a proper rejection of a claim for being indefinite, which of the following expressions in the claims must be supported by a specification disclosing a standard for ascertaining what the inventor means to cover?

(A) "relatively shallow."
(B) "of the order of."
(C) "similar" in the following claim preamble: "A nozzle for high-pressure cleaning units or similar apparatus."
(D) "essentially" in the following phrase following the claim preamble: "a silicon dioxide source that is essentially free of alkali metal."
(E) All of the above.

24. Claims 1 through 5 in a patent application read as follows:

1. A computer comprising:
   (i) a microprocessor having a maximum clock rate of 350 megahertz;
   (ii) a random access memory chip coupled to said microprocessor;
   (iii) a read only memory chip coupled to said microprocessor; and
   (iv) a case enclosing said microprocessor, said random access memory chip, and said read only memory chip.
2. The computer of claim 1, wherein said case has an outer surface comprised of plastic.
3. The computer of claims 1 or 2, further comprising a peripheral controller chip coupled to said microprocessor.
4. The computer of claim 1, wherein said memory chip has eight million storage locations.
5. The computer of claim 2, wherein said microprocessor has a maximum clock rate of 400 megahertz.

Which of the following is/are proper dependent claims(s) in accordance with 37 CFR §1.75?

(A) Claims 2 and 3.
(B) Claim 4 only.
(C) Claims 2 and 5.
(D) Claim 2 only.
(E) None of the above.

25. Gonnagetrich Corporation asked you to represent, before the PTO, some of its employees who have invented an apparatus. On Tuesday, August 17, 1999, you deposited a nonprovisional patent application containing a specification with ten claims drawn to the apparatus via hand delivery to the PTO. At that time, you neither supplied the names of any of the actual inventors with the application, nor did you file with the application drawings necessary to understand the invention. The specification refers to the drawings. You sent the drawings by first class mail to the PTO on Wednesday, September 13, 1999, and the PTO received them on Wednesday, September 15, 1999. On Wednesday, September 29, 1999, using the "Express Mail Post Office to Addressee" service of the U.S. Postal Service, and so certifying in compliance with 37 CFR § 1.10, you deposited with the U.S. Postal Service a declaration pursuant to 37 CFR § 1.63 signed by all the actual inventors. On Friday, October 1, 1999, the PTO received the signed declaration. What will be the earliest filing date given to the application by the PTO?

(A) August 17, 1999.
(B) September 13, 1999.
(C) September 15, 1999.
(D) September 29, 1999.
(E) October 1, 1999.

26. X invented a laminate which is most broadly disclosed in a patent application as containing a transparent protective layer and a light-sensitive layer, without an intermediate layer. The prior art included a laminate containing a transparent protective layer and a light-sensitive layer held together by an intermediate adhesive layer. Which of the following claims would overcome a 35 USC § 102 rejection based on the prior art?

- (A) 1. A laminate comprising a transparent protective layer and a light-sensitive layer.
- (B) 1. A laminate comprising a transparent protective layer and a light-sensitive layer which is in continuous and direct contact with the transparent protective layer.
- (C) 1. A laminate comprising a transparent protective layer and a light-sensitive layer, but not including an adhesive layer.
- (D) (A) and (B).
- (E) (B) and (C).

27. On April 21, 1998, a patent was issued to Belinda on a novel switching circuit. Shortly after receiving the patent grant, Belinda assigned 50% of her right, title and interest in her patent to Ace and 25% of the right, title and interest to Duce. After the assignments were recorded in the PTO, Belinda discovered that her claim coverage is too narrow because her patent attorney did not appreciate the full scope of her invention. Today, November 3, 1999, Belinda consults you about filing a reissue application. The reissue oath must be signed and sworn to by:

- (A) Belinda, Ace and Duce.
- (B) Belinda only.
- (C) Belinda and either Ace or Duce.
- (D) Ace and Duce only.
- (E) the attorney or agent of record.

28. A patent specification can be altered by interlineation before it is filed in the PTO. Such alterations are permitted if each interlineation is initialed and dated by the:

- (A) registered practitioner who prepared the specification, even if the applicant is available to sign the oath or declaration.
- (B) applicant, before the oath or declaration is signed by the registered practitioner.
- (C) applicant, at any time after the oath or declaration is signed.
- (D) applicant, before the oath or declaration is signed by the applicant.
- (E) registered practitioner who prepared the specification before the oath or declaration is signed by the applicant.

29.   On January 2, 1999, Billie files a U.S. patent application that discloses forming a naturally occurring composition X by a chemical reaction of compounds A, B and C under specified ranges of temperature and pressure. The application includes a statement "The most common meaning of the term 'fluid' includes both gases and liquids. However, it has been determined that the present invention properly operates when B is in a gaseous, fluid, or solid state, so long as temperature of the solid B is above 2°C. Below that temperature, it is believed the chemical reaction will not occur. Thus, in the context of the present invention, the term 'fluid' means 'gaseous', 'liquid', and/or certain solid states." However, research conducted in 1998 by Greene in England shows that the desired chemical reaction would occur with solid compound B at a temperature of 1°C. Greene also showed the reaction with compound B in a liquid and gaseous states. Greene submitted his research results to a British technical journal in November 1998, and they were published on January 5, 1999. Originally filed Claim 1 of Billie's application is directed to "[a] method for forming composition X comprising mixing compound A with fluid compound B at a temperature between 0°C and 10°C". Examiner Redd locates the published Greene research results that disclose the identical method set forth in Billie's Claim 1. Which rejection of Claim 1 is in accordance with proper PTO practices and procedures?

(A)   Claim 1 is rejected under 35 U.S.C. § 112, paragraph 2 as being indefinite because the meaning of the term "fluid" is unclear. Billie is encouraged to clarify the claim by deleting "fluid" and inserting --liquid-- in its place.

(B)   Claim 1 is rejected under 35 U.S.C. § 102(a) as being anticipated by Greene because, although the research results were published after Billie's filing date, the research results were submitted to the British technical journal before the filing date and were therefore known in the art.

(C)   Claim 1 is rejected under 35 U.S.C. § 112, paragraph 1 as being based on an insufficient specification because the claim does not specify a pressure at which A and B are mixed and, depending on that pressure, compound B could be either a gas or a liquid at the recited temperature range.

(D)   Claim 1 is rejected under 35 U.S.C. § 101 as being directed to non-statutory subject matter because composition X occurs naturally.

(E)   Claim 1 is rejected under 35 U.S.C. § 112, paragraph 2 as being based on an incorrect theory of operation because the theory of operation disclosed in the specification is inconsistent with the claim.

30.   Which of the following may not properly apply for a patent on an invention?

(A)   A child.
(B)   A convicted felon.
(C)   A British subject.
(D)   A current employee of the PTO.
(E)   A scientist who has assigned to his employer all rights to the invention.

31.   An international application under the Patent Cooperation Treaty (PCT), which designated the United States, was filed on November 1, 1996. The application claimed priority of a prior French national application filed on December 6, 1995. A copy of the international application was communicated to the United States as a designated office on June 20, 1997. A demand for international preliminary examination, in which the United States was elected, was filed on June 5, 1997. Accordingly, the thirty month period of PCT Article 39(1)(a) expired at midnight on June 6, 1998. The applicant submitted the basic national fee to enter the United States national stage on June 2, 1998. On August 3, 1998, the applicant timely submitted a translation of the international application and a declaration of the inventors in compliance with PCT regulations in reply to a Notice of Missing Requirements. Also, on August 10, 1998, the applicant timely submitted a translation of amendments under Article 19 of the PCT in reply to the Notice of Missing Requirements. On August 29, 1998, a Notice of Acceptance was mailed to the applicant. The national stage application issued as a U.S. patent on October 13, 1999. What is the effective date of the U.S. patent as a reference under 35 U.S.C. § 102(e)?

(A)   November 1, 1996.
(B)   June 2, 1998.
(C)   August 3, 1998.
(D)   August 10, 1998.
(E)   October 13, 1999.

32.   A client comes to you and tells you that he has been informed by his competitor that he is infringing the competitor's patent. Your client tells you that the competitor's invention was well known in the field at the time the application for the patent was filed. Your client shows you several published articles, two United States patents, and two written statements by experts in the field which clearly support his conclusion. Upon further investigation, you find that the published articles and patents were not considered by the examiner during the prosecution of the patent application. Your client informs you that he would like to avoid litigation, and have the PTO take action to invalidate the patent. Which of the following choices would be an appropriate course of action to take on behalf of your client?

(A)   Petition the Commissioner of Patents and Trademarks to revoke the patent.
(B)   File a request and fee for reexamination of the claims in the patent relying on the published articles and the U.S. patents as the basis for reexamination, and include all statements, information, and documents required by PTO rules for initiating reexamination proceedings.
(C)   File a protest in the PTO with copies of the published articles, patents and the written statements from the experts, along with an explanation of their pertinence to the claims of the patent.
(D)   File in the PTO copies of all of the documents provided to you by your client and request that they be made of record in the patented file.
(E)   (B) and (C).

33.   Ann invented an electrical signal filter for obtaining increased signal-to-noise ratios in certain electrical systems. Ann filed a first non-provisional patent application on May 1, 1997, fully disclosing and claiming one embodiment of her invention, a capacitor. The sole claim stated: "a capacitor for filtering electrical signals, comprising: a first terminal connected to a first plate; a second terminal connected to a second plate; and an electrical insulator between said first plate and said second plate." The first application also disclosed that even better results could be obtained if the capacitor were coupled to a resistor. Ann wanted to file a second application in the future specifically claiming the combination of the capacitor and resistor. On February 1, 1999, while Ann's first application was still pending, Ann filed a continuation application under 37 CFR § 1.53(b). The continuation application contains the following single claim: "a capacitor for filtering electrical signals, comprising: a first terminal connected to a first plate; a second terminal connected to a second plate; an electrical insulator between said first plate and said second plate; and a resistor, connected to said first terminal." Ann received a non-final Office action wherein the claim in the continuation application was provisionally rejected under the judicially created doctrine of double patenting over the claim drawn to a capacitor in Ann's copending first application. The rejection correctly stated that the subject matter claimed in Ann's continuation application was fully disclosed in her copending first application and would be covered by a patent granted containing the claim in the first application. Neither application was ever assigned to anyone. The rejection may be properly overcome by a timely reply:

(A)   traversing the rejection and arguing that since the first application had not yet matured into a patent, a double patenting rejection was unfounded.

(B)   arguing that rejections of this type are no longer warranted for continuation applications, since any utility application filed on or after June 8, 1995, will expire 20 years from its filing date, and therefore Ann's continuation application, which gets the benefit of the filing date of the first application, would expire at the same time as the first application, anyway.

(C)   arguing that the claim in the continuation application is patentably distinct and unobvious from the claim in the first application.

(D)   including a terminal disclaimer, signed by Ann, disclaiming any portion of the term of any patent granted on the continuation application beyond twenty years from May 1, 1997, and including a provision in the terminal disclaimer that any patent granted on the continuation application shall be enforceable only for and during such period that said patent is commonly owned with the first application.

(E)   including the filing of a terminal disclaimer, signed by Ann, disclaiming any portion of the term of any patent granted on the continuation application beyond twenty years from May 1, 1997.

34.   Your client, Vada, disclosed the following information to you. While vacationing on a desert island, she discovered a salt lake where the water was a solution saturated with NaCl. Vada experimented with the solution and determined that it could be used to cure skin rashes if applied directly to the skin. By further experimentation, Vada determined that the best results could be obtained if the solution were first heated to an ideal temperature (T_i) equal to skin temperature (T_s) plus the square of the difference between room temperature (T_r) and skin temperature (T_s). Vada documented her findings in the form of the following equation: $T_i = T_s + (T_r - T_s)^2$. Vada further experimented and found that she could obtain the exact same solution that she discovered while vacationing, by mixing NaCl with water followed by heating the mixture to 212°F and cooling it to 80°F. You draft a patent application with a specification including all the information disclosed to you by Vada. Which, if any, of the following claims, included in the application, would provide the proper basis for a rejection pursuant to 35 U.S.C. § 101?

(A)   A composition comprising: water saturated with NaCl.
(B)   A composition for restoring youth.
(C)   A composition and method for treating skin rashes, comprising: a solution of water saturated with NaCl; heating said solution to a temperature defined by skin temperature plus the square of the difference between room temperature and skin temperature; and applying said solution to skin rashes.
(D)   An expression comprising: $T_i = T_s + (T_r - T_s)^2$.
(E)   All of the above.

35.   Which, if any, of the following statements is true according to PTO rules and procedure?

(A)   If a claim is cancelled by an amendment and a new claim is added in the amendment, then the new claim should be numbered using the number previously assigned to the canceled claim.
(B)   A claim which recites the best mode of carrying out the invention can only properly incorporate by reference the limitations having the essential material into the claim, for purposes of satisfying the requirements of 35 U.S.C. § 112, second paragraph, if the reference is made to a U.S. patent or U.S. patent application.
(C)   For fee calculation purposes, a multiple dependent claim which refers directly to independent claims and dependent claims will always be considered to be the number of independent claims to which direct reference is made therein.
(D)   The subject matter disclosed in a first claim which is part of the original disclosure in a nonprovisional patent application may be relied upon for purposes of enabling a second claim in the application in order to satisfy the requirements of 35 U.S.C. § 112, first paragraph, even if the detailed description and drawings, taken alone, are inadequate to satisfy the requirements of 35 U.S.C. § 112, first paragraph, with respect to the second claim.
(E)   None of the above.

36.   A patent application includes a specification describing a mechanical fastener that attaches a rubber heel to the bottom of a shoe. The particular structure of the fastener allows the heel to maintain a secure attachment to the shoe while providing a cushioning effect when the shoe is worn. The specification includes a drawing clearly illustrating the fastener. The written portion of the specification accurately explains the structure of the fastener, the manner in which the fastener attaches the heel to the shoe, and how the cushioning effect is obtained. Additionally, the last paragraph of the specification states "It should be understood that the present invention is not limited to the preferred embodiment described above, and that changes may be made without departing from the spirit or scope of the invention. For example, an adhesive may be used in conjunction with the mechanical fastener to more securely attach the heel to the shoe." No specific formulation of adhesive is given in the specification, but such adhesives are well known in the art. Claim 1 of the application reads:

1.   A system for securely attaching a rubber heel to the bottom of a shoe and providing a cushioning effect when worn, said system comprising cushioning means for mechanically fastening said heel to said shoe.

Which of the following statements is correct?

(A)   Claim 1 is a "means plus function" claim subject to the provisions of 35 U.S.C. § 112, paragraph 6 and is therefore construed to cover the corresponding structure disclosed in the specification for performing the recited function and equivalent structures. Thus, claim 1 is properly construed to cover only the specific mechanical structure of the fastener described in the specification and equivalents of that mechanical structure.

(B)   Claim 1 is a "means plus function" claim subject to the provisions of 35 U.S.C. § 112, paragraph 6 and is therefore construed to cover the corresponding structure disclosed in the specification for performing the recited function and equivalent structures. Thus, claim 1 is properly construed to cover both (a) the specific mechanical structure of the fastener described in the specification and equivalents of that mechanical structure; and (b) the specific mechanical structure of the fastener described in the specification together with an adhesive and equivalents of that mechanical structure together with an adhesive.

(C)   Claim 1 is indefinite because it covers every conceivable means for achieving the stated result.

(D)   Claim 1 is not supported by an enabling specification because the claim covers every conceivable means for achieving the stated result.

(E)   Because claim 1 is drafted in means plus function language, proper claim interpretation under 35 U.S.C. § 112, paragraph 6 requires that there be a specific description in the specification of an acceptable adhesive formulation.

37.   Fred files a patent application disclosing and claiming an electrical circuit. The disclosed circuit has, in series, (i) a DC current source capable of producing a variable current of 10-30 amperes, preferably 18-22 amperes; (ii) a resistor having a value in the range of 10-20 ohms, preferably 14-16 ohms; and (iii) a fixed capacitor in the range of 3-8 microfarads (mf), preferably 5-6 mf. The application includes the following four original claims:

Claim 1.   An electrical circuit comprising, in series, a DC current source, a resistor and a capacitor, wherein said DC current source is capable of producing current of 18-22 amperes, said resistor has a value in the range 10-20 ohms, and said capacitor has a value in the range of 5-6 mf.

Claim 2.   The electrical circuit of claim 1, wherein said resistor has a value in the range of 14-16 ohms.

Claim 3.   The electrical circuit of claim 1, wherein said capacitor has a value in the range of 3-8 mf.

Claim 4.   The electrical circuit of claim 1, wherein the DC current source produces variable current in the range of 18-22 amperes.

Barry's Canadian patent, published thirteen months before the effective filing date of Fred's application, discloses an electrical circuit having, in series, a DC current source which produces 20 ampere current, a 12 ohm resistor, and a 6 mf capacitor. Which of the following statements regarding the claims is correct?

(A)   Each of Claims 1- 4 is patentable over Barry's Canadian patent.
(B)   Claim 1 is unsupported by a sufficient written description because the specification does not set forth the claimed combination of component values in a single disclosed embodiment.
(C)   Claim 2 is an improper dependent claim.
(D)   Claim 3 is an improper dependent claim.
(E)   Claim 4 is an improper dependent claim.

38.   Assuming that each of the following claims is in a different utility patent application, and each claim is fully supported by the disclosure in the preceding claims or in the application in which it appears, which of the claims properly presents a process claim?

(A)   A process for using monoclinal antibodies to isolate and purify interferon.
(B)   A process of using paint to cover a surface comprising applying paint to a surface and removing any excess paint.
(C)   A use of a metallic fibrous compound having a proportion of metallic granules as a motor compression part subject to stress by sliding friction.
(D)   The use of a sustained release therapeutic agent in a human body wherein said sustained release therapeutic agent comprises a painkiller absorbed on a polymeric surface.
(E)   All of the above.

39. You prepared a patent application on behalf of inventors Jo and Tommie. Jo invented a new and unobvious technique for inexpensively manufacturing a known chemical compound. Tommie invented a new and unobvious technique that uses the chemical to clean-up toxic waste spills. Both inventions have been assigned to Ace Chemical Company. The patent application fully discloses and claims both inventions. Both inventors approve the application, but Tommie is unavailable to sign an inventors' oath before an upcoming statutory bar date. In accordance with instructions, you to immediately file the application under 37 CFR §1.53(b) without an executed oath, but with an information sheet to identify the application. Tommie was inadvertently left off the list of inventors on the information sheet, which listed Jo as a sole inventor. After receiving a Notice to File Missing Parts, you submit an oath executed by both Jo and Tommie. No paper was filed to change the named inventive entity. You later receive an Office action restricting the application between Jo's invention, and Tommie's invention. In response, you elect Jo's invention, cancel the claims directed to Tommie's non-elected invention, and immediately file a divisional application directed to Tommie's invention together with an inventor's oath executed by Tommie only. The divisional application includes a specific reference to the original application. Which of the following statements is correct?

(A)   Because the original application as filed named only Jo as an inventor, Tommie's divisional application is not entitled to the filing date of the original application because there is no common inventor between the original application and the divisional application.

(B)   The incorrect inventorship listed on the information sheet of the original application was never properly corrected and, therefore, any patent issuing on that application will be invalid under 35 U.S.C. § 116 unless the inventorship is later corrected.

(C)   After canceling the claims to Tommie's non-elected invention, it is necessary to change the named inventive entity in the original application by filing a petition including a statement identifying Tommie as being deleted and acknowledging that Tommie's invention is no longer being claimed in the application, and an appropriate fee.

(D)   Written consent of Ace Chemical Company is required before any change of inventorship can be made.

(E)   It is necessary in the divisional application to file a petition including a statement identifying Jo as being deleted as an inventor and acknowledging that Jo's invention is not being claimed in the divisional application, and the appropriate fee.

40. Which of the following factors would **not** be indicative of an experimental purpose for testing a utility invention?

(A) Testing is conducted over a substantial period of time to determine the operativeness of the invention.

(B) Testing is conducted under the supervision and control of the inventor.

(C) Testing to determine product acceptance or market testing.

(D) The nature of the invention was such that any testing had to be, to some extent, public.

(E) The inventor regularly inspected the invention during the period of experimentation.

41. Your client has invented a miniature vacuum tube comprising a capacitor having a capacitance of 0.003 to 0.012 µf, preferably 0.006 µf. You draft a patent application directed to your client's invention and satisfying the requirements of 35 U.S.C. § 112. You draft the following independent claim:

1. A miniature vacuum tube comprising a capacitor having a capacitance of 0.003 to 0.012 µf.

Which of the following would not be a proper dependent claim if presented as an original claim in the application when the application is filed in the PTO?

(A) 2. The miniature vacuum tube of Claim 1 wherein the capacitor has a capacitance of 0.006 µf.

(B) 2. A miniature vacuum tube as in Claim 1 wherein the capacitor has a capacitance of 0.006 to 0.012 µf.

(C) 2. A miniature vacuum tube as in Claim 1 wherein the capacitor has a capacitance of about 0.003 to 0.011 µf.

(D) 2. The miniature vacuum tube of Claim 1 wherein the capacitor has a capacitance of between 0.005 and 0.012 µf.

(E) (C) and (D).

42. A multiple dependent claim may not properly depend upon _____.

(A) an independent claim.

(B) another dependent claim.

(C) any other multiple dependent claim.

(D) a claim containing Markush language.

(E) a claim which is in Jepson-type format.

43. In which of the following situations, considered independently of each other, does the event described below not constitute a statutory bar to the granting of a patent on an application filed August 30, 1999, claiming a bottle cap?

(A) The inventor reduced the invention to practice in June, 1998, and sold the claimed bottle caps to a bottling company on July 30, 1998. The sale was conditioned on the bottling company's satisfaction. The inventor and the company are located in New York.

(B) The inventor reduced the invention to practice in June, 1998, sold the claimed bottle caps to bottling companies beginning on July 30, 1998. Although the inventor sold the bottlecaps to commercially exploit his invention, the inventor's manufacturing and overhead costs exceeded his income from the sales and the inventor did not profit from the sales. The inventor and the companies are located in New York.

(C) The inventor reduced the invention to practice in June, 1998, and on July 30, 1998, assigned to Company X his patent rights to the claimed bottle cap invention for good and valuable consideration. The inventor and Company X are located in New York.

(D) The inventor reduced the invention to practice in June, 1998, and on July 30, 1998, the inventor offered to sell his inventory of the claimed bottle cap to a bottling company. The sale was not consummated until September 3, 1999. The inventor and the company are located in New York.

(E) The inventor reduced the invention to practice in June, 1998, and the inventor's offer, on July 30, 1998, to sell the claimed bottle caps to a bottling company was delayed in the mail and not received by the company until September 10, 1998. The inventor and the company are located in New York.

44. G is the sole inventor in a patent application filed in the PTO describing and claiming a surgical instrument. H is the sole inventor in a patent application filed in the PTO describing G's surgical instrument, as well as describing and claiming a modified embodiment of G's surgical instrument. Following proper PTO practices and procedures, under which circumstance is it most likely that you will need to overcome a provisional 35 U.S.C. § 102(e)/103 rejection in G's application?

(A) G's application is filed in the PTO before H's application, and they do not have a common assignee.

(B) H's application is filed in the PTO before G's application, and they do not have a common assignee.

(C) G's application is filed in the PTO on the same date as H's application, and they have a common assignee.

(D) G's application is filed in the PTO after H's application, and they have a common assignee.

(E) G's application is filed in the PTO before H's application, and they have a common assignee.

45.   You have been asked to draft a patent application based on Figures 1 and 2 provided below. The inventor has provided you with a written disclosure which states that the invention is directed to a toy building element which may be mounted as a dump body on a toy vehicle. According to the inventor's description, the toy building element comprises an open container part and a bottom, said container part and bottom being hingedly interconnected, said bottom being moreover provided with coupling means for coupling with other toy elements. Referring to Figure 1, the inventor's description states that the toy building element (1), which is just called a dump body, consists of two parts which are interconnected via a hinge (2) viz a container part (3) and a bottom (4). The written description further provides that the container part (3) is formed by an upwardly open, box-like unit having a substantially square bottom and four side walls, one of which is considerably lower than the others. In the embodiment shown, the bottom of the container is provided with coupling studs (5) on which toy building elements may be coupled. As described by the inventor, the bottom (4), which is square in its base face, has a plane surface on which the container part (3) rests along its entire circumference when it is tilted down. The surface of the bottom (4) may be provided with well-known means for detachably retaining (not shown) the container part (3) so that "it just takes a small force to tilt the container part." Referring to Figure 2, the inventor's description states "Figure 2 shows the dump body (1) mounted to tilt rearwardly on a toy truck (6), which comprises a bottom (7), wheels (8), and a driver's cab (9)." It is further provided that "on the chassis at the rear end of the truck (6), the truck bottom (7) is equipped with a square, plane face provided with well-known coupling means (not shown) which meet with the well-known coupling means (not shown) positioned on the underside of the bottom (4) of the dump body (1).

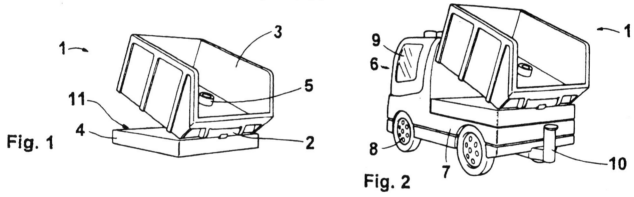

Fig. 1   Fig. 2

Based on the drawings and description provided above, which of the following claims, if any, are in accordance with proper PTO practice and procedure?

(A)   A toy building element for use as a dump body (1) for a toy vehicle, said toy building element comprising an open container part (3) and a bottom (4).

(B)   A toy building element for use as a dump body (1) for a toy vehicle, said toy building element comprising an open container part (3) and a bottom (4), said container part (3) and bottom (4) being hingedly interconnected by a hinge (2).

(C)   A toy building element comprising an open container part and a bottom, said open container part and bottom being hingedly interconnected, said bottom being provided with coupling means for coupling with other toy building elements.

(D)   (A), and (B).

(E)   (A), (B), and (C).

46. On June 22, 1999, you receive a final Office action, dated June 17, 1999, rejecting numerous claims in a patent application that you filed in the PTO. The Office action did not set a shortened statutory period for reply. Following proper PTO practices and procedures, under which circumstances is it most likely your submission of new evidence under 37 CFR § 1.129(a) in support of patentability, along with the appropriate fee, will result in the automatic withdrawal of the finality of the final rejection?

(A) The application is filed on June 8, 1995, it has an effective filing date of June 8, 1993, and you file the submission on October 14, 1999, one month after you file a Notice of Appeal to the Board of Patent Appeals and Interferences.

(B) The application is filed on June 7, 1995, it has an effective filing date of June 8, 1993, and you file the submission on October 14, 1999, one month after you file an appeal brief to the Board of Patent Appeals and Interferences.

(C) The application is filed on June 8, 1995, it has an effective filing date of June 7, 1993, and you file the submission on December 20, 1999.

(D) The application is filed on June 7, 1995, it has an effective filing date of June 7, 1993, and you file the submission on the same day you file an appeal brief to the Board of Patent Appeals and Interferences.

(E) (A) and (C).

47. You filed a patent application for a client containing a claim to a composition wherein X is defined as follows: "X is a member selected from the group consisting of elements A, B, and C." The claim is properly rejected under 35 U.S.C. § 102(b) as being anticipated by a reference describing the same composition invention wherein X is element A. The rejection may be properly overcome by:

(A) Amending the claim by canceling elements B and C because the reference is concerned only with element A.

(B) Arguing that the reference is not relevant because it lacks elements B and C.

(C) Amending the claim by canceling element A from the Markush group.

(D) Amending the claim by changing "consisting of" to "consisting essentially of."

(E) Amending the claim to redefine X as "being a member selected from the group comprising elements A, B, and C."

276

48.   Which of the following statements is in accordance with proper PTO practice and procedure?

    (A)   A claim to a computer which recites that various components, such as motherboard and RAM, which are old in the art, as well as a novel disc drive, is unpatentable under 35 U.S.C. § 102(f) inasmuch as the inventor derived one or more components, and did not himself invent each of the components of the claimed computer.

    (B)   Where a patent granted to Able discloses subject matter being claimed in an application filed by Baker undergoing examination, the designation of Able as the sole inventor in Able's patent raises a presumption of inventorship with respect to the subject matter disclosed but not claimed in the patent.

    (C)   A terminal disclaimer overcomes a rejection under 35 U.S.C. § 102(e).

    (D)   When Able's patent application, filed on June 2, 1999, is rejected based on unclaimed subject matter of a patent granted to Smith on July 6, 1999, on Smith's application filed on February 18, 1997, and the unclaimed subject matter is Able's own invention, Able may overcome a prima facie case by showing that the patent discloses Able's own previous work.

    (E)   All of the above.

49.   In preparing an application claiming only apparatus to be filed in the PTO, you inadvertently forgot to include a figure in the drawings. While, you did include a brief description of the figure in the written description of the invention in the specification nevertheless the invention of Claim 10 cannot be understood without the omitted figure in the drawings. Only after the application had been filed in the PTO did you realize that the figure was omitted. The application as filed included a proper declaration under 37 CFR § 1.63 signed by the inventor. What document(s), if any, must be filed in the PTO to obtain the original filing date in accordance with proper PTO practice and procedure?

    (A)   An amendment deleting the description of the figure and Claim 10, and a petition with the proper fee to have the application accepted without the omitted figure.

    (B)   An amendment filed before the first Office action deleting all references to the omitted figure and Claim 10 to have the application accepted without the omitted figure.

    (C)   A petition and an amendment to add the figure to the application as soon as possible, and a supplemental declaration stating the omitted figure accurately illustrates and is part of the applicant's invention.

    (D)   The omitted figure along with a supplemental oath or declaration stating that the omitted figure accurately illustrates and is part of the applicant's invention.

    (E)   An amendment adding the figure to the application.

50.   Prior art references have been combined to show obviousness of the claimed invention under 35 U.S.C. § 103. Which of the following most correctly completes the statement: "In establishing obviousness, _____

(A)   a suggestion to modify the art must be expressly stated in one of the references used to show obviousness."

(B)   a suggestion to modify the art must be expressly stated in all the references used to show obviousness."

(C)   a suggestion to modify the art may be inherently or implicitly taught in one of the references used to show obviousness."

(D)   a suggestion to modify the art is unnecessary unless the patent applicant presents evidence or argument tending to show unobviousness."

(E)   a suggestion to modify the art can come from recent nonanalogous prior art references."

Examination for Registration to Practice in Patent Cases
Before the U.S. Patent and Trademark Office
November 3, 1999

Afternoon Session Model Answers

1.   ANSWER: (A). MPEP § 2173.05(b). The term "substantially" has been held as definite, given sufficient guidelines contained in the specification. *In re Mattison*, 509 F.2d 563, 184 USPQ 484 (CCPA 1975). (B) is incorrect because the narrow range within the broad range using the term "preferably" will likely render the claim indefinite. MPEP § 2173.05(c). (C) - (E) are incorrect because each is narrower in scope than (A).

2.   ANSWER: (D). 35 U.S.C. § 251; 37 CFR §§ 1.111; 1.173; 1.176; and MPEP §§ 706.03(o), 1411.02, and 1440. (A) is wrong because the statute pertains to a patent wherein the "patentee [is] claiming...less than he had a right to claim," as opposed to a patentee being entitled to enlarge the scope of the content of the patent. (35 U.S.C. § 251). (B) and (C) are wrong because the amendment will be entered even if it contains new matter, inasmuch as the reissue application is examined in the same manner as the original application and the amendment, being a reply to a non-final first office action, is entitled to be entered. (37 CFR §§ 1.111 and 1.176, and MPEP 1440). (C) is also wrong because no petition and fee are needed. (E) is wrong because the 3.0 to 4.5 ohm range is outside the scope of the broadest range of resistance disclosed in the patent.

3.   ANSWER: (D). It would not be proper to make final a first Office action in a continuing application where that application contains material that was presented in the earlier application after final rejection, and the material was denied entry because new issues were raised that required further consideration and/or search. MPEP § 706.07(b). Since the Amendment After Final Rejection was denied entry, a first Action final rejection in the CPA is improper. (A) is incorrect because it is based on the false premise. The determination that the amendment presented new issues requiring further consideration or search did not state that Claims 1-10 that the revisions failed to place Claims 1-10 in condition for allowance. In any event, proper PTO practice and procedure does not prevent the Examiner from reconsidering such a determination, even if it had been made, and allowing the claims. (B) is incorrect because proper PTO practice and procedure does not prevent the Examiner from determining in the CPA application that the revisions do not overcome the rejection of claims 11-20 made in the parent application. There is no requirement that the Examiner reject Claims 11-20 on grounds that differ from the grounds that these claims were rejected in the parent application due to the determination in the parent application that the Amendment After Final Rejection presented new issues. (C) is incorrect because the applicant may request that the amendment after final be entered in the CPA before issuance of an Office action. See 37 CFR § 1.53(d)(3)(ii); MPEP § 201.06(d), "FILING FEE." (E) is incorrect because (B) is incorrect.

4.   ANSWER: (A). MPEP § 714.13, and 1207.

5.   ANSWER: (E). (A) and (B) are incorrect because a broadened claim can be presented within two years from the grant of the original patent in a reissue application. MPEP § 1412.03. (C) is incorrect because it would involve an attempt to recapture claimed subject matter deliberately canceled in a patent application. MPEP § 1412.02. (D) is incorrect because it improperly relies on new matter. The given facts state that "all leg members must be parallel."

Although the specification of the nonprovisional application was later amended to state that the leg member could be substantially parallel, this is new matter, even in the absence of an objection to entry of new matter in the nonprovisional application. There was no support in the original disclosure for "substantially parallel," where the specification requires the legs "must be parallel." Therefore, amending the claim in the reissue application to replace "parallel" with "substantially parallel" is not likely to be allowed. MPEP § 1411.02.

6.   ANSWER: (D). The claim (A) recites sufficient acts performed on subject matter, e.g. passing the signal through the filter. See MPEP § 2173.05(q) and *Ex parte Porter*, 25 USPQ2d 1144 (Bd. Pat. App. & Int. 1992) cited therein. Therefore, (A) appropriately claims a process. (B) recites the act of polymerizing an organic compound. Therefore, (B) appropriately claims a process. The claim in (C) is not a proper process claim because it does not recite an act specifying how a use or process is accomplished. Therefore, this claim would be rejected as indefinite under 35 U.S.C. § 112 or as an improper definition of a process under 35 U.S.C. § 101. See MPEP § 2173.05(q); *Ex parte Erlich*, 3 USPQ2d 1011 (Bd. Pat. App. & Int. 1986) (claim to "A process for using monoclonal antibodies of claim 4 to isolate and purify human fibroblast interferon" was held indefinite because it merely recited a use without any active, positive steps delimiting how this use is actually practiced); *Clinical Products Ltd. v. Brenner*, 255 F.Supp. 131, 149 USPQ475 (D.D.C. 1966) (claim to "The use of a sustained release therapeutic agent in the body of ephedrine absorbed upon polystyrene sulfonic acid" is not a proper process claim under 35 U.S.C. § 101). (E) is incorrect because (C) is incorrect.

7.   ANSWER: (D). 37 CFR §§ 1.97; 1.98; 1.607(c); and 10.23(c)(7). (A), (B) and (C) are not correct because they do not identify the number of the patent claim that has been copied. (E) is not the most proper course of action to take. The IDS does not identify the QED patent from which the claim was copied. Arguing that Claim 6 of the QED patent is an obvious improvement to the instant invention would not be considered relevant. 37 CFR § 1.98(a)(3).

8.   ANSWER: (A) is the most correct answer. 37 CFR § 1.131; and MPEP § 715.03. See *In re Spiller*, 500 F.2d 1170, 182 USPQ 614 (CCPA 1974). (B) and (C) are incorrect. To overcome a reference indirectly, as in (B) and (C), a showing of prior completion of a different species should be coupled with a showing that the claimed species would have been an obvious modification of the species completed by applicant. *In re Spiller, supra; In re Clark*, 148 USPQ 665 (CCPA 1966); *In re Plumb*, 176 USPQ 323 (CCPA 1973); *In re Hostettler*, 356 F.2d 562, 148 USPQ 514 (CCPA 1966), MPEP § 715.03. (D) is incorrect because the declaration cannot be used to antedate a statutory bar, and the reference is a statutory bar under 35 U.S.C. § 102(b) inasmuch as it issued more than one year before the Jones application was filed. 37 CFR § 1.131. (E) is incorrect because the declaration is ineffective to overcome a U.S. patent where there is no patentable distinction between the claims of the application and of the patent. *In re Hidy*, 303 F.2d 954, 133 USPQ 650 (CCPA 1962); MPEP §§ 715.05 and 2308.01.

9.   ANSWER: (D). MPEP § 713.05.

10.   ANSWER: (B). *Ex parte Markush*, 1925 CD 126 (Comm'r Pat. 1925) sanctions claiming a genus as a group "consisting of" elements connected by "and." MPEP § 2173.05(h), item I., Markush Groups. (A) is not the most correct answer inasmuch as the elements are improperly

connected by "or." (C) and (D) are not the most correct answers. It is improper to use the word "comprising" instead of "consisting of. *Ex parte Dotter*, 12 USPQ 283 (Bd. App. 1931); MPEP § 2173.05(h).

11. ANSWER: (E). 37 CFR § 1.8(a); and MPEP § 512. (A) is incorrect because the response would not be timely, even if the August 6th date is given to the response. The six month statutory period for response is measured from the date of the Office action, not the date the action was received. The response was mailed beyond the six month statutory period for response. (B) is incorrect because the U.S. Postal Service certificate of mailing does not comply with 37 CFR § 1.8(a). (C) is incorrect. The date of the certificate of mailing is after the statutory six month period for response. Therefore the response is not shown by the certificate to be timely mailed. (D) is incorrect because (A) and (C) are incorrect. (E) is correct because (A), (B), (C) and (C) are not correct.

12. ANSWER: (B). MPEP § 2173.05(b). (A) is incorrect because the claim interpretation of one possessing ordinary skill level is relevant. MPEP § 2173.02. (C) is incorrect because the guidelines in the specification may be sufficient. MPEP § 2173.05(b). (D) is incorrect since it relies on the improper addition of new matter. (E) is incorrect since (B) is correct.

13. ANSWER: (B). MPEP §§ 710.04, and 710.04(a).

14. ANSWER: (D). Claim 1 provides antecedent basis for Claim 2 of answer (D). 35 U.S.C.§ 112, second paragraph. (A) is incorrect. Claim 1, which is drawn to a "modular telephone plug crimping tool," provides no antecedent basis for "[t]he modular telephone" required by Claim 2. MPEP § 2173.05(e). (B) is incorrect because it fails to incorporate all the limitations of the claim to which it refers. Caim 1, requiring the secondary body part have a fixed length, provides not antecedent basis for the limitation of claim 2, that the second party part have an ajustable length. 35 U.S.C. § 112, fourth paragraph. (C) is incorrect because it improperly recites a process without setting forth any steps in the process. MPEP § 2173.05(q). (E) is incorrect because (D) is correct.

15. ANSWER: (E). 37 CFR §§ 1.131, and 1.132; and MPEP §§ 706.02(b), 715, and 716.

16. ANSWER: (E). Both (B) and (C) are proper dependent claims and are supported by the specification. 37 CFR § 1.75. (A) is incorrect. The use of the phrase "at least" has no upper limit and could include temperatures greater than that set forth in the specification, i.e. "when exposed to a temperature of from about 10°C. to 15°C." MPEP § 2163.05. (D) is incorrect. MPEP § 2111.03 provides that "A claim which depends from a claim which 'consists of' the recited elements or steps cannot add an element or step." As such, (D) seeks to add primary and secondary amines in violation of this caveat.

17. ANSWER: (C). The amendment points out two words occurring in line 6 that are to be deleted, and two words that are to be inserted in place of the deleted words. 37 CFR § 1.121(a)(2)(i). (A) is incorrect because "dihydric" appears on line 4 and not line 3. (B) is incorrect because "alcohols" does not occur in line 4 of claim 1. (D) is incorrect because "cooling" appears on line 9 and not line 8. (E) is not correct because (B) is incorrect.

18. ANSWER: (C). The scope of Claim 1 is enlarged, or broadened by the deletion of "from the local pool subset" from the claim. As presented in (C), the reissue application is filed less than two years after the original patent was granted and the application seeks to enlarge the scope of Claim 1. As such, a reissue application may be properly granted containing the claim. 35 U.S.C. § 251. (A) and (B) are incorrect. The scope of Claim 1 is enlarged by the proposed amendment. Claims cannot be enlarged or broadened in a reexamination application regardless of when the application is filed. 35 U.S.C. § 305; 37 CFR § 1.552(b). (D) and (E) are also incorrect given that the scope of Claim 1 is broadened by the proposed amendment. As such, the reissue application cannot be filed more than two years from the grant of the original patent. 35 U.S.C. § 251.

19. ANSWER: (B). In *Racing Strollers Inc. v. TRI Industries Inc.*, 11 USPQ2d 1300 (Fed. Cir. 1989) the in banc Federal Circuit stated that for design patents "the 'best mode' requirement of the first paragraph of §112 is not applicable, as a design has only one 'mode' and it can be described only by illustrations showing what it looks like (though some added description in words may be useful to explain the illustrations)." 35 U.S.C. § 171 indicates that the provisions of the Patent Act relating to utility inventions apply to designs "except as otherwise provided." MPEP § 1504.04. The Patent Act, the Rules of Practice in Patent Cases, and the pertinent case law do not exempt designs from the written description, definiteness and independent claim requirements of 35 U.S.C. § 112. Accordingly, inasmuch as (B) is correct, (E) is incorrect. (A), (C), and (D) are incorrect because the written description, definiteness and independent claim requirements of 35 U.S.C. § 112 apply to design applications.

20. ANSWER: (D). MPEP § 402.10.

21. ANSWER: (A). 37 CFR § 1.11; and MPEP §§ 103, and 201.09.

22. ANSWER: (E). The transitional phrase "consisting of" in Claim 1, excludes any element not specified in the claims. MPEP § 2111.03. When the phrase "consisting of" appears in a clause of the body of a claim, rather than immediately following the preamble, it limits the elements set forth only in that clause, but other elements are not excluded from other clauses in the claim as a whole. Id. Here, the phrase "consisting of" in the base claim limits the output device to a video monitor. Thus, in Claim 4 the recitation of "a printer" as an output device is improper. Moreover, the recitation of the same limitation found in Claim 1, i.e., "a video monitor," does not further limit the base claim. 35 U.S.C. § 112, paragraph 5, 37 CFR § 1.75(c). Claim 5, depends on improper Claim 4, and they are improper. A claim, which depends from an improper base claim, is itself improper. MPEP § 608.01(n). Answer (A) is incorrect because Claim 2 properly refers to a prior claim, Claim 1, it includes all the limitations of Claim 1, and it further limits claim 1. 35 U.S.C. § 112, paragraph 4, 37 CFR § 1.75(c). Answer (B) is incorrect because Claim 3 properly refers to, in the alternative, prior claims (claim 1 or claim 2), it includes all the limitations of Claim 1 or Claim 2, and it further limits Claim 1 or Claim 2. 35 U.S.C. § 112, paragraph 5, 37 CFR § 1.75(c). As discussed above, Claim 2 is a proper dependent claim. Answer (C) is incorrect because, as discussed above, Claim 3 is a proper dependent claim. Answer (D) is incorrect because, as discussed above, Claim 4 is also an improper dependent claim. Thus, the most correct answer is Answer (E).

23. ANSWER: (E) is the most correct answer. MPEP § 2173.05(b), "Reference To An Object That Is Variable May Render A Claim Indefinite," items B, C, and F. Each expression has been found to require support in the specification disclosing a standard for ascertaining what the inventor meant.

24. ANSWER: (A). 37 CFR § 1.75, and MPEP § 2173.05(b). The limitation, "the outer surface of said case" does not lack antecedent basis since it is an inherent part of the case. (B) is incorrect because claim 1 recites two different memory chips and the recitation of "said memory chip" therefore renders the claim indefinite. MPEP § 2173.05(e). (C) is incorrect because claim 5 does not further limit claim 1. (D) and (E) are incorrect because (A) is correct.

25. ANSWER: (C). 37 CFR §§ 1.10(a), and 1.53(b). "The filing date of an application for patent filed under this section, is the date on which a specification as prescribed by 35 U.S.C. § 112 containing a description pursuant to § 1.71 and at least one claim pursuant to § 1.75, and any drawing required by § 1.81(a) are filed in the Patent and Trademark Office."

26. ANSWER: (E) is correct because (B) and (C) are correct. (A) does not overcome the prior art because the broad "comprising" language permits the laminate to have additional layers, such as an intermediate adhesive layer. MPEP § 2111.03. (B) overcomes a § 102 rejection on the basis of the prior art by reciting that the transparent protective layer and the light-sensitive layer are in actual contact therewith, eliminating the possibility of an intermediate adhesive layer. (C) also avoids the prior art by using a negative limitation to particularly point out and distinctly claim that X does not claim any laminate including an adhesive layer. MPEP § 2173.05(i).

27. ANSWER: (B). 37 CFR § 1.172.

28. ANSWER: (D). 37 CFR § 1.52(c), and MPEP § 605.04(a).

29. ANSWER: (A). 35 U.S.C. §112, paragraph 2; and MPEP §§ 2173.05(a), and 706.03(d). A patentee can be his own lexicographer and may use a term in a manner contrary to or inconsistent with one or more of the term's ordinary meanings. However, a term may not be given a meaning repugnant to its usual meaning. MPEP § 2173.05 (third italicized subject). Here, the use of "fluid" to mean "solid" is repugnant to its ordinary meaning. Also, when there is more than one definition for a term, it is incumbent on the applicant to make clear which definition is relied upon. Until the meaning of the claim is clear, a rejection under the second paragraph of 35 U.S.C. § 112 is appropriate. Here, "fluid" is inconsistently defined. In the specification, it must be "above 2° C." in the specification, whereas it is "0° to 10° C. in the claim. *See also* MPEP § 2106 (in context of computer related inventions). If an applicant asserts that a term has a meaning that conflicts with its art-accepted meaning, the applicant should be encouraged to amend the claim to better reflect what is intended to be claimed as the invention. MPEP § 2106. (B) is incorrect because the Greene research results were published after Billie's filing date and the research occurred in Great Britain. Thus, this research does not constitute prior art under 35 U.S.C. § 102(a). (C) is incorrect because it confuses the concept of enablement with definiteness. (D) is incorrect because whether the composition that results from the claimed process occurs naturally is immaterial to whether a method for forming that

composition is statutory subject matter. (E) is incorrect because an applicant need not understand how an invention works or recite the theory in a claim.

30. ANSWER: (D). 35 U.S.C. § 4; and MPEP § 309.

31. ANSWER: (C). August 3, 1998, was the date on which the requirements of 35 U.S.C. § 371(c)(1), (2), and (4) were completed. PCT Articles 11 and 20; PCT Rule 47.1(c); and 35 U.S.C. § 102(e) which states that a person shall be entitled to a patent *unless* "the invention was described in a patent granted on...an international application by another who has fulfilled the requirements of paragraphs (1), (2), and (4) of section 371(c) of this title before the invention thereof by applicant for patent."

32. ANSWER: (B). 37 CFR §§ 1.291, and 1.501; MPEP §§ 2202, and 2203.

33. ANSWER: (D). 37 CFR § 1.321(c); and MPEP § 804.02. (A) is incorrect because provisional rejections between copending applications based on the judicially created doctrine of double patenting are provided for in MPEP § 804, item 1B. (B) is incorrect because the rejection is still applicable even though the continuation application gets the filing date of the first application. MPEP § 804.02. (C) is incorrect because the rejection is proper. Applicant voluntarily filed a second application without a restriction requirement by the Examiner. *In re Schneller*, 158 USPQ 210 (CCPA 1968) and MPEP § 804. (E) is incorrect because it omits the provision concerning common ownership. 37 CFR § 1.321(c).

34. ANSWER: (E). (A) is incorrect because the composition naturally occurring. MPEP 2106. (B) is incorrect because patentability of a product claimed by a product-by process claim is based on the product itself. MPEP § 2106. Since the product is naturally occurring, the claim provides the basis for a proper rejection under 35 U.S.C. § 101. (C) is incorrect because it drawn to more than one statutory class of invention, i.e., a product and a process, in the same claim and is therefore not within one of the statutory classes set forth by 35 U.S.C. § 101. The claim is properly rejectable under 35 U.S.C. § 112, second paragraph. MPEP § 2173.05(p). (D) is incorrect because mathematical equations alone are not patentable subject matter. MPEP § 2106. (E) is correct because (A) - (D) are incorrect.

35. ANSWER: (D). MPEP § 608.01(l). (A) is incorrect because the original numbering of the claims must be preserved throughout the prosecution. 37 CFR § 1.126. (B) is incorrect and nonsensical. (C) is incorrect because a multiple dependent claim will always be considered to be the total number of claims (dependant and independent) to which direct reference is made therein. 37 CFR § 1.75(c). (E) is incorrect because (D) is correct.

36. ANSWER: (D). Claim 1 is a "single means claim" which is not subject to the interpretive rules of §112, paragraph 6 (which applies only to claims for combinations). Answers (A), (B) and (E) are incorrect for at least that reason. According to *In re Hyatt*, 708 F.2d 712, 218 USPQ 195 (Fed. Cir. 1983), the proper basis for rejecting a single means claim is the first paragraph of §112 (enablement) rather than the second paragraph (definiteness). *See also* MPEP § 2181. Therefore, answer (C) is not the correct answer

37. ANSWER (D). Claim 3 is improper because does not further limit the claim from which it depends, in violation of 35 U.S.C. § 112, paragraph 4 and 37 CFR §1.75(c). (A) is wrong because the Barry patent anticipates only claims 1, 3 and 4. (B) is wrong at least because Claim 1 is an original claim and an original claim provides its own written description. *In re Anderson*, 471 F2d 1237, 176 USPQ 331 (CCPA 1973). (C) is wrong because claim 2 is a proper dependent claim that further restricts the scope of claim 1 by narrowing the resistance value range. Similarly, (E) is incorrect because claim 4 specifies that the DC current source produces variable current, a limitation not in claim 1, and therefore properly narrows the scope of that claim.

38. ANSWER: (B). 35 U.S.C. §§ 101 and 112, second paragraph; and MPEP § 2173.05(q). The claim in (B) recites two positive steps of using paint. The first step is applying the paint to a surface. The second step is removing the excess paint. (A), (C) and (D) are not proper process claims because they do not recite a positive step specifying how the use is accomplished. For example, (A) does not set forth the step(s) by which the antibodies isolate interferon.

39. ANSWER: All answers accepted.

40. ANSWER: (C). 35 U.S.C. § 102; and MPEP §§ 2133.03(e)(4), and 2133.03(e)(6).

41. ANSWER: (C). (C) is correct because it fails to comply with 37 CFR § 1.75(c), which states: "One or more claims may be presented in dependent form, referring back to and further limiting another claim or claims in the same application." In the present case, Claim 2 refers back to Claim 1, but fails to properly limit the capacitance recited in Claim 1 because it recites the term "about" immediately before the capacitance range. The term "about" allows for a range slightly above 0.011 μf or below 0.003 μf. A range below 0.003 is outside the scope of Claim 1. See MPEP 2144.05. Therefore, the claim in (C) does not properly limit Claim 1. (A), (B), and (D) are wrong because they are proper dependent claims. They further limit Claim 1 by limiting the capacitance to values within the scope of Claim 1, and therefore, comply with 37 CFR § 1.75(c). In (D), the applicant may rely upon the original claim for the description of the range of capacitance. MPEP § 608.01(l). (E) is wrong because (D) is a proper dependent claim.

42. ANSWER: (C). 37 CFR § 1.75(c); and MPEP 608.01(n).

43. ANSWER: (C). 35 U.S.C. § 102(b); and MPEP § 2133.03(b), item D, states "An assignment or sale of the rights, such as patent rights, in the invention is not a sale of 'the invention' within the meaning of section 102(b). The sale must involve the delivery of the physical invention itself. *Moleculon Research Corp. v. CBS, Inc.*, 793 F.2d 1261, 1265, 229 USPQ 805, 809 (Fed. Cir. 1986)." (A) is incorrect. MPEP § 2133.03(b), item I (A), states, "An invention may be deemed to be 'on sale' even though the sale was conditional. The fact that the sale is conditioned on buyer satisfaction does not, without more, prove that the sale was for an experimental purpose. *Strong v. General Elec. Co.*, 434 F.2d 1042, 1046, 168 USPQ 8, 12 (5th Cir. 1970)." (B) is incorrect. MPEP § 2133.03(b), item I (B), states, "A 'sale' need not be for profit to bar a patent. If the sale was for the commercial exploitation of the invention, it is 'on sale' within the meaning of 35 U.S.C. 102(b). *In re Dybel*, 187 USPQ 593, 599 (CCPA 1975)

('Although selling the devices for a profit would have demonstrated the purpose of commercial exploitation, the fact that appellant realized no profit from the sales does not demonstrate the contrary.')." (D) is incorrect. MPEP § 2133.03, item IIB, states, "It is not necessary that a sale be consummated for the bar to operate. *Buildex v. Kason Indus.*, 849 F.2d 1461, 1463-64, 7 USPQ2d 1325, 1327-28 (Fed. Cir. 1988) (citations omitted)." (E) is incorrect. MPEP § 2133.03, item II (A), states, "Since the statute creates a bar when an invention is placed 'on sale,' a mere offer to sell is sufficient commercial activity to bar a patent. *In re Theis*, 610 F.2d 786, 791, 204 USPQ 188, 192 (CCPA 1979)... In fact, the offer need not even be actually received by a prospective purchaser. *Wende v. Horine*, 225 F. 501 (7th Cir. 1915)."

44. ANSWER: (D). "Applications for patents shall be kept in confidence by the Patent and Trademark Office and no information concerning the same given without authority of the application or owner unless necessary to carry out the provisions of any Act of Congress or in such special circumstances as may be determined by the Commissioner." 35 U.S.C. § 122. However, when the applications share a common assignee, an examiner may provisionally reject claims, under 35 U.S.C. § 102(e)/103, in the later filed application, when appropriate. MPEP § 706.02(k). Here, G's application and H's application share a common assignee. Answers (A) and (E) are incorrect because a provisional rejection, under 35 U.S.C. § 102(e)/103, in any of these circumstances would not maintain the confidence of G's application or H's application. 35 U.S.C. § 122. Thus, in neither of the circumstances presented in these answers will you most likely need to overcome the rejection. Answer (B) is incorrect. Inasmuch as there is no common assignee, the confidential status of applications under 35 U.S.C. § 122 must be maintained, and no rejection can be made using or relying on the earlier filed application as prior art. MPEP 706.02(g), item II. Answer (C) is incorrect because a provisional rejection under 35 U.S.C. § 102(e)/103, cannot be properly made when the applications have the same filing date. A provisional double patenting rejection may be proper. Answer (E) is incorrect because the examiner may not properly reject claims in an earlier filed application over the claim of a later filed application. 35 U.S.C. § 102(e)/103; MPEP § 706.02.

45. ANSWER: (E). 35 U.S.C. § 112, first and second paragraphs. Interconnection of the elements as described in the written description provided by the inventor and as disclosed in the drawings is no longer required.

46. ANSWER: (A). An applicant in a patent application filed on or before June 8, 1995, and which has an effective filing date of June 8, 1993 or earlier, is entitled to have new evidence in support of patentability entered and considered (and the finality of the final rejection withdrawn), provided the submission (along with the appropriate fee) is filed prior to the filing of an appeal brief to the Board of Patent Appeals and Interferences or abandonment of the application. 37 CFR § 1.129(a); MPEP § 706.07(g). Here, the application is filed on June 8, 1995, it has an effective filing date of June 8, 1993, and the submission (along with the appropriate fee) is filed prior to the filing of the appeal brief to the Board of Patent Appeals and Interferences or the abandonment of the application. Answers (B) and (D) are incorrect because the submission was not filed prior to the filing of the appeal brief to the Board of Patent Appeals and Interferences. 37 CFR § 1.129(a); MPEP § 706.07(g). Answer (C) is incorrect because the submission was not filed prior to the abandonment of the application on December 18, 1999. 37 CFR § 1.129(a); and MPEP § 706.07(g). Answer (E) is incorrect because Answer (C) is incorrect.

47. ANSWER: (C). 35 U.S.C. 102(b); and MPEP §§ 715.03, 2111.03, and 2173.05(h). Deletion of the anticipated element from the claim leaves an invention, which is no longer anticipated by the reference. (A), (D), and (E) are incorrect because despite the amendments, the claim remains anticipated since the claim is still directed to the invention described in the reference wherein X is element A. For example, in (D) and (E), element A would still be a member of the group and the claim would still be anticipated by the prior art. (B) is incorrect because the argument does not change the fact that the claim remains anticipated by the same invention described in the reference wherein X is element A. (E) is incorrect because "comprising" cannot be used in a proper Markush group.

48. ANSWER: (D). MPEP § 2136.05. (A) is incorrect. MPEP § 2137. "The mere fact that a claim recites the use of various components, each of which can be argumentatively assumed to be old, does not provide a proper basis for a rejection under 35 U.S.C. 102(f)." *Ex parte Billottet*, 192 USPQ 413, 415 (Bd. App. 1976). Derivation requires complete conception and communication by another to the applicant. *Kilbey v. Thiele*, 199 USPQ 290, 294 (Bd. Pat. Inter. 1978). (B) is incorrect. MPEP § 2137, third paragraph. The designation of inventorship in a patent does not raise a presumption of inventorship with respect to subject matter disclosed, but unclaimed in the patent. (C) is incorrect. MPEP § 2136.05. A terminal disclaimer does not overcome a 35 U.S.C. § 102(e) rejection. *In re Bartfeld*, 925 F.2d 1450, 17 USPQ2d 1885 (Fed. Cir. 1991). (E) is incorrect because (A), (B) and (C) are incorrect.

49. ANSWER: (B). 37 CFR § 1.53; and MPEP §§ 601.01, and 601.01(g). The only way to retain the original filing date of the application is to delete all reference to the omitted figure and comply with the requirements set forth in MPEP § 608.02.

50. ANSWER: (C) is the most correct answer. 35 U.S.C. § 103; *In re Napier*, 55 F.3d 610, 613, 34 USPQ2d 1782, 1784 (Fed. Cir. 1995); *In re Grasselli*, 713 F.2d 731, 739, 218 USPQ 769, 775 (Fed. Cir. 1983); and MPEP § 2112. (A) and (B) are incorrect because a suggestion to modify the art to render obvious the claimed invention need not be expressly stated in one or all of the references. *In re Napier, supra*. (D) is incorrect. The burden is on the examiner to show that the prior art suggests modifying the art to render obvious the claimed invention. If the examiner sustains his burden of proof only then does the burden shift to the applicant to present rebuttal evidence. *Hodosh v. Block Drug Co., Inc.*, 786 F.2d 1136, 229 USPQ 182 (Fed. Cir. 1986), and MPEP §§ 2141, and 2143.01. (E) is incorrect because only analogous art can be used in a 35 U.S.C. § 103 rejection.

The Best Test Preparation and
Review Course

PATENT
BAR
EXAM

Guide for the
Preparation of
Patent Drawings

Selected Rules of Practice Relating to Patent Drawings

35 U.S.C. 113. Drawings.

The applicant shall furnish a drawing where necessary for the understanding of the subject matter sought to be patented. When the nature of such subject matter admits of illustration by a drawing and the applicant has not furnished such a drawing, the Commissioner may require its submission within a time period of not less than two months from the sending of a notice thereof. Drawings submitted after the filing date of the application may not be used (i) to overcome any insufficiency of the specification due to lack of an enabling disclosure or otherwise inadequate disclosure therein, or (ii) to supplement the original disclosure thereof for the purpose of interpretation of the scope of any claim.

37 CFR 1.71. Detailed Description and Specification of the Invention.

(d) A copyright or mask work notice may be placed in a design or utility patent application adjacent to copyright and mask work material contained therein. The notice may appear at any appropriate portion of the patent application disclosure. For notices in drawings, see § 1.84(s). The content of the notice must be limited to only those elements provided for by law. For example, "©1983 John Doe" (17 U.S.C. 401) and "*M* John Doe" (17 U.S.C. 909) would be properly limited and, under current statutes, legally sufficient notices of copyright and mask work, respectively. Inclusion of a copyright or mask work notice will be permitted only if the authorization language set forth in paragraph (e) of this section is included at the beginning (preferably as the first paragraph) of the specification.

37 CFR 1.81. Drawings Required in Patent Application.

(a) The applicant for a patent is required to furnish a drawing of his or her invention where necessary for the understanding of the subject matter sought to be patented; this drawing, or a high quality copy thereof, must be filed with the application. Since corrections are the responsibility of the applicant, the original drawing(s) should be retained by the applicant for any necessary future correction.

(b) Drawings may include illustrations which facilitate an understanding of the invention (for example, flow sheets in cases of processes, and diagrammatic views).

(c) Whenever the nature of the subject matter sought to be patented admits of illustration by a drawing without its being necessary for the understanding of the subject matter and the applicant has not furnished such a drawing, the examiner will require its submission within a time period of not less than two months from the date of the sending of a notice thereof.

(d) Drawings submitted after the filing date of the application may not be used to overcome any insufficiency of the specification due to lack of an enabling disclosure or otherwise inadequate disclosure therein, or to supplement the original disclosure thereof for the purpose of interpretation of the scope of any claim.

37 CFR 1.83. Content of Drawing.

(a) The drawing must show every feature of the invention specified in the claims. However, conventional features disclosed in the description and claims, where their detailed illustration is not essential for a proper understanding of the invention, should be illustrated in the drawing in the form of a graphical drawing symbol or a labeled representation (e.g. a labeled rectangular box).

(b) When the invention consists of an improvement on an old machine the drawing must when possible exhibit, in one or more views, the improved portion itself, disconnected from the old structure, and also in another view, so much only of the old structure as will suffice to show the connection of the invention therewith.

(c) Where the drawings do not comply with the requirements of paragraphs (a) and (b) of this section, the examiner shall require such additional illustration within a time period of not less than two months from the date of the sending of a notice thereof. Such corrections are subject to the requirements of § 1.81(d).

37 CFR 1.84. Standards for Drawings.

(a) **Drawings.** There are two acceptable categories for presenting drawings in utility patent applications:

(1) **Black ink.** Black and white drawings are normally required. India ink, or its equivalent that secures black solid lines, must be used for drawings, or

(2) **Color.** On rare occasion, color drawings may be necessary as the only practical medium by which to disclose the subject matter sought to be patented in a utility patent application or the subject matter of a statutory invention registration. The Patent and Trademark Office will accept color drawings in utility patent applications and statutory invention registrations only after granting a petition filed under this paragraph explaining why the color drawings are necessary. Any such petition must include the following:

(i)   The appropriate fee set forth in § l.17(h);

(ii)   Three (3) sets of color drawings; and

(iii)   The specification must contain the following language as the first paragraph in that portion of the specification relating to the brief description of the drawing:

"The file of this patent contains at least one drawing executed in color. Copies of this patent with color drawing(s) will be provided by the Patent and Trademark Office upon request and payment of the necessary fee."

If the language is not in the specification, a proposed amendment to insert the language must accompany the petition.

Properly executed drawings are of the utmost importance in a patent application; therefore, it is critical that the drawings be executed in an accurate manner that graphically communicates the invention of the applicant(s). The quality of a patent drawing must meet high standards in order to clearly reproduce on the printed patent, which is an essential tool used as prior art by the Examiner in determining patentability of pending patent applications.

In order to facilitate the understanding of the full scope of the patent invention, the drawing also serves the patent practitioners as a necessary tool in graphically comprehending the claims in the patent.

Drawings may be freehand work, per se, provided they meet the same standards as drawings prepared with the aid of drafting instruments.

The Office will accept computer-generated drawings provided that the drawings are substantially equivalent in quality to ink drawings having black solid lines. In computer-generated drawings, lines must be so distanced as to prevent lines touching and thereby resulting in a single heavy line. Jagged and wavy lines, characteristic in some computer-generated drawing systems, must be kept to an absolute minimum to retain the intent of 35 U.S.C. 112.

For color drawings, a petition is required because the special handling necessary is time consuming and the Office cannot permit such a special procedure unless the circumstances are exceptional. Color drawings are not acceptable until petition is granted.

Utility patents are not printed in color; therefore, three sets of color drawings are necessary for proper distribution within the Office. One set will be attached to the Letters Patent for routing to the applicant. The remaining two sets will be routed to (1) the patent file and (2) the Office of Publication and Dissemination, Patent and Trademark Copy Sales, for copying purposes.

Computer-generated color drawings require use of the same standards as applied to black ink drawings.

(b) Photographs.

(1) Black and white. Photographs are not ordinarily permitted in utility and design patent applications. However, the Office will accept photographs in utility and design patent applications only after granting a petit/on filed under this paragraph which requests that photographs be accepted. Any such petition must include the following:

(i) The appropriate fee set forth in § 1.17(h); and

(ii) Three (3) sets of photographs.

Photographs must either be developed on double weight photographic paper or be permanently mounted on bristol board. The photographs must be of sufficient quality so that all details in the drawing are reproducible in the printed patent.

Patent practitioners are cautioned that photographs can no longer be removed from applications pending in the Office. Therefore, practitioners should make sure they retain an original set of photographs.

The Office is willing to accept black and white photographs or photomicrographs (not photolithographs or other reproductions of photographs made by using screens) developed on double weight photographic paper in lieu of ink drawings to illustrate inventions which are incapable of being accurately or adequately depicted by ink drawings. However, photographs are not acceptable until a petition is granted. The photographs or photomicrographs must show the invention more clearly than they can be shown by ink drawings and otherwise comply with the rules concerning such drawings. Examples of acceptable categories of photographs are: crystalline structures, metallurgical microstructures, textile fabrics, grain structures, and ornamental effects.

(2) Color. Color photographs will be accepted in utility patent applications if the conditions for accepting color drawings have been satisfied. See paragraph (a)(2) of this section.

Patent practitioners are cautioned that photographs can no longer be removed from applications pending in the Office. Therefore, practitioners should make sure they retain an original set of photographs.

There are instances where photographs are produced through use of equipment such as tunneling electron microscopy (TEM). For example, in areas such as solid state electronics, wherein single atoms or single atomic layers can be the invention, only TEM or comparable equipment images can resolve single atoms or radicals. In such instances, the Office will not necessarily object to the images for not being completely sharp if the content of such TEM's adds to the understanding of the invention and the TEM's can be adequately reproduced in the printed patent.

Photographs taken with such specialized equipment must meet the same standards as photographs which do not require such specialized equipment. Images produced through use of specialized equipment may not always appear with secure black solid lines, however, the drawing review will consider such limitations and accept full tone photographs that meet the specified requirements.

(c) Identification of drawings. Identifying indicia, if provided, should include the application number or the title of the invention, inventor's name, docket number (if any), and the name and telephone number of a person to call if the Office is unable to match the drawings to the proper application. This information should be placed on the back of each sheet of drawings a minimum distance of 1.5 cm. (5/8 inch) down from the top of the page.

While such indicia is not required, the Office does encourage applicants to provide identifying information on the reverse of each sheet of drawings so that the Office can ascertain that drawing sheets are matched with the proper application. This suggestion is based upon the fact that the Office handles approximately one-half million papers yearly, and while very few of these go astray, such indicia significantly aid in the rare event that a drawing does become separated from the application file. Applications will not be objected to by the Office if such identifying information is not present; however, when drawings become separated, delays will result in matching the drawings with the application. When applying identification, care should be exercised so that there is no bleed through onto the drawing.

(d) Graphic forms in drawings. Chemical or mathematical formulae, tables, and waveforms may be submitted as drawings, and are subject to the same requirements as drawings. Each chemical or mathematical formula must be labeled as a separate figure, using brackets when necessary, to show that information is properly integrated. Each group of waveforms must be presented as a single figure, using a common vertical axis with time extending along the horizontal axis. Each individual waveform discussed in the specification must be identified with a separate letter designation adjacent to the vertical axis.

(e) Type of paper. Drawings submitted to the Office must be made upon paper which is flexible, strong, white, smooth, non-shiny, and durable. All sheets must be free from cracks, creases, and folds. Only one side of the sheet shall be used for the drawing. Each sheet must be reasonably free from erasures and must be free from alterations, overwritings, and interlineations. Photographs must either be developed on double weight photographic paper or be permanently mounted on bristol board. See paragraph (b) of this section for other requirements for photographs.

The requirement of the drawing being reasonably free from erasures, alterations, etc., is that upon reproduction in the printing of the patent grant, the drawings can be made to be clear and understandable.

In the interest of protecting the drawings, practitioners are encouraged to transmit drawings to the Office sent flat, protected by a sheet of heavy binder's board, or rolled for transmission in a suitable mailing tube, but never folded. If received creased or mutilated, new drawings will be required. An alternative to this suggested transmission is to handcarry the drawings to the Office.

(f) Size of paper. All drawing sheets in an application must be the same size. One of the shorter sides of the sheet is regarded as its top. The size of the sheets on which drawings are made must be:

(1) 21.6 cm. by 27.9 cm. (81/2 by 11 inches), or

(2) 21.0 cm. by 29.7 cm. (DIN size A4).

(g) Margins. The sheets must not contain frames around the sight, i.e., the usable surface. The following margins are required:

Rules of Practice Relating to Patent Drawings

(1) On 21.6 cm. by 27.9 cm. (8 1/2 by 11 inch) drawing sheets, each sheet must include a top margin of 2.5 cm. (1 inch) and bottom and side margins of .64 cm. (1/4 inch) from the edges, thereby leaving a sight no greater than 20.3 cm. by 24.8 cm. (8 by 9 3/4 inches).

(2) On 21.0 cm. by 29.7 cm. (DIN size A4) drawing sheets, each sheet must include a top margin of at least 2.5 cm., a left side margin of 2.5 cm., a right side margin of 1.5 cm., and a bottom margin of 1.0 cm., thereby leaving a sight no greater than 17.0 cm. by 26.2 cm.

Although the Office accepts four sizes of paper, the sight is the same for two of the paper sizes, i.e., 21.6 cm. by 33.1 cm. (8 1/2 by 13 inches), or 21.6 cm. by 35.6 cm. (8 1/2 by 14 inches).

(h) Views. The drawing must contain as many views as necessary to show the invention. The views may be plan, elevation, section, or perspective views. Detail views of portions of elements, on a larger scale if necessary, may also be used. All views of the drawing must be grouped together and arranged on the sheet(s) without wasting space, preferably in an upright position, clearly separated from one another, and must not be included in the sheets containing the specifications, claims, or abstract. Views must not be connected by projection lines and must not contain center lines. Waveforms of electrical signals may be connected by dashed lines to show the relative timing of the waveforms.

(1) Exploded views. Exploded views, with the separated parts embraced by a bracket, to show the relationship or order of assembly of various parts are permissible. When an exploded view is shown in a figure which is on the same sheet as another figure, the exploded view should be placed in brackets.

Each element on a view must be identified by a reference number, except on design drawings.

(2) Partial views. When necessary, a view of a large machine or device in its entirety may be broken into partial views on a single sheet, or extended over several sheets if there is no loss in facility of understanding the view. Partial views drawn on separate sheets must always be capable of being linked edge to edge so that no partial view contains parts of another partial view. A smaller scale view should be included showing the whole formed by the partial views and indicating the positions of the parts shown. When a portion of a view is

298

enlarged for magnification purposes, the view and the enlarged view must each be labeled as separate views.

(i) Where views on two or more sheets form, in effect, a single complete view, the views on the several sheets must be so arranged that the complete figure can be assembled without concealing any part of any of the views appearing on the various sheets.

(ii) A very long view may be divided into several parts placed one above the other on a single sheet. However, the relationship between the different parts must be clear and unambiguous.

(3) Sectional views. The plane upon which a sectional view is taken should be indicated on the view from which the section is cut by a broken line. The ends of the broken line should be designated by Arabic or Roman numerals corresponding to the view number of the sectional view, and should have arrows to indicate the direction of sight. Hatching must be used to indicate section portions of an object, and must be made by regularly spaced oblique parallel lines spaced sufficiently apart to enable the lines to be distinguished without difficulty. Hatching should not impede the clear reading of the reference characters and lead lines. If it is not possible to place reference characters outside the hatched area, the hatching may be broken off wherever reference characters are inserted. Hatching must be at a substantial angle to the surrounding axes or principal lines, preferably 45°. A cross section must be set out and drawn to show all of the materials as they are shown in the view from which the cross section was taken. The parts in cross section must show proper material(s) by hatching with regularly spaced parallel oblique strokes, the space between strokes being chosen on the basis of the total area to be hatched. The various parts of a cross section of the same item should be hatched in the same manner and should accurately and graphically indicate the nature of the material(s) that is illustrated in cross section. The hatching of juxtaposed different elements must be angled in a different way. In the case of large areas, hatching may be confined to an edging drawn around the entire inside of the outline of the area to be hatched. Different types of hatching should have different conventional meanings as regards the nature of a material seen in cross section.

Section lines should be designated by numbers corresponding to the view number and not by letters.

Hatching, as set forth herein, and shading, paragraph (m), are not the same. Hatching is the showing of sectioned elements and is a regular array lining which often denotes the material of which a sectioned element is made. Appendix 4 contains examples of several forms of hatching and the materials that these hatchings represent, as well as the use when encountered as exceptions to the rule for regions of ribonucleic acid (RNA)/deoxyribonucleic acid (DNA).

(4) Alternate position. A moved position may be shown by a broken line superimposed upon a suitable view if this can be done without crowding; otherwise, a separate view must be used for this purpose.

(5) Modified forms. Modified forms of construction must be shown in separate views.

(i) Arrangement of views. One view must not be placed upon another or within the outline of another. All views on the same sheet should stand in the same direction and, if possible, stand so that they can be read with the sheet held in an upright position. If views wider than the width of the sheet are necessary for the clearest illustration of the invention, the sheet may be turned on its side so that the top of the sheet, with the appropriate top margin to be used as the heading space, is on the right-hand side. Words must appear in a horizontal, left-to-right fashion when the page is either upright or turned so that the top becomes the right side, except for graphs utilizing standard scientific convention to denote the axis of abscissas (of X) and the axis of ordinates (of Y).

One view is not to be superimposed within the outline of another. Words must appear in a horizontal, left-to-right fashion when the page is either upright or turned so that the top becomes the right side. This expands the possibilities for presenting graphs to conform to standard scientific conventions, while using a format which is compatible with automated patent searching displays, such that drawings can be viewed on a monitor so that words/numbers appear either in the upright position or when rotated 90° to the right.

(j) View for *Official Gazette*. One of the views should be suitable for publication in the Official Gazette as the illustration of the invention.

Applicant's are encouraged to provide and suggest a view for the Official Gazette which clearly represents the scope of the invention. The selected view should be at a scale that will clearly illustrate details after being subjected to as much as a two-thirds reduction.

(k) Scale.

(1) The scale to which a drawing is made must be large enough to show the mechanism without crowding when the drawing is reduced in size to two-thirds in reproduction. Views of portions of the mechanism on a larger scale should be used when necessary to show details clearly. Two or more sheets may be used if one does not give sufficient room. The number of sheets should be kept to a minimum.

(2) When approved by the examiner, the scale of the drawing may be graphically represented. Indications such as "actual size" or "scale 1/2" on the drawings, are not permitted, since these lose their meaning with reproduction in a different format.

(3) Elements of the same view must be in proportion to each other, unless a difference in proportion is indispensable for the clarity of the view. Instead of showing elements in different proportion, a supplementary view may be added giving a larger-scale illustration of the element of the initial view. The enlarged element shown in the second view should be surrounded by a finely drawn or "dot-dash" circle in the first view indicating its location without obscuring the view.

(l) Character of lines, numbers, and letters. All drawings must be made by a process which will give them satisfactory reproduction characteristics. Every line, number, and letter must be durable, clean, black (except for color drawings), sufficiently dense and dark, and uniformly thick and well-defined. The weight of all lines and letters must be heavy enough to permit adequate reproduction. This requirement applies to all lines however fine, to shading, and to lines representing cut surfaces in sectional views. Lines and strokes of different thicknesses may be used in the same drawing where different thicknesses have a different meaning.

To further illustrate the character of lines, visualize the use of:

- A continuous thick line for edging and outlining views and cross sections.

- A continuous thin line for leading lines, hatching, outlining parts of adjoining elements, fictitious lines of intersection of surfaces connected by curved or rounded edges.

- A continuous thin line drawn freehand for delimiting views, part sections or interrupted views.

- A thin broken line made up of short dashes for hidden edges and contours.

- A dot-dash thin line for axes and planes of symmetry, extreme positions of movable elements, in front of a cross section.

- A thin line terminating in one heavy line for outlines of cross sections.

(m) Shading. The use of shading in views is encouraged if it aids in understanding the invention and if it does not reduce legibility. Shading is used to indicate the surface or shape of spherical, cylindrical, and conical elements of an object. Flat parts may also be lightly shaded. Such shading is preferred in the case of parts shown in perspective, but not for cross sections. See paragraph (h)(3) of this section. Spaced lines for shading are preferred. These lines must be thin, as few in number as practicable, and they must contrast with the rest of the drawings. As a substitute for shading, heavy lines on the shade side of objects can be used except where they superimpose on each other or obscure reference characters. Light should come from the upper left comer at an angle of 45°. Surface delineations should preferably be shown by proper shading. Solid black shading areas are not permitted, except when used to represent bar graphs or color.

To eliminate the possibility of any confusion regarding the difference between shading and hatching, keep in mind that hatching is applied to sectioned portions of an object, while shading is used to indicate the surface of an element.

(n) Symbols. Graphical drawing symbols may be used for conventional elements when appropriate. The elements for which such symbols and labeled representations are used must be adequately identified in the specification. Known devices should be illustrated by symbols which have a universally recognized conventional meaning and are generally accepted in the art. Other symbols which are not universally recognized may be used, subject to approval by the Office, if they are not likely to be confused with existing conventional symbols, and if they are readily identifiable.

To aid practitioners, commonly-used graphical symbols are set forth in Appendix 3. The entire list of such symbols is too extensive to include in this publication. Refer to the American National Standards Institute, 1430 Broadway, New York, NY 10018, for further information. Since such symbols are subject to updating and change, the patent specification still needs to include a complete description of the subject matter disclosed.

(o) Legends. Suitable descriptive legends may be used, or may be required by the Examiner, where necessary for understanding of the drawing, subject to approval by the Office. They should contain as few words as possible.

Drawings must not contain text matter, except a single word or words when absolutely indispensable such as "water," "steam," "open," "closed," "section on AB," and in the case of electric circuits and block schematics or flow sheet diagrams, a few short catch words indispensable for understanding. Any words used shall be so placed that if translated, they may be pasted over without interfering with any lines of the drawings. Words should not be used to describe the figure itself, such as "this is a bar graph." All text legends must be approved by the Office. The elements for which such labeled representations are used must be adequately identified in the specification.

Drawings must not contain the following:

-      Expressions or drawings contrary to morality.

-      Expressions or drawings contrary to public order.

-      Trademarks and service marks unless the applicant is shown to have a proprietary interest in the mark.

—   Any statement or other matter obviously irrelevant or unnecessary under the circumstances.

(p) Numbers, letters, and reference characters.

(1) Reference characters (numerals are preferred), sheet numbers, and view numbers must be plain and legible, and must not be used in association with brackets or inverted commas, or enclosed within outlines, e.g., encircled. They must be oriented in the same direction as the view so as to avoid having to rotate the sheet. Reference characters should be arranged to follow the profile of the object depicted.

(2) The English alphabet must be used for letters, except where another alphabet is customarily used, such as the Greek alphabet to indicate angles, wavelengths, and mathematical formulas.

(3) Numbers, letters, and reference characters must measure at least .32 cm. (1/8 inch) in height. They should not be placed in the drawing so as to interfere with its comprehension. Therefore, they should not cross or mingle with the lines. They should not be placed upon hatched or shaded surfaces. When necessary, such as indicating a surface or cross section, a reference character may be underlined and a blank space may be left in the hatching or shading where the character occurs so that it appears distinct.

(4) The same part of an invention appearing in more than one view of the drawing must always be designated by the same reference character, and the same reference character must never be used to designate different parts.

(5) Reference characters not mentioned in the description shall not appear in the drawings. Reference characters mentioned in the description must appear in the drawings.

While the rules do not specifically prohibit such practice, the use of primed reference characters should be kept to the very minimum. Single primed characters for designating the same element in different embodiments, if used sparingly, can aid in easily understanding the invention and its different embodiments, but the overuse of primed numbers tends to obfuscate the drawings and should be avoided.

The same holds true for subscript and superscript numbers.

While the rules do not specifically prohibit (other than to put a lower limit, 1/8 inch, on the size of reference characters), the use of subscripts and superscripts, tends to obfuscate the drawing and should be avoided.

(q) Lead lines. Lead lines are those lines between the reference characters and the details referred to. Such lines may be straight or curved and should be as short as possible. They must originate in the immediate proximity of the reference character and extend to the feature indicated. Lead lines must not cross each other. Lead lines are required for each reference character except for those which indicate the surface or cross section on which they are placed. Such a reference character must be underlined to make it clear that a lead line has not been lea out by mistake. Lead lines must be executed in the same way as lines in the drawing. See paragraph (1) of this section.

Note that in one of the examples, the lead lines were purposely left long so that the reference characters are all columnized. While an objection will not be entered for such, shorter lead lines are preferred because extended lead lines could tend to confuse the drawing.

(r) Arrows. Arrows may be used at the ends of lines, provided that their meaning is clear, as follows:

(1) On a lead line, a freestanding arrow to indicate the entire section towards which it points;

(2) On a lead line, an arrow touching a line to indicate the surface shown by the line looking along the direction of the arrow; or

(3) To show the direction of movement.

(s) Copyright or Mask Work Notice. A copyright or mask work notice may appear in the drawing, but must be placed within the sight of the drawing immediately below the figure representing the copyright or mask work material and be limited to letters having a print size of .32 cm. to .64 cm. (1/8 to 1/4 inches) high. The content of the notice must be limited to only those elements provided for by law. For example, "©1983 John Doe" (17 U.S.C. 401) and "*M* John Doe" (17 U.S.C. 909) would be properly limited and, under current statutes, legally sufficient notices of copyright and mask work, respectively. Inclusion of a copyright or mask work notice will be permitted only if the authorization language set forth in § 1.71(e) is included at the beginning (preferably as the first paragraph) of the specification.

(t) Numbering of sheets of drawings. The sheets of drawings should be numbered in consecutive Arabic numerals, starting with 1, within the sight as defined in paragraph (g) of this section. These numbers, if present, must be placed in the middle of the top of the sheet, but not in the margin. The numbers can be placed on the right-hand side if the drawing extends too close to the middle of the top edge of the usable surface. The drawing sheet numbering must be clear and larger than the numbers used as reference characters to avoid confusion. The number of each sheet should be shown by two Arabic numerals placed on either side of an oblique line, with the first being the sheet number, and the second being the total number of sheets of drawings, with no other marking.

For example, the numbering at the top of the sheet would indicate that sheet to be the second sheet of a total of six sheets. If the arrangement of the view is rotated as set forth in section (i), the sheet number must remain as set forth in this section (t).

(u) Numbering of views.

(1) The different views must be numbered in consecutive Arabic numerals, starting with 1, independent of the numbering of the sheets and, if possible, in the order in which they appear on the drawing sheet(s). Partial views intended to form one complete view, on one or several sheets, must be identified by the same number followed by a capital letter. View numbers must be preceded by the abbreviation "FIG." Where only a single view is used in an application to illustrate the claimed invention, it must not be numbered and the abbreviation "FIG." must not appear.

(2) Numbers and letters identifying the views must be simple and clear and must not be used in association with brackets, circles, or inverted commas. The view numbers must be larger than the numbers used for reference characters.

Each sectional view must be capable of being quickly identified, especially where several cross sections are made on the same view, by marking each end of the cross section line on the diagram with a single Arabic numeral. This number must be the same as the Arabic numeral identifying the view in the application where the section is illustrated.

(v) Security markings. Authorized security markings may be placed on the drawings provided they are outside the sight, preferably centered in the top margin.

Security markings are primarily the responsibility of the Office; however, the applicant might identify the drawings with the security designations such as NATO, TS, S, or C.

(w) Corrections. Any corrections on drawings submitted to the Office must be durable and permanent.

Special products for corrections, such as white masking fluid, may be used provided they are indelible and comply with all other requirements.

(x) Holes. The drawing sheets may be provided with two holes in the top margin. The holes should be equally spaced from the respective side edges, and their center lines should be spaced 7.0 cm. (2 3/4 inches) apart.

(See § 1.152 for design drawings, § 1.165 for plant drawings, and § 1.174 for reissue drawings.)

37 CFR 1.85. Corrections to Drawings.

(a) The requirements of § 1.84 relating to drawings will be strictly enforced. A drawing not executed in conformity thereto, if suitable for reproduction, may be admitted for examination but in such case a new drawing must be furnished.

(b) The Patent and Trademark Office will not release drawings in applications having a filing date after January 1, 1989, or any drawings from any applications after January 1, 1991, for purposes of correction. If corrections are necessary, new corrected drawings must be submitted within the time set by the Office.

(c) When corrected drawings are required to be submitted at

the time of allowance, the applicant is required to submit acceptable drawings within three months from the mailing of the "Notice of Allowability." Within that three-month period, two weeks should be allowed for review of the drawings by the Drafting Branch. If the Office finds that correction is necessary, the applicant must submit a new corrected drawing to the Office within the original three-month period to avoid the necessity of obtaining an extension of time and paying the extension fee. Therefore, the applicant should file corrected drawings as soon as possible following the receipt of the Notice of Allowability. The provisions with respect to obtaining an extension of time relates only to the late filing of corrected drawings. The time limit for payment of the issue fee is a fixed three-month period which cannot be extended as set forth in 35 U.S.C. 151.

37 CFR 1.123 Amendments to the Drawing.

No change in the drawing may be made except with permission of the Office. Permissible changes in the construction shown in any drawing may be made only by the submission of a substitute drawing by applicant. A sketch in permanent ink showing proposed changes, to become part of the record, must be filed for approval by the examiner and should be a separate paper.

37 CFR 1.151 Rules Applicable.

The rules relating to applications for patents for other inventions or discoveries are also applicable to applications for patents for designs except as otherwise provided.

This rule is included to show that unless a requirement is specifically mentioned in either this section or in 37 CFR 1.152, the provisions of 37 CFR 1.84 are controlling for the content and quality of drawings for design patent applications.

Note that 37 CFR 1.151 specifies that drawings for Design applications must meet all the requirements for utility patents unless 37 CFR 1.152 specifically states otherwise.

37 CFR 1.152 Design Drawing.

The design must be represented by a drawing that complies with the requirements of § 1.84 and must contain a sufficient number of views to constitute a complete disclosure of the appearance of the article. Appropriate surface shading must be used to show the character or contour of the surfaces represented. Solid black surface shading is not permitted except when used to represent color contrast. Broken lines may be used to show visible environmental structure, but may not be used to show hidden planes and surfaces which cannot be seen through opaque materials. Alternate positions of a design component, illustrated by full and broken lines in the same view are not permitted in a design drawing. Photographs and ink drawings must not be combined in one application. Photographs submitted in lieu of ink drawings in design patent applications must comply with § 1.84(b) and must not disclose environmental structure but must be limited to the design for the article claimed. Color drawings and color photographs are not permitted in design patent applications.

Since there is no detailed specification supporting the disclosure in a design application, it is essential that the drawing be so clear and complete that no portion of the design is left to conjecture. This may require a number of views to constitute a complete disclosure of the appearance of the article. These views must show the claimed design in solid lines, and these views must be consistent in all details of the design, appropriately shaded to show clearly the character and/or contour of the surfaces represented.

Shading is of particular importance in the showing of three-dimensional articles, where it is necessary to delineate plane, concave, convex, raised and/or depressed surfaces of the article, and to distinguish open and solid surfaces. Transparent and translucent surfaces should be indicated by oblique line shading, as shown in Appendix 4.

Broken lines may not be used to show movement or alternate positions in a design drawing, or to show hidden structure through opaque surfaces. Broken lines may be included to show environmental structure. Only the claimed design may be shown in solid lines in the drawing, unclaimed subject matter may only appear in broken lines. Legends and reference characters identifying portions of the design may not be used in a design drawing. Alternate positions are not permitted in design drawings.

Rules of Practice Relating to Patent Drawings

Broken lines may not be used to indicate unimportant or immaterial features of the design. There are no features of a claimed design which are unimportant or immaterial. (This issue was determined by court decisions: *In re Blum*, 153 USPQ 177 (CCPA 1967); *In re Zahn* 204 USPQ 988 (CCPA 1980).)

Color drawings are not permitted for any reason in design patent applications. However, color may be illustrated in design patent drawings by means of shading utilizing specific drafting symbol patterns. When such shading patterns are used in design patent drawings, special descriptions are required in the specification.

Caution is advised when submitting photographs in design applications since reproductions of photographic drawings tend to result in vague and indefinite disclosures.

37 CFR 1.161 Rules Applicable.

The rules relating to applications for patent for other inventions or discoveries are also applicable to applications for patents for plants except as otherwise provided.

This rule is included to show that unless a requirement is specifically mentioned in either this section or 37 CFR 1.165, the provisions of 37 CFR 1.84 are controlling for the content and quality of drawings for plant patent applications.

Note that 37 CFR 1.161 specifies that drawings for plant applications must meet all the requirements for utility applications unless 37 CFR 1.165 specifies otherwise.

37 CFR 1.165 Plant Drawings.

(a) Plant patent drawings should be artistically and competently executed and must comply with the requirements of § 1.84. View numbers and reference characters need not be employed unless required by the examiner. The drawing must disclose all the distinctive characteristics of the plant capable of visual representation.

(b) The drawing may be in color and when color is a distinguishing characteristic of the new variety, the drawing must be in color. Two copies of color drawings or color photographs must be submitted.

The terms drawing and photograph are used interchangeably herein as they are both acceptable means of illustration under 37 CFR 1.165 for plant patent applications filed under 35 U.S.C. 161.

There are no restrictions in combining both ink drawings and photographs or any combination thereof in an application, except for size of paper.

Color drawings may be made either in permanent water color or oil, or in lieu thereof may be photographs made by color photography or properly colored on sensitized paper.

Plant patent drawings must show the most distinguishing characteristics of the plant. Color drawings must reasonably closely correspond to the color values set forth in the specification and must accurately depict the true coloration of the plant parts so illustrated.

Care should be taken to assure that the subject is well centered and clearly in focus. Leaves, stems, flowers, whole and cut fruit (or nuts) may appropriately be shown in various combinations in a single drawing. Distinguishing characteristics occurring at different seasons should be illustrated, and may be depicted in different sheets or figures. Flower and seed parts not particularly distinguishing may still be included (if convenient) for the sake of completeness. Photographic drawings should not be retouched or amended/altered by the addition of color, as such drawings cannot be faithfully reproduced by the printer.

Drawings should avoid the inclusion of superfluous information or material(s) such as tags or stickers (unwarranted and improper advertising) which add little if anything in the way of further definition to the plant. However, scale definition means such as rulers, etc., in intimate proximity to the plant are acceptable. Drawings should be of such scale and clarity that necessary detail can still be discerned even with a fifty percent reduction in scale as may happen upon printing of same should the application mature into a Plant patent.

Drawings should not be limited to a single plant part, i.e. the fruit, nut, flower, or leaf as applicable, but should also depict the entire plant, even if the single plant part may be the entirety of what is viewed by applicant as being novel. Where flowers, foliage, fruit, etc., of the claimed plant are not depicted in sufficient scale in a whole plant drawing or view, this view should be supplemented with a close-up view of specific parts. Typical of what is sought and may be necessary on a case-by-case basis in this supplemental view would be:

– Ornamental flowering plant. Views at bud, early bloom, and late bloom stage showing bloom shape and character. Flower parts may be shown separated from whole flowers, i.e., to depict color differences between top and bottom surfaces of petals or leaves, differences in coloration of petals from basal to terminal portions, and color and shape differences between petals from different locations of the flower and different ages. Foliage and stems (bark) may also be so depicted. Where there is characteristic variation in leaf shape, each characteristic shape should be depicted. For perennial, deciduous plants, the drawing should include a showing of the plant in a dormant state to illustrate details of bark and branching.

– Fruit or nut bearing plant. Views depicted at different attitudes, with fruit (or nut) split in different directions to show details and coloration of seeds, stone, stone well, core, flesh coloration, skin ground coloration, blush and pubescence (as applicable). Bloom may also be shown along with foliage.

Fingerprint information may also be presented as a figure of the drawing and should include identifying information. Such drawings should be given view numbers, as appropriate. These illustrations may be mechanical in nature, or in the case of isozyme banding, be presented as a black-and-white photograph, even if other drawing figures are in color.

Where the pedigree of the plant is disclosed in the form of a detailed flow chart, this must be made a drawing view and not appear in the specification, as per 37 CFR 1.58(a), the printer will not print same in the body of the specification proper.

Where a claimed plant is a sport of a known variety, every effort should be made to Photograph the sported plant in a side-by-side relationship with the parental variety and such parental variety should clearly be identified as "Prior Art." This applies to plant parts, such as color sports of flowering plants (i.e., roses or chrysanthemums) or fruit (i.e., apples or nectarines).

NOTE 1:

Duplicate formal drawings should be filed concurrently with the application papers. Examination of drawings for content, detail, scale, and color fidelity is critical to the effective examination of a 35 U.S.C. 161 plant patent application. Filing of informal or single copies of said drawings will result in delay of prosecution of the application (for example, applications otherwise in condition for allowance will not normally be forwarded to the Publishing Division, Office of Publication and Dissemination, prior to receipt and evaluation of formal drawings). The drawing(s) may be in color and when color is a distinguishing characteristic of the new variety, the drawing(s) must be in color (37 CFR 1.165(b)).

NOTE 2:

The number of drawing views (and sheets) in plant patent applications should be limited to the minimum number necessary to adequately depict the distinctive botanical characteristics of the claimed plant which are capable of being visually represented (37 CFR 1.165(a)). The views may be given view numbers as appropriate, so long as any view numbers set forth in the drawings find corresponding reference in the written specification.

37 CFR 1.171 Application for Reissue.

An application for reissue must contain the same parts required for an application for an original patent, complying with all the rules relating thereto except as otherwise provided, and in addition, must comply with the requirements of the rules relating to reissue applications. The application must be accompanied by a certified copy of an abstract of title or an order for a title report accompanied by the fee set forth in § 1.19(b)(4), to be placed in the file, and by an offer to surrender the original patent (§ 1.178).

37 CFR 1.174. Drawings.

(a) The drawings upon which the original patent was issued may be used in reissue applications if no changes whatsoever are to be made in the drawings. In such cases, when the reissue application is filed, the applicant must submit a temporary drawing which may consist of a copy of the printed drawings of the patent or a photoprint of the original drawings of the size required for original drawing.

(b) Amendments which can be made in a reissue drawing that is, changes from the drawing of the patent, are restricted.

An original drawing can be used as a reissue drawing; however, even a slight modification would require a new complete drawing.

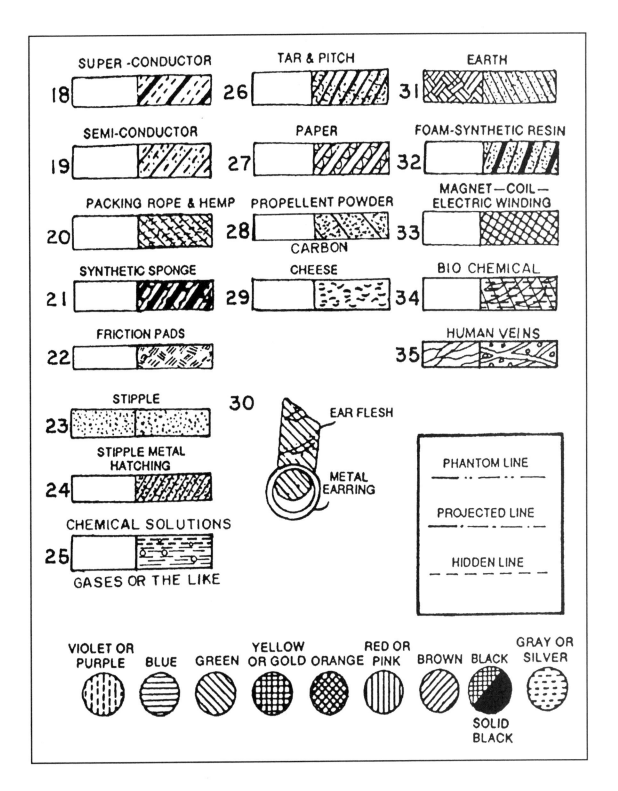

Notes:

1. **Porous sintered metal:** Powdered metal fused together—use stipple metal hatching.
2. **Dielectric:** is non conducting material, e.g., plastic, rubber, etc.
3. **Abscissa:** Horizontal line. —
4. **Ordinate:** Vertical line. |

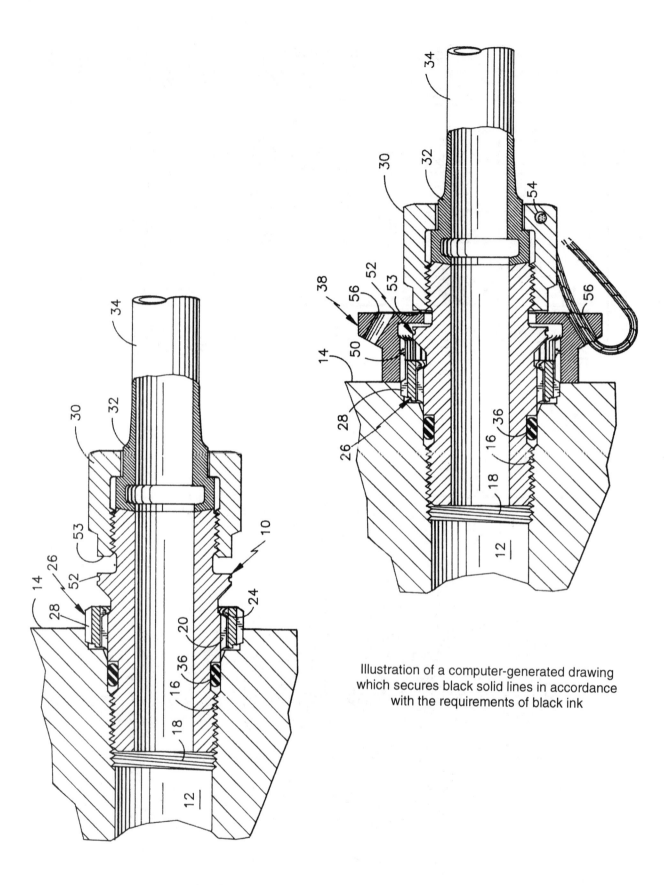

Illustration of a computer-generated drawing
which secures black solid lines in accordance
with the requirements of black ink

316

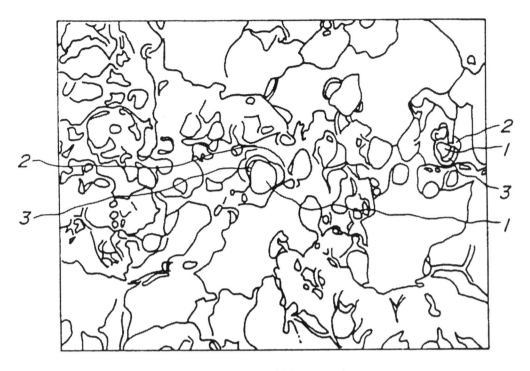

Illustrative View of Photograph

(1) Fuel Electrode
(2) Thin Filmy Tissue
(3) Gap

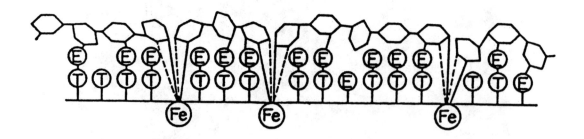

T: Triazine dithiol
E: Epoxy compound

Illustration of chemical formulae
which may be submitted as drawings

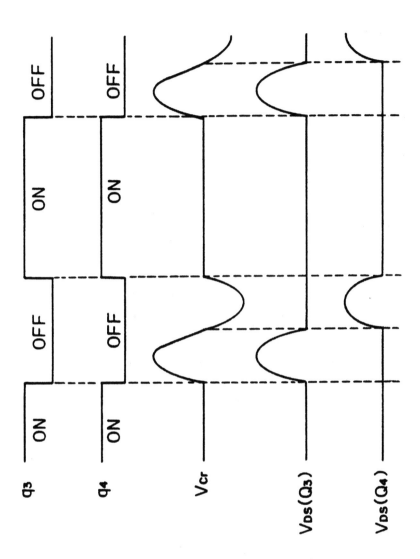

Illustration of waveforms with lead lines

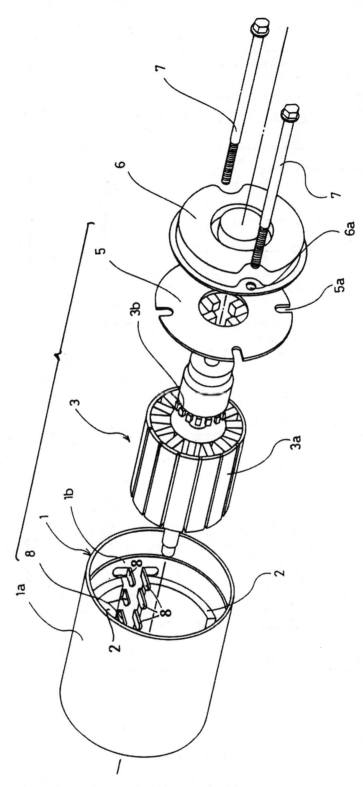

Illustration of an exploded view which
may be submitted as a drawing

320

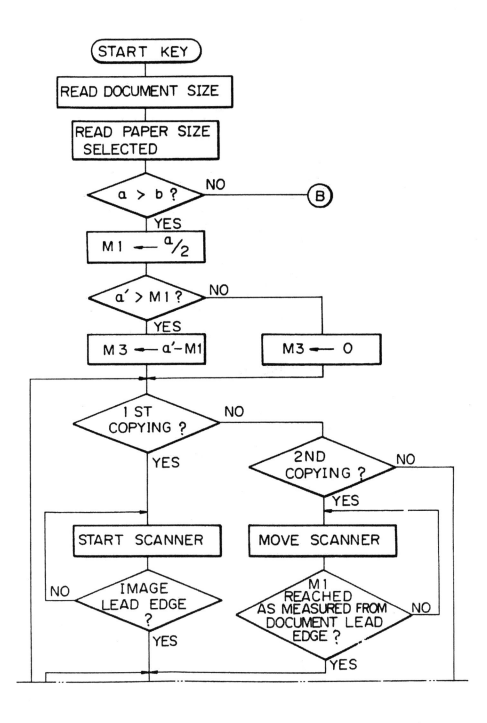

Illustration of a partial view

321

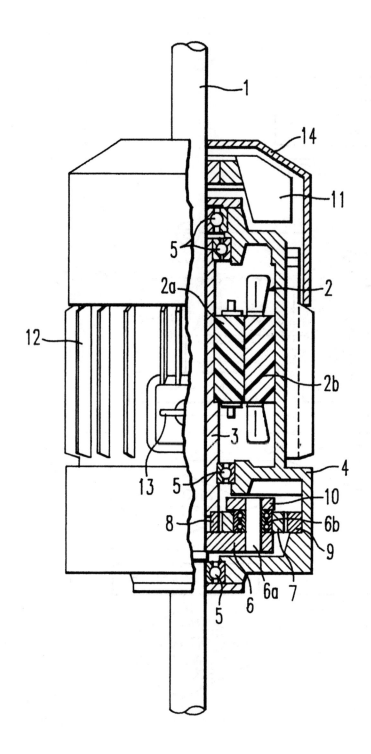

Illustration of the character of lines and numbers in a drawing
and specifically illustrates a continuous thick line for edging
and outlining views and cross-sections

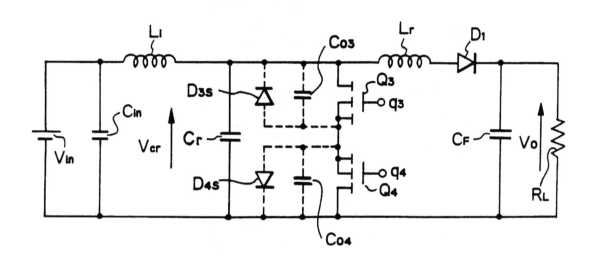

Illustration of a drawing which depicts acceptable symbols

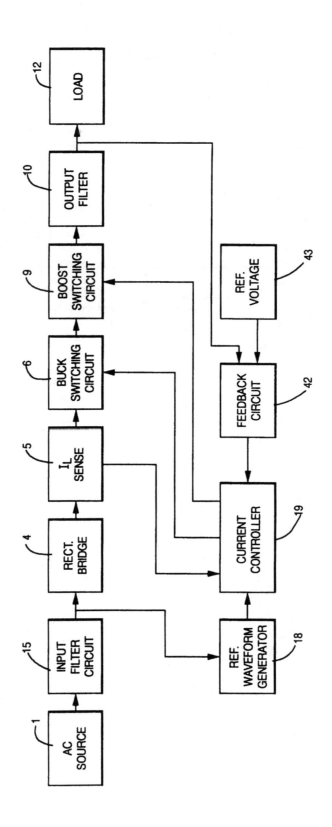

Illustration of a drawing which depicts
acceptable descriptive legends

324